More Praise for
ECONOMIC PUPPETMASTERS

"Larry Lindsey's remarkable new book is a must-read insider's account of economic policy for those of us on the outside. Drawing on the insights and world views of some of the leading figures of our time, Lindsey provides a highly readable and entertaining guide to economics from which all citizens, policymakers, and even his fellow economists can profit."

—Robert E. Litan, Director, Economic Studies Program, The Brookings Institution

"A riveting look ahead at how those who pull the strings of the world economy will affect our policies and our investments...Refreshing because it is written by a wise and balanced economist who knows enough about what he is talking about to be able to write plainly enough for the rest of us."

—Lamar Alexander, Former Governor of Tennessee and U.S. Education Secretary

"Anyone wondering how the world fell into its current financial predicament needs to listen to Larry Lindsey. With unmatched clarity and insight, he explains how economies come to ruin and what we can do to help them recover. His book is a sometimes frightening, always fascinating tour of economic decisionmaking at the highest level. In this time of financial turmoil, policymakers, investors, and voters would do well to listen to his analysis and advice."

—The Honorable Richard Armey, Majority Leader, U.S. House of Representatives

"Larry Lindsey has traveled from the ivory tower of Harvard to the White House to the real citadel of power in this world...the Federal Reserve Board. In his new book, he walks us through the corridors of power, not only in Washington and New York, but in Tokyo and Bonn. And he guides us through the even trickier maze of national and international economic policy on the eve of the millennium. [This is] the best book about the 21st century available in the 20th century."

—James Pinkerton, Columnist for *Newsday* and Lecturer at the Graduate School of Political Management, The George Washington University

R

Economic Puppetmasters

Lessons from the Halls of Power

Lawrence B. Lindsey

The AEI Press

Publisher for the American Enterprise Institute

WASHINGTON, D.C.

1999

n the AEI Press, c/o Publisher Re-
vd., P.O. Box 7001, La Vergne, TN
269-6267. Distributed outside the
United States by arrangement with Eurospan, 3 Henrietta Street, London WC2E 8LU England.

1 3 5 7 9 10 8 6 4 2

THE AEI PRESS
Publisher for the American Enterprise Institute
1150 17th Street, N.W., Washington, D.C. 20036

Printed in the United States of America

To Troy and Emily,
who let Daddy use the computer,
even when they had something else to do on it.

Contents

Foreword

This is a work of contemporary history. The events being described are continuing, and the global economic landscape is changing at an even faster pace than we are accustomed to. But the reader will still find the analysis quite current. That is so because the decisionmakers portrayed in this book, and their successors, are driven by a logic that is both historically continuous and inescapable.

The contrarian, Alan Greenspan, has seen the economy for which he is responsible turn for the worse since he was interviewed for this book. But both the direction of the economy and his reaction to it were eminently predictable from his comments. Eisuke Sakakibara has seen both Japan deteriorate and bureaucratic power slip gradually from his fellow mandarins. But the underlying power vacuum between elected politicians unskilled in policymaking and bureaucrats who have lost the Mandate of Heaven continues unfilled, to the detriment of both Japan and the world. Chancellor Kohl was thrown out of office in late September 1998, but not after he completed his mission. Europe will be struggling with his legacy—a single European currency—and the deep historical forces that drove him to change Germany and Europe for years to come.

The pages of history write themselves, but that is not the case with a book. I am deeply grateful for the help of many people, especially the subjects. Alan Greenspan not only cooperated in the formal sense of being interviewed, but also provided invaluable insights and lessons over the more than five years during which I was his colleague. He is both an outstanding student of economic history and its shaper. I am also grateful to both Eisuke Sakakibara and George Soros for their insights. They were most generous with the scarcest of resources—time. I would also like to thank the entire Kohl family for giving me such a glimpse into their lives and their souls, and especially to Walter Kohl, who made it possible.

My deepest thanks are also extended to those who slogged through the early drafts and whose frank comments turned the book into something readable. They include Tim Adams, Dick Alford, Jeff Gedmin, Mark Groombridge, Walter Kohl, Susan Lindsey, John Makin, Allan Meltzer, Tomo Sugita, and Donald Van de Mark. I would also thank the many people whose names adorn the jacket and front of the book for their generous comments: Lamar Alexander, Richard Armey, John Ashcroft, George W. Bush, Lou Dobbs, Martin Feldstein, Steve Forbes, John Kasich, Robert Litan, Gene Ludwig, James Pinkerton, and William Simon.

I was especially fortunate to have outstanding assistants help me manage the entire process. First and foremost, my thanks to Janet Walker, who made sure the trains ran on time during the entire process, even if it meant she had to stoke the engines herself. I would also like to thank Katherine Carothers, Brandon Garson, Frank Goldberg, and Ryan Holston for their research, editing, and fact-checking efforts, and Ryan in particular for his help with the charts.

The American Enterprise Institute has been wonderfully supportive of my writing efforts. Special thanks are owed to Chris DeMuth and David Gerson who have made AEI what it is today—a preeminent think tank. Leigh Tripoli has been the best of all editors with a light but firm touch. Many others at AEI have provided a variety of assistance, including Virginia Bryant, Alice Anne English, Susanna Huang, Nancy Rosenberg, Stanley Thawley, and Murray White. My deepest thanks to them all.

"All service ranks the same with God:
With God, whose puppets, best and worst,
Are we; there is no last nor first."

—Robert Browning, Pippa Passes, *part iv*

1

Masters of the System—Or Its Servants?

In my country, as in yours, public men are proud to be the servants of the State and would be ashamed to be its masters.
—Winston Churchill to a joint session of the U.S. Congress, December 26, 1941[1]

So, this is a global economy? It sure doesn't look like anyone's in charge. In America, until recently, we talked of a New Era. Wall Street continuously set new records, having doubled in the past three years and risen more than tenfold since the bull market began in 1982. For the first time in its history, the United States has had a sixteen-year expansion punctuated only by one short and shallow recession in 1991. The lowest unemployment rate in three decades was coupled with the near absence of inflation. Optimists tell us this is just the beginning—that we have two decades of prosperity ahead and that the Dow Jones Industrial Average is undervalued even at historically high levels.[2] Meanwhile, pessimists worry about a break in the market leading to another depression. At this writing in the fall of 1998, the pessimists were looking better. And, once you leave America, there is plenty to worry about.

In Asia, we are witnessing what one leading bank's strategist described to me as a "train wreck in slow motion." Japan, the world's second largest economy, is officially in recession, with no end in sight. Its banking system is on the brink of collapse. There is talk of $1 trillion in bad loans on the balance sheets of the banks, with the nation's insurance companies and other financial institutions also in deep trouble. Elsewhere in Asia, things only get worse. Some estimates suggest the dollar value of Korea's GNP will fall by one-third in 1998.[3] In Hong Kong the stock market and property markets are plunging. In the year since Hong Kong left British protection, the fall in those markets has wiped out $300 billion of wealth, the equivalent of all the bank accounts in the territory.[4] Further south still, Indonesia saw its president of thirty-two years resign as economic pressures and a falling currency wiped out the savings of tens of millions of Indonesians. The price of food has spiraled, and many face hunger after years of prosperous growth.

Meanwhile, Europe seems preoccupied with itself. Much of Europe has the highest unemployment since the end of the Second World War. But European financial markets act like their American cousins and seem to ignore the grim reality of the unemployment lines. European leaders are focused on a new project—currency union—giving their electorates the assurance that this will solve Europe's problems.

In short, the world's three major economies—America, East Asia, and Europe—seem to be confronting radically different conditions. We don't see much that is "global" about today's world economic picture.

During eight years in government, split between the White House and the Federal Reserve Board, I got to see how decisions are made on the inside. In the past eighteen months, I have traveled the world as a scholar and consultant, meeting with the world's economic decisionmakers to try to make sense of it all.

Among the questions my clients raise: Will Asia collapse? Will it drag down the rest of the world with it? Is America really in a New Era, and if so, why? How will the Euro, Europe's new currency, work out? And most often, how can I make money on it all?

This book is a work of contemporary history, written as events unfold. We don't know how today's events will end, but without a doubt, they pose the greatest challenge since the Second World War to those in the corridors of power who are responsible for the world's economic health.

About one year after I left the Federal Reserve Board of Governors to follow those events from the private sector, I remarked to a friend in government, one generation ahead of me, that it had been the most interesting year in history to have been following global markets. My friend's sage rejoinder: "No. Things were about this interesting seventy years ago. It's just that none of us remember."

This book is a guide to how the world's economic decisionmakers think, what drives them, and what limits their scope of action. It takes you, the reader, inside the corridors of power and inside the heads of some of the individuals who pull the strings. In particular, the book introduces the thinking of four key individuals: Alan Greenspan, chairman of the U.S. Federal Reserve Board, Eisuke Sakakibara, vice minister of finance in Japan, Helmut Kohl, former chancellor of Germany, and George Soros, arguably the world's leading financier. The choices these men make as this crisis unfolds will largely determine how many economic dominoes actually fall and how the world will go about picking up the pieces if they do fall.

I've written the book for three types of readers. First is the modern investor who wants to make a killing in the market—or at least avoid being killed by it. We'll journey behind the day's headlines and resulting market volatility. Headlines come and go. This book explains how decisionmakers will respond to today's headlines and thus will help to write tomorrow's.

The second type of reader is the student of political economy striving to understand why decisions are made the way they are. Political scientists often refer to this as the "path dependence" argument. In simple English, does history make the individual or does the individual make history? Can one man make a difference? Are these men masters of their system or its servants? As we shall learn, even a puppetmaster can move in only a few directions or he will find his strings becoming completely tangled.

The third type of reader is the informed voter. This book is about systems of political economy put in place half a century ago that are now showing signs of outliving their usefulness. One likely consequence of the current crisis is that voters in much of the world will be asked to adopt new decisionmaking systems. To do so, they'd better understand why our current systems are breaking down.

The remainder of this chapter introduces today's key decisionmakers and considers how history will ultimately view them. Investors, political scientists, and voters will all recognize the roles we ask them to play: to preside over prosperity if they succeed or to become the system's scapegoats if they fail. We—as investors or voters or simply men and women driven by human nature—naturally seek others to assume responsibility for results that we do not wish to shoulder ourselves. Are our leaders prepared for their task? What is the reasoning behind their decisions? Are we safe with what we've got, or should we tear it down and begin anew?

The book then turns to the puppetmasters themselves, looking at the environment in which they must make decisions and how it helps determine what actions they must take. We begin with America and Alan Greenspan, now in his third term as chairman of the Federal Reserve Board, the man most likely to keep America above the fray. We then turn to Japan and Dr. Eisuke Sakakibara, who exemplifies the governing tradition of that country—what we shall call the mandarin model. No man influences foreign exchange markets more than he does. Then we turn to former Chancellor Kohl to see what motivated that man, who led Germany longer than any other individual save Bismarck. The book concludes its conversations with the puppetmasters with an interview with George Soros, world famous financier and hedge fund operator. The final section of the book puts those pieces together to make some sense of our global economy.

Did They See It Coming?

The best place to begin our world tour is from where they've seen it all before. The Old Lady of Threadneedle Street—the Bank of England—sits in the middle of the tangle of streets known as the City of London. From here, a collection of some of Her Majesty's most talented servants have managed the financial affairs of a kingdom turned global empire, then social welfare state, and finally Thatcherite land of opportunity, now governed by "New" Labour. But the Bank of England has stood there through it all, conveying a sense of financial permanence in a world wracked by crises. The bank has survived the South Sea Bubble, the American Revolution, Napoleon's conquest of Europe, the collapse and rebirth of the British textile industry during and after the American Civil War, and all the calamities the twentieth century has wrought.

The bank's issue serves as the planet's oldest continuously circulating currency, the universally recognized generic name of which, "sterling," conveys the permanence of value that only precious metal was once thought to provide.[5] The debt backed by the bank—"gilts," in effect British government bonds—also conveys by their very name the historic notion of security and permanence of value associated with something made of gold.

The Bank of England exposes a visitor to that sense of long-standing tradition as soon as he or she crosses the threshold. Men in morning coats colored a distinctive soft red escort the guest to one waiting area, then, through a maze of corridors as complex as the streets of the city, to another. The furniture is classic and well used. The visitor temporarily ends his journey when directed to a chair whose seat has been well and permanently shaped by the many visitors who have sat there over the decades.

On the wall is a cartoon from the *Chicago Tribune* at the start of the 1930s. It shows Uncle Sam nailing down everything he can and locking up the U.S. gold stock. In the background, a bearded gentleman, Montague Norman, then head of the Bank of England, is striding off a boat. The caption says, "Mr. Norman's back in town." The cartoon is a reminder of yet another crisis: the outbreak of the Great Depression when England and America were wrestling with the currency crisis of that moment—the gold standard. A closer look at Norman's caricature reveals the anti-Semitic bias of the cartoonist. It is a reminder that hard economic times often create social and political perils as well—even in the United States.

So it was appropriate that here, on November 25, 1997, over lunch in one of the bank's many private dining rooms, I heard the globe's unfolding crisis placed unforgettably in historic context. My host, Mervyn King, was chief economist and is now deputy governor at the Bank of England. Trained at Kings' College Cambridge and Harvard University, a former professor at the London School of Economics and Harvard, he developed an academic reputation for cogent insight on both sides of the Atlantic. He moved to the bank in 1990 under a Tory government, but he has the respect of the current Labour government as well, as indicated by his reappointment and promotion.

We spoke of world events. Suddenly King made a historical leap that caused me to set down my silverware. "They weren't as stupid as we thought during the 1930s, were they? I'll bet they saw it coming, too," King remarked. It was as if the ghosts who inhabited this venerable institution had forced their way into the conversation.

King did not, of course, base his insight on any formal historic research but on one man's day-to-day frustration of watching a global financial crisis unfold and feeling powerless to stop it. Over the previous few months he had seen the Thai currency crisis lead to problems in Southeast Asia. He had witnessed the American government's seeming paralysis as it tried to shift away from its total preoccupation with maximizing American exports. King knew that more was on the way. One month later, in December, the world's eleventh largest economy, Korea, effectively collapsed and was declared in default on its loans. Bank regulators from New York to Frankfurt took the dramatic step of telling the banks under their control to roll over their Korean loans even though many of those loans were technically in default. Here was an uncharacteristic act of desperation. The regulators, unprepared for the crisis, faced the choice of turning a blind eye to credit quality or watching the global banking system unravel in a spreading series of defaults.

As 1998 unfolded, the economic dominoes continued to shake. Some toppled. Indonesia's President Suharto ended his thirty-two-year grip on power just weeks after he was reelected to a seventh term in office. Emerging economies from Brazil to Russia saw dramatic declines in their stock markets and attacks on their currencies. The International Monetary Fund, which had failed to foresee the crisis, quickly depleted its reserves and was forced to ask for more money. Its threat if Congress was not forthcoming with the funds: it had nothing left if a Brazil or a Russia should run into trouble.

By mid-1998 the world watched as the planet's second largest economy, Japan, seemed on the verge of suffering an economic implosion. Japan's government had proposed no fewer than six economic rescue packages since the fall when I met with Mervyn King. Official government purchases were shoring up the Japanese stock market. The yen had collapsed on world markets after having fallen 80 percent since its high of eighty to the dollar in 1995.[6] America uncharacteristically intervened in the market to help the Japanese currency, but even that help proved short-lived as the yen soon plunged to new lows. In mid-July Japan's voters sent the ruling party a loud message of discontent.

But still the "train wreck in slow motion" continued, seemingly unstoppable.

A Look Backward from the Future at Today's Puppetmasters

In the future, historians and students of political economy will debate why our current set of decisionmakers took the actions they did. If our society and economy fail to provide the preconditions for the continued ascent of democratic capitalism, economists will ask why the individuals in charge today were doomed to make the same kind of mistakes as the leaders of the 1930s. Were the 1990s' leaders reckless? Did they base their decisions on the wrong economic model? Did they simply lack information, or were markets and events simply moving too fast for them to act appropriately? Did public-sector decisionmakers need more power, or did they need more knowledge? Did they need both? Or is there something more fundamental about the nature of uncertainty and the capacity of limited government?

Mervyn King's comments at the Bank of England suggest that we should be a little more reflective on that point. For what we may soon be seeing as this crisis unfolds is the most natural historical corollary to not solving problems—finding scapegoats. As students, we, of course, presumed that the ignorance or the irresponsibility of the decisionmakers of the 1930s led to the Great Depression. In the hand-me-down fashion of retail political history, Herbert Hoover has been demonized as a bumbling incompetent, though any scholarly look at his resume or his actions shows that he was not.

Finding historical scapegoats is a particularly comforting action for a society because citizens can falsely assume that eliminating those scapegoats eliminates the chance that history will repeat itself. Presumably, newer, wiser heads have taken charge, and they would not and could not make the same mistakes. The process of scapegoating causes more than just a mere injustice to innocent men. It locks society into a misreading of its own history.

Consider the following description of why the Federal Reserve chose to cut interest rates in August 1927. Bear in mind that this description was written in 1931 and therefore possessed at least some modest benefit of hindsight:

> This action had been taken for the most laudable motives: several of the European nations were having difficulty in stabilizing their currencies, European exchanges were weak, and it seemed to the Reserve authorities that the easing of American money rates might prevent the further accumulation of gold in the United States and thus aid in the recovery of Europe and benefit foreign trade.[7]

Now, let us move that explanation forward in time. Substitute *Asia* for *Europe,* simply to reflect the development of that region and its rising importance in international trade. Second, recall that the world was on the gold standard in 1927, so that the modern manifestation of the "accumulation of gold" would be the flight of capital to the United States. Today, the foreign purchases of U.S. bonds would reflect the same behavior. In light of that, consider the following quotations from the *Wall Street Journal* in December 1997 and January 1998 about likely Federal Reserve policy in 1998: "To be sure, many investors are streaming into bonds as part of a flight to quality, amid continuing difficulties in . . . Asian markets." And "[t]he recent Asian market turmoil will only add to the attractiveness of [bonds], said Vic Thompson, who manages $150 billion in bonds for State Street Global Advisors. 'You think about the general backdrop, people are interested in dollar-denominated assets,' Mr. Thompson said."[8] In short, modern investors were seeking safety in American assets just as surely as their predecessors sent their gold to America seventy years ago in search of a safe haven.

Fed policymakers are candid about their present concerns. Vice Chairman Rivlin said in December 1997 in a direct echo of the thinking of 1927, "If we were not presently engulfed by the worldwide currency crisis, I think we'd be worrying very considerably at the Federal Reserve about the economy overheating and incipient inflation, though we haven't seen any" of the latter.[9]

Some economists actually see good news in that for the United States:

> "This is the immaculate slowdown," says Joel Prakken, chairman of Macroeconomic Advisers LLC, a forecasting firm based in St. Louis. By cooling things off without a Fed move, the Asian crunch "allows us to project lower interest rates into the future, which is very good for potential growth," he adds. "This could actually be a boon to us."[10]

As we shall see in this book, it could be too much of a boon, turning our expansion into an asset "bubble."

One should not jump to conclusions about whether the Fed took the "correct" action in 1927, or whether the present Fed is taking the "correct" action in its recent decisions. In retrospect, the seemingly well-intentioned move in 1927 probably helped fuel speculative fires that caused the stock market to rise to even more ridiculous levels and ultimately produced the stock market crash in 1929. The Federal Reserve Board in 1927 was performing a classical function: *it was buying time.* At the time, that seemed a perfectly reasonable thing to do. Is the Fed just buying time today?

In light of such parallels, Mervyn King's comment can be a two-edged sword. Just as we may have been a little hurried in our judgment about the foolishness of our predecessors, are we not potentially also wrong about the omniscience of our current institutions? One can certainly make the case that "we" did not see the current crisis coming either. Consider, for example, what happened at the International Monetary Fund in December 1997, when events unfolding in Asia simply made its earlier estimates "inoperative." As reported in the *Wall Street Journal* on December 22, 1997:

> The IMF updated its World Economic Outlook, last released in September, to reflect the financial crisis that has enveloped Southeast Asia and South Korea since then. Gone is the ebullience of the earlier report, which predicted the global economy would enter its best five-year stretch in the past 25 years. In its place is a new humility—and a host of downward revisions in global growth.[11]

In September 1997 the IMF simply did not see a crisis that effectively started the very next month. U.S. Treasury Secretary Rubin confessed similar myopia before Congress in January 1998 when, in response to a congressman's question regarding what could be done to prevent a crisis from happening, he replied, "I think there is [a] . . . limit to . . . prognostication. [T]he prediction of what is going to happen either in markets or economies is an extremely uncertain thing at best."[12] One can only wonder whether Secretary Rubin's predecessors felt equally blindsided by events seventy years ago.

The key point is that decisionmakers may never be the *masters* of the systems over which they hold sway, no matter how much they delude themselves and the public into believing that they are. More typically, they are the system's *servants.* They are constrained by the prejudices of existing theory, the information flow that has developed in the bureaucracies they oversee, and the constraints that other decisionmaking forces impose on them.

That is what makes the process of scapegoating so enticing for a society. It presumes that the scapegoat was really the master of the system in the first place. The system is now safe because a new "master" is allowed to take his place without any fundamental reforms' occurring. Of all the world's major economies, no one has ritualized the process of scapegoating better than Japan. Whenever there is a scandal or major policy failure, a top official simply resigns, sometimes offering a tearful apology. Japan got rid of its finance minister, Hiroshi Mitsuzuka, and the head of its central bank, Yasuo Matsushita, early in 1998 once the public realized that the nation was in the midst of the economic crisis. Heads rolled. Scapegoats were created. Nothing changed.

Protecting the system is the reason that, in a crisis, complicity in finding a scapegoat is extraordinarily widespread. Even people (particularly the governing elites) who are closest to the process and who therefore know better are often involved. We may make scapegoats out of those individuals and institutions, but we do not do so because of their behavior but because of the system's need to protect itself. Those individuals, and the institutions they represent, were simply at the wrong place at the wrong time as the world learned the limits of economic management. So, for the sake of future historians, as well as ourselves, let us look at some of the individuals and decisionmaking institutions that are now in place. If things go badly, will we, the American people, do the same? If we do, we shall commit the ultimate injustice, for the responsibility really belongs to us. The men who now hold office are eminently qualified. They head institutions that have survived the test of time. Most important, those institutions are behaving precisely as we, the voters, have demanded that they act.

In Defense of Modern Decisionmakers

As an innoculation against this scapegoating process, we should establish that our current decisionmakers are neither irresponsible nor foolish, nor ignorant nor impotent, for they patently are none of those things. To do that convincingly, we need to take a close look at who those decisionmakers are and how they operate. While it is probably an exaggeration to personify the decisionmaking apparatus of a country in the personality of a single individual, the complexities of individual human strengths, weaknesses, biases, and objectives often closely mimic those of the systems in which they operate.

Three men, who over their careers have risen to the top of their fields in their respective nations, exemplify the various decisionmaking models around the world. They are the economic puppetmasters. In this book we shall give them nicknames—the contrarian, the mandarin, and the historian—which also reflect the paradigms or the systems they represent. Each of these men, Alan Greenspan, chairman of the U.S. Federal Reserve, Eisuke Sakakibara, vice minister of the Japanese Ministry of Finance, and Helmut Kohl, former chancellor of Germany, have been the key players in the world economy as the millennium approaches.

Greenspan, the contrarian, is the product of two distinctly American markets for ideas: the political market of Washington and the financial market of New York. He has been a quintessentially successful entrepreneur in both. Sakakibara, the mandarin, conquered the Japanese academic system, graduating at the institutional top of a system that has been labeled the educational equivalent of hell in the stress that it places on students. He then went on to rise to the very pinnacle of the Japanese bureaucracy, not known for its tolerance of either the timid or the foolish. Helmut Kohl, the historian, was the longest-serving elected chancellor in the history of Germany, until losing office in September 1998. His years of electoral success were matched by a mastery of statecraft that is historically exceptional: he managed to reunite a country physically divided for nearly a half century by the most powerful armies on earth. He did so without firing a single shot and on terms that can only be described as his own. No, these men, and those they tolerate around them, are not fools.

Nor is it reasonable to assume that these men, or the coterie of individuals around them, are ignorant of global events. This is a world of instantaneous global communications. Greenspan sits with two computers on his desk from which he can glean any price for any currency, stock, or bond anywhere, as well as the latest news headlines from the wire services. He has a small television nearby to get a physical picture of events and arrives two hours before Board meetings to pore over at least four newspapers. Should any of that fail to bring him the information he needs, he has a staff of hundreds that is recruited exclusively from the top graduate schools of the country.

Sakakibara sits facing a tote board high on the wall—roughly three feet by eight feet in size—from which he can observe price fluctuations from anywhere in his office. Like Greenspan, he is supported by a bureaucracy that recruits only the top university graduates. Kohl, like many other of the world's political leaders, dispensed with the computer and the instantaneous price updates. But the television, which provides the same view of the world as his electorate receives, is politically indispensable. As in the U.S. Federal Reserve and the Japanese Ministry of Finance, the men and women who serve the chancellor in the bureaucracy are among the best and the brightest the nation can produce. So it would also be unreasonable in the extreme to view those men as either ill-informed or poorly advised.

Continuing down our list of potential failings, one also cannot say that these men, as individuals, lack power. Certainly, they are not autocrats. But Greenspan is said to occupy a position second only to that of the president of the United States. Indeed, one of the president's campaign advisers, James Carville, was complaining because many of the policies he espoused were vetoed on the grounds that the bond market would not like them. Carville said he hoped to be resurrected as the bond market,[13] which in turn, waits with bated breath for the very next syllable to be uttered by Greenspan. By implication of this White House insider, Greenspan is at least as powerful as the president's advisers, if not the president himself. As chairman of the Board of Governors and the Federal Open Market Committee, he has never lost a vote on monetary policy, nor even really come close to losing a vote.

Sakakibara, like Greenspan, has been known to move markets with a mere sentence. Unlike Greenspan, he has shown little reticence in doing so. Nor can one underestimate the powers of the former chancellor of Germany, who, by virtue of his position as chairman of the Christian Democratic Union Party, headed a coalition that controlled a guaranteed majority in the lower house of the German Parliament.

Not only does none of these men lack power, intellect, or information, none of these men, or the institutions they head, has so far failed in the missions assigned them. Far from it. Alan Greenspan has presided over a decline in U.S. inflation and unemployment that is unprecedented in American history. The Federal Reserve is the preeminent macroeconomic institution on the planet, and Greenspan's own credibility and prestige are at an all-time high. Eisuke Sakakibara's pronouncements on the foreign exchange value of the yen have a credibility that one can earn only by multiple successes at picking its prospective level. Helmut Kohl succeeded both in reuniting his country in an alliance with the West and in linking Germany inextricably closer to the European Union. By most standards of success, these men not only have attained lofty positions personally but have used those positions in a manner that their predecessors could only admire.

If it is not recklessness, ignorance, or a lack of information or power that can explain current events, what can? We can dismiss the reasoned underpinnings of any scapegoating theory, but we still run into what psychologists call the "just-world theory." Most of us believe that bad things simply don't happen—and especially that bad things don't happen to us personally owing simply to the randomness of life. Instead, we seek a reason. If these individuals are such successes, why do we face even the possibility of a global economic crisis?

The answer lies not with the individuals involved. Powerful in their own right, the individuals elevated to responsible positions in those systems are in fact the servants of the systems in which they operate. They are, therefore, constrained to pursue objectives that are not necessarily the same ones that are most likely to avert a crisis.

Thus, this book will suggest that it is not these individuals' shortcomings but the limitations inherent in the decisionmaking systems in which they operate that can potentially lead to global problems. Economic management is not, and cannot be, unlimited in its scope. If that were not the case, the Berlin Wall would never have fallen, for omniscient and omnipresent control was what Communism was supposed to be all about. Instead of celebrating democratic capitalism, we would be celebrating the triumphant efficiencies of bureaucratic central planning.

So "blaming the system" is not right, either. In a sense, doing so is no more useful than finding an individual to name as "scapegoat." The system, with all its flaws and weaknesses, is the way it is because we have chosen it, by trial and error, as the least-worst alternative: "The fault, dear Brutus, is not in our stars, but in ourselves."[14]

The Systems Bequeathed by History

Greenspan the contrarian, Sakakibara the mandarin, and Kohl the historian are the quintessential representatives of their systems because their personalities embody the traits that the world's various governing systems demanded. In turn, these governing systems are successful improvisations from the crises that created them: depression, global war, and cold war. They are the way they are for the most pragmatic of reasons: they filled society's need at that time. As a result, each role was demanded by, or at least had its continued existence sanctioned by, the democratic institutions of their respective countries, even though, in many respects, the role being demanded had undemocratic aspects. Democracies demanded those institutions and tolerated their undemocratic natures because they solved a problem for which no other solution was offered.

The contrarian was the product of an Anglo-Saxon wish for economic stabilization, a product of the Great Depression. But, by its very nature, stabilization requires a contrarian—someone to act in a way contrary to that of the majority. If a society's stabilizer is within the public sector, that creates a fundamental conflict between the stabilizer's doing its proper job and the wishes of democratic government. Alan Greenspan is successful at his job because he found a way of taking unpopular actions without arousing sufficient wrath to cause elected officials to curtail his power.

That is a remarkable achievement. So impressive, in fact, that many societies around the globe sought to create domestic Alan Greenspans and failed. As a result, many chose to hire the real thing—by pegging their currencies to the U.S. dollar. As we shall see, that expedient action often proved only temporarily successful. Currency arrangements designed to import the monetary discipline of others are unsustainable unless governments are also willing to take actions to bring their economies into line with monetary realities. Where that did not occur, the seeds of crisis became deeply planted. The challenge of creating successful stabilizing institutions—a global coterie of contrarians—is one facing not just Anglo-Saxon voters but all the economies of the world.

The mandarin in his most undiluted form was largely the product of centuries of Asian political development. Confucius extolled the virtues of the educated bureaucrat governing in concert with other like-minded souls in the name of the emperor. But conquering armies also easily coopted the model to meet their own objectives. Certainly, the British governance of Hong Kong (and earlier of India) was compatible with that model. Of more direct relevance to our current story was the relation of that model to MacArthur's occupation of Japan. Although it was among the most benign occupations in military history, the political institutions MacArthur left behind based their legitimacy on his writ, not on a popular mandate.

Some advantages offset that lack of legitimacy. The capacity of a mandarinate to gather and process information, mobilize financial capital, and stimulate the growth of human capital gave it a potential edge in this process. An otherwise poor electorate might therefore gratefully give its democratic blessing to a mandarinate, despite its undemocratic characteristics. Furthermore, the mandarin is not just ensconced in power in East Asia. Americans and Europeans will easily recognize his function in political guarantees of "cradle to grave" security in the arms of the nanny state. But after fifty years of elections, even a mandarinate governs with democratic legitimacy, although it is by no means itself democratic.

The historian possesses the most democratic persona, at least superficially. The motivating forces behind his governance are not just personal history but the history of his nation. The personal tragedies in his own life story may have shaped his objectives and motives, but that story is one shared by millions. Unfortunately, history is ultimately written in grand designs, and grand designs are not easily made by the direct consent of millions, but by a relative few. Kohl the historian was a preeminent builder of political coalitions, but, in practice, the coalitions that he built were often coalitions of "princes," not of people, because that is what history demands. Further, the focus of a system based on a reaction to history is by definition backward-looking. It is designed to make sure that the European past is not also Europe's future. But Kohl and his given set of talents were what the people of Germany chose. He, his successors, and their counterparts in Europe have the democratic legitimacy to make the choices they do.

Democratic Triumph—Democratic Default

In America a president who promised to reverse the international focus of his predecessor and deal with our day-to-day problems was generally hugely popular despite a vast array of scandals. Similarly, Japanese voters, for reasons we shall examine later, continuously reelected the status quo. Even their surprise vote against the long-ruling Liberal Democratic Party in July 1998 still left the LDP in charge. The German public elected Chancellor Kohl four times. Now, in the midst of crisis, that may be changing. The ruling parties of Japan and Germany lost elections, and President Clinton seems in serious trouble. In this age of democracy, it is not in the hands of the contrarian, the mandarin, or the historian to redefine the institutional mission of government. It is in the hands of the people. Things are the way they are because, as voters, we wanted them that way. It may be a sad commentary that we voters wait for things to fall apart before we opt for change.

The historic irony of the current crisis is deeper. Politically, we discover that just at the moment when democracy seems triumphant around the globe, popular interest in the affairs of government is at a low ebb, and our distaste for government soars. Today's economic crisis is inextricably linked to a crisis in democratic confidence. We see widespread estrangement of electorates from the institutions that we have created to guarantee our liberty and our hard-won peace. Trust in government's ability to solve problems is clearly ebbing, after a century of accumulating state power. Voter turnout is plummeting in nearly every established democracy. In the United States the turnout fell from 63 percent in 1960 to 49 percent in 1996. The decline in Japan was substantial: from 71 percent to 60 percent over the same time period. Over a comparable period of time, turnout has fallen in England by 12 percent, in France by 19 percent, in Germany by 20 percent, and in Italy by 9 percent.[15]

Why? It may be the case that we, the individuals who comprise those electorates, do not appreciate the variety of our options. Usually the choices are at the margin, a little bit more of this, a little bit less of that. Only rarely do we have truly decisive choices, and having made the big decisions, the rest pretty much fall into place. Consider the case of Italy. Professor Marco Vitale of Bocconi University argues:

> Italy has really only had one election. It was in 1946. The choice was whether we wanted to be governed by the Communists, and to the surprise of many, the Communists lost. After that decision to stick with the West, we really only had one option, because the big choice had already been made.[16]

Voters around the world may well feel that, as in Italy, the important choices have already been made in some previous election and that participation in the current one is not worth the effort. That really reflects a satisfaction with the existing order, a willingness to let the contrarian, the mandarin, and the historian continue to lead.

Politicians may also be compliant in this process and by so doing encourage us to believe that big changes are not possible. In the United States one of the key questions in polls indicating support for the president is whether he "understands problems of people like [me]." This desire to have one's national leadership concerned about day-to-day problems may lead the political establishment to narrow its focus. Successful politicians will devote their energy and political resources to keeping cigarette vending machines away from children or deciding how many days someone with a certain ailment should spend in the hospital. They will avoid tackling big issues that may not be so easily soluble and for which finding a solution may not be what the voters say they care about.

We seem to base our electoral choices on relatively minor matters and not on affairs of state—what the political consultant, Dick Morris, refers to as "bite-size" or "incremental" achievements. In an October 1994 poll, voters said, according to Morris, that they were "prepared to believe in [Clinton's] smaller achievements and these are . . . more than enough to move their votes back to [Clinton]."[17]

As voters, we have rewarded those we elect for ignoring the big picture of global events and paying attention to our personal concerns. But we may be about to pay a price. Many in Anglo-American policy circles seem to have been caught daydreaming. We may have allowed our leaders to be lulled into a self-indulgent preoccupation with our own success. Most alarmingly, we have permitted our own political institutions to neglect the big picture and, in the process, have become driven by overnight polls and focus groups. We forgot that government can do only a finite number of things well at any one time. And in the global context, there are some things that only the American government, and particularly the American president, can do. The economic principle of opportunity cost—by spending time on one set of concerns we are, of necessity, neglecting others—may come back to haunt us.

As Brad DeLong, former Clinton aide, now a professor at the University of California at Berkeley, said in a *Wall Street Journal* story, "[T]he late 1990s may resemble the late 1920s, when a 'wave of currency crises and devaluations that destroyed the financial systems came as a complete surprise' to policy makers."[18] DeLong, from his insider perspective, gives one possible answer to the question about whether *they* saw it coming: they didn't. Just as in the 1920s, the political process was still committed to "a chicken in every pot," in addition to two cars in every garage.

The main reason our systems are the way they are is that they have worked well over a long period of time. They won the cold war. Today we must realize that we achieved this triumph of capitalist democracy because it created institutions that could survive a long-term battle with Communism. That is a tribute to the system. But being better than the alternatives does not mean being the "best."

Today, we must understand that some of these institutions were compromises: democratic institutions that were less than democratic; supposedly capitalist institutions that relied on rigged markets. Democrats and capitalists accepted those compromises for five decades because democracy and capitalism were on a war footing. Today, these vestigial institutions remain as relics of the cold war, which, along with Communism, should be relegated to the dustbin of history. They stand there ready to fight the battles of the late twentieth century but are incapable of leading the world to a truly capitalist and democratic twenty-first century. Our societies and systems still possess vast quantities of political capital and goodwill. The test of them in the present situation is whether they can move beyond their cold war roles to transcend their historical mission.

The Ultimate Historic Irony

This discussion of our institutions and the individuals who lead them highlights the ultimate irony in our current situation. We begin with individuals of remarkable competence who perform admirable jobs in their assigned roles. We then find that these roles, though not democratic, have a democratic legitimacy well grounded in historical success. Finally, we note that these individuals and the institutions they head have just triumphed in a global conflict lasting at least half a century over a competing model. Democracy and capitalism, the unifying political and economic principles of the American contrarian, the Japanese mandarin, and the German historian, have triumphed at just the moment that the world's democracies find themselves in crisis.

The triumph of democracy in the fight against communism has left us with a democratic dilemma. Only the voters have the option of creating a new mission statement for their governing institutions, one that takes into account the changing world around us. But the voters are in no mood to issue such a mission. There's little understanding of what that mission statement should look like.

Five decades of record-setting economic performance, victory in the cold war, and talk of "miracle economies" and "New Ages" have led to a sense of security that is incompatible with requiring change. This means that our fates are in the hands of systems that we inherited and did not choose—systems created at another time to meet other challenges. That fact is politically what puts us all most at risk in the current crisis. The global triumph of democracy has coincided with a democratic "default" on how to proceed.

Overcoming that default is the real challenge facing our political leaders. Our economic puppetmasters are starting to find that their strings are getting tangled up. Prosperity in a new century will require action to get them untangled. One must hope that as in the past, democracy has the ability to produce leaders who will take the necessary steps, for as former Prime Minister Margaret Thatcher often said, "There is no alternative."

2

The Contrarian at the Center

> *[I]deas of economists and political philosophers, both when they are right and when they are wrong, are more powerful than is commonly understood. Indeed the world is ruled by little else.*
>
> —*John Maynard Keynes*[1]

In June 1997 in Denver, Colorado, the leaders of the United States acted as rather rude hosts to the annual world summit of the seven industrial nations—the G-7, to which Russia has been added. American participants couldn't stop lecturing their guests on the success of the American economy. At the summit, one American official rather impolitely described the United States as the "world's only economic superpower."[2] While such breast beating is almost certainly inappropriate diplomatically, one of the reasons that the claims were so impolite was that they had a ring of truth. America (and its philosophical cousin, the United Kingdom) seemed to have learned some lessons that Japan and the nations of continental Europe could usefully adopt.

Learning is never easy, and the lessons of political economy can be particularly painful. The current Anglo-Saxon economic success is all the more stunning because just two decades ago America and the United Kingdom were among the economies about which informed opinion was the most pessimistic. America suffered under record-setting peacetime inflation and high unemployment, while economic life in the United Kingdom was dimming visibly under electrical production cutbacks produced by a nationwide coal strike. When two of the most dull students suddenly move to the head of the class, it is quite natural to sit up and take notice.

One man—Alan Greenspan—has presided over most of the period during which America has regained its global leadership. Appointed in 1987, he has seen America through a sharp, but very short, stock market crash. He, in large measure, oversaw the reorganization of the American banking system, which had problems similar to those now faced in Japan. His conduct of monetary policy during the banking overhaul turned a potentially protracted economic slowdown into a short and very mild recession. Furthermore, he has presided over an economy that has brought both unemployment and inflation to thirty-year lows. In a world in which so much is going wrong, a good place to start is by visiting a man who has gotten so much right.

In the 2000 block of Constitution Avenue sits yet another of Washington's many imposing marble structures. The close observer would detect that the exterior is a bit less shabby than the half-vacant Interior Department building next door and that the grounds are a bit better maintained. But there is no outward sign that in this building is the center of American macroeconomic stabilization policy.

Anonymity suits the Board of Governors of the Federal Reserve just fine. You will rarely see tourists snapping photos and certainly no queue waiting for a tour. There aren't any school buses outside that have brought in their precious cargo to get a bit of a real-life civics lesson. In fact, it is sometimes possible to find a parking space on the street, a feat that is truly rare in the nation's capital. It's not that the Board actually prevents tourists from seeing their government at work. The Board actually provides a very nice tour, and the grounds outside are certainly suitable for a photo opportunity. Let's just say the Fed doesn't advertise, and the American public by and large missed that chapter in their civics text (if it was there in the first place) about the functions of the nation's central bank.

This lack of knowledge is reinforced by the tour buses that go by outside spouting their fifteen-second sound bite about the Fed. It's usually wrong. Some tell visitors to America's capital that the Fed is where their money is stored in giant vaults. It isn't. In fact, the Board of Governors building is probably the only building in the Fed system that doesn't store any money. Tourists wishing to see stacks of money should visit any of the twelve district banks spread around the country or even one of the twenty-five branches of those district banks. Or, to see the money printed, visitors should go to another giant stone building down on 14th Street—the Bureau of Engraving and Printing, which isn't even managed by the Fed. Absent stacks of money, the Fed building is just another office building from a tourist point of view, and the tour guides quickly turn to more interesting subjects, like the Vietnam Memorial, across the street and set back along the 2100 block of Constitution Avenue.

But the view from the Fed is a key one for understanding the developing global economic crisis and the limits on what current economic management is and is not capable of controlling. The Fed building has been likened to a temple,[3] and a visit there involves a ritual that can only reinforce that perception. The guard will check your name at the C Street entrance, and you will enter a hall that would make a Greek god proud. As in any temple, the intended architectural effect is to instill silence and reverence in the guest. High above the visitor is his objective—the entrance to the hall containing the offices of the Board of Governors. To get there he must scale either of the thirty-two-step staircases that flank the sides of the hall. Silence is a must unless one wishes to make his every syllable reverberate off the nearly naked marble walls. The visitor who makes it to the top then enters "The Oval," where a guard will direct him to a large sitting room on the left.

There, you will be treated most courteously by either Pam or Diane. They will take your coat, get you coffee, and chat about the day's events if you like. Or, if you prefer, you can sit and read any number of newspapers of record displayed on the coffee table. But do sit down. This is not the hurried pace of Wall Street. It is not the frantic bustle of the White House or Capitol Hill. Here, at the intersection point of politics and economics, time moves with the slow, deliberate pace of an eighty-five-year-old institution that has long ago learned that deliberate actions work best. After all, what's the rush when the lags between your actions and their effects are best described as "long and variable"?

It is not that the Fed isn't punctual. Board meetings begin at 10:00 A.M., and governors and staff entering at 10:01 A.M. will find the door closed. Latecomers are not formally reprimanded but given the distinct impression of interrupting already ongoing business. A new governor will quickly learn that it pays to arrive around 9:58 A.M.

Nor will you as a guest be asked to wait long. The businesslike pace of the institution will ensure that you will be in your meeting with the chairman at the appointed hour. You will be ushered down the hall, past the boardroom into the first open door on your left where Anne, his secretary of many years, will say, "You can go in now," and signal you to proceed through the one closed door in her three-door office.

For the uninitiated, entering that door is a bit of a mystical experience. Here sits a man whose job has been described as the second most powerful in America. The office is tasteful but nothing spectacular. It has an L-shaped work area with a desk facing the front of the room and a computer table with multiple screens at the side. The desk is invariably cluttered, the result of hundreds of pages of incoming documents and memoranda that the chairman must process each week. Newspapers add to the clutter. Greenspan reads not just the *Washington Post* and the *New York Times*, but the financial press and even the industry publications that focus on the latest news in the auto, steel, or banking industries. The office has a small half-bath and a modest walk-in closet, two large floor-to-ceiling windows, a desk, and a sitting area. In the kind of logic that makes sense only after you've been at the Fed a while, the chairman's office is almost the same as that of each of the other governors, with a single notable exception, which proves that the chairman really is *primus inter pares*. He, and he alone, has a door that leads right into the boardroom.

When I mention to Greenspan that he is probably considered the best Fed chairman in history, he shifts uncomfortably in his chair and puts on the customary grimace that signals that he doesn't like the way the conversation is going.[4] But Greenspan has been successful enough to have been appointed by three different presidents. He has been appointed by both Republican and Democratic presidents and confirmed by both Democratic and Republican Senates. Interestingly, he has managed to appease both parties at the same time, with the president appointing him always of a different party from the Senate that confirmed him. His modest answer to all of this is that "I was just in the right place at the right time. Someone like Volcker went through a really tough time."

Alan Greenspan is the thirteenth chairman of the Federal Reserve.

To most, he is a riddle wrapped in a mystery inside an enigma. This was Churchill's view of Russia,[5] and indeed a whole industry of Fed watchers has emerged, like the Kremlin watchers of old, to parse every syllable coming from insiders. In that regard, Greenspan is the insider of all insiders and has developed a style of sentence construction that leaves the Fed watcher with plenty of syllables, not to mention whole clauses, to parse.

He is usually described as an intensely private man, even shy. But few men have a private history that melds so seamlessly into their public personae. It is the job of the Fed chairman to be above the political fray of Washington, yet sensitive to its every nuance. That may seem a paradox, but it is one that Greenspan, in many ways a paradoxical man, accomplishes by using a powerful analytic detachment that allows him an objective view of the economic and political events that swirl around him.

How does one detach himself from politics in the heart of the nation's capital? How can anyone detach himself from the economy when every news commentator links his behavior to the economy's performance? The starting point for Greenspan is information: "We have sources of information not available generally. Companies and member banks, for example, won't speak to their competitors, but they speak to us."

Greenspan's point about information is revealing on a number of fronts. First, it debunks one of the bases for the scapegoating that we discussed in the previous chapter—that policymakers simply don't know what is happening. They do, perhaps better than anyone else. A widespread claim among the Fed's critics is that it operates in an ivory tower. Perhaps, but it is the best–plugged-in ivory tower in existence.

The second revealing point about Greenspan's reliance on information is that *he* seeks out an objective confirmation of his superior position to make judgment calls. Having enormous power is a huge responsibility. Some men shoulder the burden of responsibility simply on the basis of their ego. For Greenspan that is not enough. Access to superior information justifies holding superior responsibility.

The Fed's relatively omniscient position helps give it some immunity from external criticism as well. Critics often cite the templelike qualities of the place as useful to maintaining the aura. Perhaps, but the aura is real, if in my view, slightly exaggerated. The view in the market that the Fed is about to move because "it knows something we don't" is regrettably widespread.

At times that view reaches utterly irrational levels. I remember taking a call on the day of the New Hampshire primary in 1992 from a reporter who had heard that the Fed was about to cut rates immediately. Why? The Fed *knew* that Pat Buchanan was running close to then-President Bush in the Republican primary votes cast so far that day and "needed to give Bush some help." That rumor missed the point on so many different assumptions that all I could do was laugh. But the most amazing part of the whole affair was the belief that the Fed "knew" how people had marked the ballots that were at that time still stuffed in ballot boxes 450 miles away.

Complete omniscience is not given to man, even to Federal Reserve officials. Yet a whole industry has sprung up to track down every rumor like the one about the New Hampshire primary. The Fed knows a lot of details that inform its decision and, as we shall see, improve its timing. But as for acting "out of the blue" because of some inside knowledge, Greenspan was clear: "It may occur sometime that we have no choice but to act precisely because we know something the rest of the world does not. But that has not happened since I've been here."

The Need for a Contrarian

Information may be necessary for achieving detachment, but the detachment is essential because the job Greenspan performs requires one not only to ignore the winds of political and economic opinion but to lean against them actively. The job of chairman of the Federal Reserve Board of Governors has evolved into being a contrarian—one whose views actively run contrary to established wisdom. Greenspan did not establish that role. Many of his predecessors—Arthur Burns with his pipe and air of academic detachment, Paul Volcker with his long cigar and immovable frame—also cultivated it. But they did not create the role, either. The role of contrarian is deeply embedded in the culture of American political economy, and no Fed chairman could successfully do anything to change that. Different actors may play the role differently, but the script is an unchanging one, written by the American economic experience of the twentieth century.

Central to that experience is the Great Depression of the 1930s and the resulting rise of the economic thinking of one man—John Maynard Keynes, who established the contrarian role for government. Keynes may posthumously need a publicity agent. He is widely perceived by his critics as a starry-eyed idealist, an egghead, if you will. In practice, he took a remarkably pragmatic view of the events surrounding him, actively pushing for realistic government policies against existing ideologues. He correctly foretold the likely consequences of the punitive reparations leveled against Germany after the First World War and opposed them. He made a fortune in the markets as an arbitrageur. He offered sensible advice at the end of his life for creating institutions to help rebuild the shattered world economy. While no one has a perfect record, the investor or policymaker of the first half of the twentieth century would have done much better heeding Keynes's advice than ignoring it.

Of course, what he is most known for is his equally sensible advice to governments confronted by the Great Depression. The business cycle had been a primary focus of Anglo-Saxon economic thinking, at least since the days of Alfred Marshall at the end of the nineteenth century. That intellectual tradition had always ascribed an important role to pseudopsychological factors such as business confidence and anticipation of the future. Keynes famously (or infamously) characterized those psychological factors as "animal spirits."[6] It was an interesting choice of words; one that won Keynes both widespread support in the elite intellectual classes and widespread mistrust among the business classes he so effectively put down.

One does not know whether Keynes's choice of words was a careless reflection of his class bias or was more deliberate. The intellectual and policymaking classes interpreted it as an appeal for action. After all, if "animal spirits" could be depressed among the business and commercial classes, then the more observant policymaking class could compensate through increased government spending. That spending could offset the diminished demand from business for investment and maintain economywide demand and employment. A successful intellectual entrepreneur would certainly not shy away from flattering the customers. The class biases of the upper ranks of the British civil service and their New Deal cousins were certainly known to Keynes, and classifying the business community in a lower order certainly fit.

Whatever the language, Keynes was making a more subtle economic point known to economists as the fallacy of composition. Put simply, it states that what may be a rational action for each individual in society may be counterproductive for society as a whole when all individuals act in the same manner. For example, when a businessman confronts falling sales, it is eminently rational for him to cut back on production and lay off workers. When all businessmen confront falling sales and each cuts production and lays off workers, household incomes fall, sales fall still further, and a vicious downward spiral ensues for the entire economy.

What is needed is for some economic agent to intervene to halt that process. In most markets, speculators usually play that role. "Buy low, sell high," the expression goes, or, "Buy on the cannon, sell on the trumpets." The assorted axioms for success in markets all involve some version of doing the opposite of what the mob is doing.

At that level, all Keynes was doing was urging government to act like a contrarian, to do for society what he did for his university's portfolio when he managed it as a speculator. In markets, successful speculators—those who buy low and sell high—tend to stabilize prices. Having government increase spending in a bust and decrease spending in a boom is an eminently sensible recipe to any pragmatic policymaker. Economies, like markets, need contrarians to provide stability and balance. Mob psychology, left unchecked, is a prescription for extreme variations in market performance.

Keynes maintained that the total amount of demand in an economy was inherently unstable, animal spirits being what they are. The discerning policymaker, above the fray, was to detect any shortfalls in demand caused by drops in consumption, or particularly in private investment, and compensate for them by creating public-sector demand. Keynes's goal was *stabilization,* and to achieve that goal required the public policymaker to act in a manner contrary to the private forces around him.

Keynes's minimal prescription was public-sector spending. In a famous critique of policy he said:

> If the Treasury were to fill old bottles with banknotes, bury them at suitable depths in disused coal mines which are then filled up to the surface with town rubbish, and leave it to private enterprise on well

> tried principles of laissez-faire to dig the notes up again, there need be no more unemployment and, with the help of the repercussions, the real income of the community and its capital wealth also, would probably become a good deal greater than it actually is. It would, indeed, be more sensible to build houses and the like; but if there are political and practical difficulties in the way of this, the above would be better than nothing.[7]

The Fed acts as a stabilizer, as a contrarian, by controlling the price of money. By doing so it is not "filling old bottles with banknotes," but by affecting the cost of borrowing to finance economic activity, the Fed is endeavoring to stimulate more sensible things, like building houses, to use Keynes's terminology. The Fed's role in that is now central to stabilization policy. The key fact is that, unlike in Keynes's day, policymakers like Greenspan, not automatic mechanisms like the gold standard, affect the price of money. As Greenspan says, "If you had a gold standard, there would be no need for monetary policy. When we intervene to affect interest rates, we are acting because we have a system of fiat money, and there is no automatic mechanism to constrain it."

Fiat money, money by law or decree, "is legal tender for all debts, public and private," as it says on our currency. That currency, Federal Reserve notes, are the liabilities of the Fed. The Fed decides on a target rate of interest for overnight money and buys and sells government bonds paid for by those liabilities. If the economy is booming, the Fed raises the target rate, selling government bonds to take back some of the money it has issued. If the economy is falling, the Fed issues more money to buy more bonds, thus lowering the overnight rate of interest.

Money creation is an admittedly indirect way of affecting the economy. Keynes preferred direct government spending. But back in the 1970s it became increasingly obvious that direct spending measures weren't working well.

In retrospect, where this otherwise successful recipe probably went wrong was on its reliance on government and the political process to play the role of contrarian. In short, politics got in the way of policies that depended crucially on their timing. Perhaps more fundamentally, it may be possible for an elite to act as a counterbalance to the prevailing sentiment but not a democratic government. Institutionally, the kind of mandarinate that the British civil service had become in the Victorian era might work as contrarians—hence Keynes's view. In modern times, however, politicians actively adopt the prejudices of mob psychology to win elections, and the contrarians are the losers.

Keynes's reliance on elected politicians to be the contrarians in the economy, while inspired in the desperate days of the 1930s, was too utopian a solution to work in the long run. Government faces some practical limitations in its ability to act, all of which damage the timing of its policies.

Government, particularly American government, is not designed to act quickly. First, it takes time for decisionmakers to realize what is going on. Economists refer to that as a "recognition lag." Typically, a recession is defined as two consecutive quarters of negative growth. The data for any single quarter are typically released four weeks after the end of the quarter. Thus, to recognize a recession officially would mean waiting, typically, seven months until after it began. By contrast, the average length of postwar recessions in the United States is only eleven months. So, by the time the politicians recognized a problem, it would be too late to act.

Next comes a decision lag. In the United States, the budget procedure is a textbook in tedium. The agencies draw up plans in the autumn of each year that the president approves in late December. He submits those plans in January, and with luck they will be implemented by the start of the fiscal year the next October. Thus, in the United States, a typical recession could have begun and ended between the time agencies make budget plans and Congress appropriates the necessary funds.

Finally, once a tax or spending change is announced, it generally takes effect over an entire year. That is known as an "implementation lag." Tax changes generally take place through paycheck adjustments (withholding). The impact on the economy is generally slow to materialize. Similarly, spending programs rarely put the appropriated funds out the door immediately. Complicated bidding and contracting procedures usually must be followed. Typically, the funds are disbursed over the course of the project being undertaken, which may consume the entire fiscal year or even longer. Thus, the median dollar of funds in an intentionally countercyclical policy move is usually disbursed six months into the fiscal year. By then, the recession may well be over.

How does Greenspan get around those problems? First, he is a natural skeptic: "I'm not wedded to a Keynesian model that you learn in

Economics 101. When the economy doesn't behave exactly the way the model predicts, I disaggregate the numbers." Of course, not everyone can have the confidence to form a judgment independent of what economic models are saying. For Greenspan, it is a bit like his faith in his superior access to information. As a basis for his independent judgment, Greenspan credits a long and varied career:

> I've spent all of my working life observing how the economy functions. I was at various times a specialist in virtually every major industry and generally knowledgeable about the remainder. When you go through every industry over your lifetime, you should know how the system works.

In short, Greenspan can try to overcome the "recognition" lag by following not only the government's data, but the tone of individual markets. That is what all those industry publications are for.

Greenspan's grasp of the facts can be a bit overwhelming to both the staff and his colleagues. I remember one instance when spring floods were making many of the bridges on the Mississippi River unusable. At the time of the weekly Board of Governors meeting, the U.S. economy was literally linked together by a single bridge. Greenspan not only knew the location of the bridge, but also the various reroutings that could be used to get merchandise there. Those types of facts fit naturally into the mind of a man who studies statistics on boxcar loadings at all the major terminals in the country. On another occasion, he humbled the staff steel expert into silence by discussing the daily output of the various Midwestern steel mills.

But Greenspan does not rely on private-sector sources alone. As he said in our formal interview, "Over the years I've learned the National Income Accounts backwards and forwards. In fact, I used to teach a class in it." This also shows up in Board meetings. He frequently instructs the staff on the nature of the seasonal adjustment involved in a particular data series. He knows what is right with it and what is wrong with it. The staff members whose job it is to follow that segment of the economy just sit there taking notes.

In short, Greenspan's mind acts like a computer model of the economy that is based on an industry-by-industry re-creation of what is actually going on. That helps him play the Keynesian contrarian without some of the problems of lags that his counterparts on the fiscal side of government may possess. For Greenspan, whose mind is a real-time model of the economy, there is no such thing as a "recognition lag."

That a brain wired in such a way is a rare, if not unique, combination of nature and nurture may give us a clue to Greenspan's shyness. One of Greenspan's comments in our formal interview summed up the self-image of a man who knows his strengths and his weaknesses and is content with both:

> Of course, there's also the fact that I've lived enough years to have had time to accumulate a lot of information. And, I'm not senile yet. Of course, I may not be able to remember the name of someone I just met. But, when it comes to numbers and statistics, it just sticks.

Greenspan's job is also well designed to overcome the "decision lag" that hamstrings fiscal policy in America. The Board of Governors can raise or lower the discount rate at which it lends to member banks at any time. The Federal Open Market Committee can raise or lower the "fed funds target rate," which is the rate at which banks lend to each other on an overnight basis at any time, although the Fed usually does so only at meetings held every six or seven weeks.

As far as prevailing at those meetings, Greenspan rarely has any trouble. As he noted in our conversation, the people on the Board are of a similar mind-set. That does not mean they all agree politically. But all are problem solvers by orientation. Esoteric and theoretical abstractions exist, but when it comes to a concrete vote, they rarely play a role. On average, there is less than one dissenter per meeting—out of twelve voting members.

Has the chairman ever been swayed by his colleagues? Well, as a good economist, yes and no:

> It's unlikely that I would be caught off base at Federal Open Market Committee meetings in the sense that I see things totally differently from everybody else. Like everyone else, I read the Beige Book and evaluate the same statistics. But it has happened that certain members have said certain things about what is going on that hadn't occurred to me. I do not recall having changed from yes to no but certainly [it] moved me from symmetric to asymmetric and back-and-forth in the meeting.

Furthermore, policy is implemented immediately upon a vote of the Board or the Federal Open Market Committee. So, when it comes to the three lags that bedevil policymakers, Greenspan, recognizing what's going on and deciding to act, is in an enviable position. At the Fed, a real-time monitoring of data eliminates recognition lags. Frequent meetings sharply cut decision lags, and because policy is changed immediately, implementation lags do not exist. That does not make the Fed perfect. It takes time for interest rate changes to alter the economy. But, to the extent that lags are controllable, the Fed has the elected branches of government beat hands down.

Congress may well recognize that fact. That is the reason it created the Fed. A story that has made its way into Fed lore about House Banking Chairman Wright Patman and Fed Chairman William McChesney Martin provides a further piece of evidence. Patman, as a good Texas populist, could give some stemwinding speeches blasting the Fed as an elite institution dominated by bankers. But he never let any anti-Fed legislation out of his committee. Over lunch, Martin asked him why. Patman allegedly responded, "If we didn't have you to blame, what would we do?"

Politics and the Contrarian

Two more problems with Keynes's reliance on politicians to act as contrarians exist. Both are "political." The major political limitation of relying on politicians to be economic contrarians is that politicians are asymmetric in their preferences and actions. Simply put, politicians will gladly spend to get the economy out of a recession but are less willing to cut spending to prevent a boom from developing. In a boom, not only will politicians adopt mob psychology, but some will struggle to get to the front of the line to lead the mob to even higher expectations. Most important, many politicians will tie their egos and their political careers to the continuing success and excess of the economy. America is now in that situation, with politicians rushing to claim credit for the economy's success. But, when it comes to countercyclical action to cool a booming economy, those politicians are nowhere to be found. The reduction in the U.S. budget deficit has been almost entirely the result of automatic increases in revenue, not discretionary moves by policymakers to try to mitigate the business cycle. In fact, the last discretionary fiscal tightening occurred in 1993, when unemployment was 50 percent higher than at present.[8]

The human emotions that drive markets to excess and propel business cycles into boom and bust are as present in politicians as they are in the rest of humanity. But the linkage in the public mind made by Keynes between public policy and economic performance has actually worsened the excesses of those emotions. Politicians' job performance is now dependent upon the maintenance of good times, even when the times are "too good." The result is a permanent bias of policymakers toward fiscal stimulus.

The other political shortcoming of politicians as contrarians has to do with timing. While politicians' egos do tend to want their entire terms in government to be the best in history, some years are more important than others. In particular, the periods leading up to elections are particularly vital. The economics profession noted the existence of a "political business cycle" more than a quarter century ago. That discovery came during the heyday of Keynesian policy dominance.

The existence of a political business cycle should be of particular concern to advocates of the Keynesian paradigm. In this case, the politicians not only shirk their responsibilities as contrarians, they actively adopt policies that will destabilize the economy to coincide with their election. Neither this "timing" issue nor the "asymmetry" issue mattered back in the 1930s. But both matter crucially for long-term economic management.

Again, Greenspan and the Fed have come to dominate elected government at playing the role of contrarian because they have mastered that political problem. Interestingly, in our interview Greenspan did not mention any of his political skills, which are enormous, when I asked him about the reason for his success. He may never have been elected to any office, but he is without question one of the most successful politicians of the late twentieth century. That is all the more surprising given his political views, which are distinctly libertarian. During the early 1950s, Greenspan was part of Ayn Rand's salon, known somewhat ironically as "The Collective."[9] While he might have shed some of the more extreme egoism of Rand, Greenspan's faith in markets and skepticism about government have remained.

Michael Lewis, in a somewhat critical biographical piece, attributes Greenspan's political success to his ability to bridge "the gap between what universities produced and what the world demanded of an economist." Greenspan became an adviser to Richard Nixon's 1968 campaign but thereafter turned down offers of formal government jobs. Lewis notes: "Most people throw themselves into political campaigns with the vague hope that they will receive an important job in government. Greenspan's interest in Nixon seems to have been more purely principled."[10] To Greenspan, it was one thing to convince those in government to do the right thing, but holding a government job was something else. Later, Greenspan joined the fray and became chairman of the President's Council of Economic Advisers under President Ford. President Reagan tapped him to chair the Social Security Commission, which engineered a difficult bipartisan compromise on Social Security in 1983. Then, in 1987, Reagan appointed him chairman of the Federal Reserve. Both Presidents Bush and Clinton reappointed him. A man trusted by five presidents is not likely to be naïve about political considerations.

In Greenspan's view, handling the politics is actually the hardest part of the job. Although nominally independent, the Fed is the creation of the elected branches of government. They can abolish or alter it as an institution at any time. How does that affect the Fed's behavior? Says Greenspan:

> We are constrained by an unwritten set of rules. From where I sit, one of the toughest jobs is to know exactly where we cross the line. We are a central bank in a democratic society that functions under an existing set of laws. We have technical independence in the sense that there is no body that has the legal capability of rescinding an action we take in the monetary area. But we cannot do things that are totally alien to the conventional wisdom in the professional community. Of course, if we simply look to the conventional wisdom to tell us what to do, we might as well go out of business and have somebody run policy by just conducting a poll.

Not that it would matter, but Greenspan would probably get high marks, if a poll were conducted, assuming the public-at-large knows who he is. Interestingly, he would garner high approval ratings for different reasons from those on which the president must focus. Greenspan doesn't pretend to care about the kind of everyday concerns the ordinary man or woman talks to pollsters about. Instead, Greenspan would score well with the public because he takes his job seriously and does it well. He has faced a variety of challenges and persevered—thereby earning the public confidence.

Most important, he is instinctively the contrarian. In 1987, after he came to office in August, the stock market cracked that October. His reaction was to provide unlimited overnight liquidity to the markets. Then, when the market was safe, he quietly drained that liquidity from the system. In the late 1980s, just as *BusinessWeek* proclaimed the business cycle to be "kinder and gentler,"[11] he led the Fed to a series of interest rate tightenings to offset the overheating economy. In the early 1990s, the United States went through a complete overhaul of its banking regulations, and with it, a credit crunch. Greenspan led the Fed to a historic lowering of official rates and was way ahead of other bank regulators in seeing the pernicious effects of some of the new regulations on the macroeconomy. He then engineered a preemptive tightening in 1994 that calmed building inflationary pressures, and he eased policy in 1995 and 1996 when the economy cooled.

Not only did he not turn over policy to a pollster or to a focus group, he showed leadership by continuously leaning against prevailing sentiment. That kind of political courage is generally lacking in the world. But, if we are going to make the kind of changes we need, it will have to become a trait more valued by electorates, for, as we shall see, Greenspan might have the right temperament to play the role of contrarian, but it is still an open question whether or not he has the right tools to take on the job.

3

Supply Shocks and Creative Destruction

You have to choose [as a voter] between trusting to the natural stability of gold and the natural stability of the honesty and intelligence of the members of the Government. And, with due respect for these gentlemen, I advise you, as long as the Capitalist system lasts, to vote for gold.
—*George Bernard Shaw*[1]

Greenspan's popularity is no doubt earned by his skill. But a dark cloud looms on the horizon. The week of my formal interview with the chairman, both the *Economist* and the *Financial Times* ran articles about the development of a bubble in the U.S. market.[2] Greenspan mentions both in our conversation:

> There are all sorts of parallels to the late 1920s. But you have to be a little careful about the 1929–1932 analogies. The problem is that if actions in 1930 and 1931 were taken differently, we might have had a fairly significant recession, but we would not have had the deep fall that we know as the Great Depression. As to the stock market crash, it could not by itself be blamed for 1932. The effect of wealth destruction on economic conditions is far more complex.

At this point, we reach something close to the limits of the Fed's and Greenspan's ability to act as a contrarian. And it is worth exploring what those limits are. The Fed has one tool—its control over the price of money. That tool must cover a variety of conditions. The Keynesian contrarian, the role Greenspan plays so well, is one who keeps his eyes on the desire of people and businesses to spend. If there are insufficient freight car loadings or if steel ingot production suddenly falls, the most likely culprit is that there aren't enough buyers. If that seems to be the case economywide, the time may have come to cut interest rates to encourage people to buy more and businesses to invest in more plant and equipment. On the other hand, if so many freight cars are being loaded that freight rates are starting to rise or if steel ingot producers are serving only their best customers, it may be time for the contrarian to tighten a bit.

Observation of and policy reaction to those conditions is standard fare at the Fed. But Greenspan is very careful to distinguish between rapid economic growth and "too much" demand: "Basically the domestic economy is now expanding at a very strong pace. But what we need to pay attention to is internal imbalances developing in the economy, with inflation being a symptom." Greenspan's statement that "there are all sorts of parallels to the late 1920s" is what is most intriguing. So is his careful separation of a strong economy from an inflationary one, for what many observers (including Greenspan) think is happening is not the traditional Keynesian cycle based on too little or too much *demand,* but on a *supply*-driven cycle. As we shall see, one of the characteristics of a supply-driven cycle is rapid growth, stable or falling prices, and a booming market for financial assets like stocks and bonds. Many economic historians point to the developments of the late 1920s as an example of another era with our economy driven by a positive supply shock.

Supply shocks are caused by changes in underlying production technology. If the changes are good ones, they involve a lowering of costs. But a lowering of costs can imply other changes in economic behavior that lead to the formation of a financial bubble, trouble in the banking system, and price collapses in certain industries that create regional economic distress, which may grow.

In practice, the process of a supply shift is one of enormous "creative destruction," a term coined by Joseph Schumpeter in 1942.[3] It sorts out those who can adapt to change quickly from those who cannot. It also separates those who experiment too dangerously and take excessive risks from those who are more prudent. This chapter details the ramifications of a supply shock on an economy. It then returns to Chairman Greenspan to see how he thinks about that problem.

The usual guideposts of monetary policy might not have their usual meaning during a supply shock. Creative destruction might cause an increase in the equilibrium real interest rate in a society because private risk factors have increased. That real interest rate is the cost of money after subtracting inflation. In a supply shock, uncertainty increases. So lenders should require a higher return for taking greater risks. In fact, a deliberately stimulative interest rate policy might not work because financial intermediaries such as banks are unwilling to take the risks entailed in lending in the uncertain business environment. We certainly experienced that in the United States in the early 1990s, and Japan suffers from that phenomenon today.

In sum, decisionmaking institutions must pay particular attention to whether or not the economy is enjoying a supply shock or a demand shock. Actions that may be appropriate under normal "demand-driven" conditions might not be appropriate in other circumstances. Certainly, one reason that the economic decisionmaking institutions of our societies are having trouble today is that many institutions continue to focus on demand-side prescriptions in a world in which the supply side is driving the course of economic events.

The starting point for analyzing how policymakers should confront creative destruction is to realize that a supply shock creates an enormous amount of economic uncertainty for workers, firms, and investors. The productive arrangements of a generation may be subject to sudden change. Jobs that seemed secure might suddenly vanish. One can imagine a father's telling his fifteen-year-old son in 1880 that "as long as we have horses, we'll always need blacksmiths." But, if the son had elected to become a blacksmith, he would have found himself unemployed just as his own wife and children relied on him the most. Dad was right, but his premise about the world's still utilizing horses so extensively was faulty. Creative destruction is the market's way of changing economic fundamentals to reflect changes in technology and consumer preferences.

Much of Schumpeter's writing occurred during the first half of the twentieth century, a time of significant creative destruction in both the global and American economies. In the United States the emergence of the automobile and radio brought about profound changes in transportation and communication that allowed a reduction in costs not unlike the one the world has been experiencing lately. In addition, millions of individuals saw their real incomes rise, and with those higher incomes came demands for new and different products.

The result was creative destruction in numerous industries. Frederick Lewis Allen, an astute observer of the 1920s and 1930s, describes the seeming paradox of failure amidst plenty in his 1931 book *Only Yesterday:*

> Not everyone could manage to climb aboard this wagon. Few agricultural raw materials were used in the new economy of automobiles and radios and electricity. And the more efficient the poor farmer became, the more machines he bought to increase his output and thus keep the wolf from the door, the more surely he and his fellows were faced by the specter of overproduction.[4]

Overproduction means falling prices for much of the economy. Obviously, some are beneficiaries of that, but others are losers. One reason grain prices fell so much in the 1920s was the automobile—more cars, fewer horses. A substantial portion of crop production had been used to feed the now-obsolete transportation infrastructure. So not only did crop producers not benefit from the boom in the auto industry, they actually lost out. One sign of supply shocks is a growing disparity between those with stakes in the new, growing sector of the economy and those stuck in the shrinking sector.

Supply Shocks and Capital

The second fact of a supply shock is the need for capital to build the new technology. A supply shock might mean that the existing capital stock is suddenly less competitive in international markets, thereby requiring new capital investment by firms to stay competitive. Or it might be driven entirely by domestic consideration. But suddenly society needs more capital. Of the three ways to get it, none is easy. The lessons of the United States during the 1980s, when our supply shock began, provide some clues as to changes that society might undertake to raise capital.

First, an economy could get rid of rules that prevent its existing capital stock from being used as efficiently as possible. It could have internal barriers to the smooth flow of funds to their best use. For example, the United States has a variety of special institutions and tax rules that channel a disproportionate amount of loanable funds into politically favored industries such as housing and away from business investment. Or it could have rules that make the efficient takeover of existing capital by a new management extremely difficult. This "market for corporate control" is crucial to making sure that managements focus on obtaining the most efficient use of the existing capital stock of society.

In the United States, many of those bottlenecks were eliminated during the 1980s. The market for corporate control was revolutionized by men like Michael Milken who introduced creative means of financing corporate takeovers and by a more aggressive assertion of shareholder power by investors like Warren Buffett and the managers of large blocks of stock in pension funds and mutual funds. But the process wasn't a pleasant one from society's point of view. Moving assets to more productive uses means that existing labor arrangements must often change, producing worker layoffs, downsizing, and intensifying economic insecurity.

The United States also began to limit its long-standing practice of channeling capital into the housing industry. Tax law changes and the reduction of inflation both served to limit the attractiveness of investment in housing, thus moving capital into industrial use, and the special treatment of the housing-oriented savings and loan industry ended. In 1979 producers' durable equipment was only 19 percent larger than residential investment. By 1989 that figure was 60 percent larger, and by 1995 it was more than twice as big.[5] Of course, part of that transition included a housing recession and an expensive taxpayer bailout of the savings and loan industry.

The second way of getting the capital needed to finance a supply shock is to increase the savings in a country. That is not so easy as it seems. The economics profession does not have any good idea about how to achieve such a policy objective. Complicating that is the fact that a sudden short-term increase in saving may produce a recession, a fact stressed by John Maynard Keynes. In the early 1980s, for example, the U.S. personal saving rate rose from 7.7 percent at the business cycle peak in 1979 to over 9 percent in 1981, the start of one of the most severe post–World War II recessions.[6] Thus, a deliberate policy of trying to increase the saving rate during a supply shock may only exacerbate the socioeconomic tensions of the transition.

Another aspect of this process is that the market cost of capital, the real interest rate, tends to rise. That is a natural process, as the demand for capital has risen faster than its supply. The higher cost is a way of rationing the existing capital to make sure that only those who need it the most (and are willing to pay the premium price for it) get the capital. A higher interest rate is the key way a market economy moves capital from slower growing areas to the fast-growing sectors that are enjoying the supply shock. But again, high interest rates are painful as they force belt tightening and occasional business failures on those who cannot afford them.

The third way of getting the capital that society may need to finance a supply shock is to import it. In a global capital market, that is a relatively easy process. If one country or region is enjoying a supply shock, the real interest rates in that region rise. Investors all around the world see the more attractive investment opportunity and thus send their capital there. During the 1980s, real interest rates in the United States rose, and investors flocked in. The United States had been a net lender to the rest of the world but became a net borrower beginning in 1976. Throughout the late 1980s, net foreign inflows of capital into the United States consistently exceeded American investments abroad.[7]

Again, there is no free lunch when it comes to capital, even imported capital. One consequence is an appreciating currency. If real interest rates are high and foreign investors want to buy into the attractive yields, they must first purchase the currency of the country involved. Again, with demand for the currency exceeding supply, the foreign exchange value of the currency rises. That may be good for consumers of imports, but it makes the lives of exporters of goods and services more difficult. The United States certainly experienced that in the 1980s when the dollar appreciated 54 percent during the early part of the decade and exports fell.[8]

Imported Capital and Exchange Rates

We see that aspect of our current global supply shock in what has happened to a number of developing countries. Some countries may try to get around that problem by pegging the exchange value of their currency to some external value. One way of doing that is a formal peg such as Hong Kong adopted in 1983 when it set the value of the Hong Kong dollar at 7.8 to the U.S. dollar. Another way is to establish a link to a basket of currencies that include all or most of the country's major trading partners. Currency boards are another more formal mechanism that many countries have adopted during the 1990s and that some advance as a "solution" to currency crises. In a currency board, the central bank prints money for the domestic economy in some fixed ratio to the value of its foreign currency holdings. So, if the exchange rate is two to the U.S. dollar and the foreign central bank has $1 billion in U.S. dollar reserves, it only prints 2 billion in domestic currency.

A currency board is really little more than a more formal and restrictive mechanism of enforcing an exchange rate peg. To maintain a peg, the central bank has to intervene in the foreign exchange market, buying domestic currency and taking it out of the market when the exchange rate gets too low and selling domestic currency into circulation when the rate gets too high. Usually, a currency gets "too low" when there is too much of it relative to foreign reserves and "too high" when there is too little. So, the distinctions here are fairly technical. Such changes could be due to domestic macroeconomic conditions or to a shift in the country's terms of trade.

The key problem with both systems is that the domestic monetary authority cannot "lean against the wind" during a supply shock. Suppose investment suddenly becomes attractive in a country with a pegged currency or a currency board. Foreign investors flock in with their U.S. dollars. The local monetary authority must print local currency to accommodate that inflow. (In a peg they do so to keep exchange rates in line; in a currency board they do so because the central bank's foreign reserves rise.) With local money relatively abundant, domestic inflation can get started, sometimes in the market for local products, but more commonly in the local real estate market.

The local boom has the potential for turning into a bubble. At first, even more foreign capital may be attracted to the country as domestic real estate investments seem particularly attractive. That exacerbates the local inflationary problem. Eventually, as domestic prices get pushed up, investment may become more expensive, and the attractiveness of the country may fade. Foreign investors begin to leave, the domestic money supply must shrink, and the local real estate or economic bubble bursts. This has become a familiar story throughout Asia during the current crisis.

So an economy has no easy way to finance a supply shock. Making more efficient use of domestic saving is probably always a good idea, but the transition costs can be quite high. Raising the domestic saving rate may also be a good idea, but it is unclear how to accomplish that objective, and the short-run effect may be a recession. Foreign borrowing offers another potential source of capital, but it may create difficulties for exporters if a currency is allowed to float on foreign exchange markets. Foreign borrowing has the capacity for creating a boom-bust cycle if the currency is pegged.

That does not mean that a supply shock is a "no-win" situation. After all, society will be better off and have a higher standard of living at the end of the process. But the transition to a supply shock may be quite painful. A look at some of the details of the supply shock financing process shows that the problems are not just at the macroeconomic level but also affect the process of investment.

Banker Meets Supply Shock

Let us turn this theory into practice by putting you, the reader, on the spot. I've come up with a cure for cancer. You're a banker. I come to you to ask to borrow some money to invest in the equipment that will make the pill that cures cancer. Because you're a banker, you don't have the problems of a policymaker who has to figure out what to do with all the unemployed doctors, nurses, and other care givers who will be out of a job. All you've got to do is decide whether or not to lend me the money.

Here are the specifics. A machine that costs $100 billion to make can take $1,000 of raw material and turn it into a pill that will cure one person's cancer. The machine will be able to churn out 5 million pills per year for ten years. The Food and Drug Administration has already approved the pill, and congressmen are so excited about the pill that they've banned any lawyers from ever suing me if it doesn't work. The only catch is that they don't want me to make "excess profits." So part of the deal for not letting any lawyers sue me involves my promising never to charge more than $5,000 per pill.

So let's recap the numbers. I charge $5,000 per pill, which covers the $1,000 of raw materials and leaves me $4,000 left over per pill to pay you back. At 5 million pills per year, I clear $20 billion per year for each of the next ten years. That's $200 billion. You pull out your calculator and find that this investment is yielding a rate of return of a bit over 20 percent. The cost of funds is running around 6 percent, so the spreadsheet on your personal computer shows that the bank would more than break even if it demanded ten annual payments of $13 billion to service the loan. That still leaves a $7 billion annual cushion, which for now will go into company "profits" but could be a reserve if something goes wrong. Besides, the guys in the Public Relations Department would love it. They could advertise that theirs is the bank that financed a cure for cancer! Visions of the corner office dance in your head!

O.K., you're the reader and not just a banker. So you know that there's a catch in here somewhere. But it's not with any of the facts I've presented. Let's fast forward to the period when the loan goes bad and the bank has lost a substantial portion of its capital. You may think that you have done nothing wrong, and you probably won't go to jail for malfeasance (unless you took a kickback from me). But, your decision on the bank loan, while arguably more exciting than most such decisions, is not atypical of what banks do.

The problem that would doom your bank if you made me the cancer cure loan described above is that other manufacturers of the pill would enter the market. The price of a cure for cancer would fall dramatically below the $5,000 prescribed maximum. Indeed, given the facts described above, a distinct possibility exists that the price could fall toward $1,000, just enough to cover the cost of the raw materials. At that level the borrower would not be clearing anything on the pills that he was manufacturing and could not service the debt.

Let's go through the development of this market in a little more detail. Curing cancer is a sure-fire winner as a product, and it turns out that the world needs more than one pill factory. As we've seen, financing probably isn't a problem. Lots of loan officers at lots of banks will lend the money. Indeed, it is hard to contemplate your holding your job after your boss found out that you had the bank pass up the chance to lend to such a guaranteed winner as the Cancer Cure Company. Besides, the numbers all seem to work. In the first year or so, before many factories get built, supply simply can't keep up with demand. The problem appears to be holding the price down to the government-set maximum of $5,000, as there are not yet enough pills being produced. There are even signs that a black market in cancer cure pills is developing.

As long as the price stays at $5,000, everyone who opens a factory has the prospect of $7 billion in profits over the life of the plant after paying back the bank, so factories begin to spring up everywhere. At some point, demand is satisfied at a price of $5,000, and the price starts to drop. Then, the economics of manufacturing begin to become an interesting point. Although the price is dropping, bankers running certain price assumptions through their spreadsheets will continue to find lending on yet another pill factory a good idea until we reach a point where the price just covers the costs of putting out more pills. In the case we have just described, that occurs at a price of $3,600—$1,000 for the raw materials and $2,600 for each of the 5 million pills produced each year to pay the bank the $13 billion it needs to service the debt. For the sake of description, let's call that the "long-run breakeven" point.

Unfortunately for the industry and the banks, it is quite unlikely that new plants will actually stop coming on line when the price hits that point. The problem is most likely to involve the time lag between when the decision to finance the factory is made and the time at which it begins to produce pills. In the case of the cancer cure pill, the price is likely to stay very close to $5,000 until just before the market price starts to crash. That is so since there is probably very little price sensitivity for the product—people will pay anything as long as they need it and pay nothing if they don't need it.

People making the decision to invest in a new plant will therefore have very little advance warning that demand has become saturated and a price collapse is imminent. One might have dozens of plants already under construction around the world, each one with financiers wanting to be repaid. Quite quickly the price falls to cover just the cost of raw materials—what economists call variable cost. After all, if you're the capitalist and can generate at least some money to repay your lenders, you probably will. So even at a price of $1,010, you can generate $50 million in extra revenue to meet your bank debt. On the other hand, at a price of $990, you can't even cover your raw material cost, and so it makes no sense to begin production. As they say, if you lose money on every unit you make, you can't make up the difference on volume. So, at the end of this cycle, the world is left with too many cancer cure pill factories, each producing output at a price that just covers the cost of production but does not leave enough margin to repay the lenders of capital. Those who financed the production are out of luck, at least for now, and the result is an awful financial mess to clean up.

Creative Destruction and Bank Loans

When congressional committees get around to investigating why banks have made bad loans, they usually tend to look for some sign of fraud. The press naturally plays up such stories as they come out. But even in the case of widespread bank failures, as in the savings and loan case, fraud plays only a very small part. In that case, leading bank analyst Bert Ely estimated that fraud played a role in only about 3 percent of the money lost by the industry.[9] Faced with the facts available at the time of the deal, the banker and the borrower usually had made a good-faith agreement.

Widespread bank failures more often result from changes in economic circumstances—what we have just introduced as the process of creative destruction. Consider, for example, the case of Texas in 1986. Banks throughout the state had based their loans on the assumption that the price of oil would stay at about $30 per barrel. That was not an unrealistic assumption. The U.S. Department of Energy made the same assumption. Instead, the price fell to roughly $10.[10] The economic circumstances of the state changed drastically, and the great majority of banks in Texas failed. Today, eight of the top ten banks in the state are owned by non-Texans.[11]

Those familiar with recent developments in Asia will note a similarity to what actually occurred there and to the financial problems we now face as a result. This story is also strikingly similar to Frederick Allen's description of the farmer in the 1920s. Indeed, this story has a significant amount of resonance in the writings of many nineteenth century economists. Karl Marx, for example, predicted that capitalism would destroy itself in a process not unlike the story of the Cancer Cure Company. So, before going on, it is important to stress that this is not an unusual story, but a very familiar tale in the history of economic development and of the business cycle. Recently, this economic argument has reentered the academic literature under the concept of "increasing returns to scale." Paul Krugman, Brian Arthur, and others have presented a more formalized description of those events.[12]

The Real Estate Cycle—
Creative Destruction without Technological Change

But the banking cycle, which drives that kind of market behavior, is not limited to new technologies or even to concepts such as return to scale. The problem comes down to human emotions. In fact, many American and Japanese readers may have even had close firsthand experience with one of those cycles: the real estate cycle. It starts when some entrepreneur notes that there are not enough office buildings downtown to meet the growing needs of the community. Usually, the developer wants something distinctive about the building to draw tenants and makes it taller or more attractive than existing space. Other developers soon figure out that maybe the first guy is onto something, and they want to make sure that their building, not his, is the tallest or prettiest in town.

Banks are often drawn into the deals by having the new buildings named after the bank. The new construction can be sold to the board of directors as a form of prestige advertising and market dominance. A classic case of that exists in Hong Kong, where the Hongkong and Shanghai Bank was the tallest in town until just around the time when Beijing's takeover of the colony was arranged. Then, the Bank of China built its headquarters next door, making sure that from the top you could *look down on* Hongkong and Shanghai. In fact, in many cities around the world, the tallest buildings are the bank buildings.

But you do not need to name buildings after banks to get a real estate cycle going. It soon becomes obvious to everyone in town that the local real estate market is hot. Owners of underdeveloped real estate begin to raise their own estimates of the value of their property. A few even sell at those high prices, and the owners are often not shy about buying some demonstration of their success—a new car, for instance. That only fans the fires of greed in others, who then go out to pursue similar deals.

In addition to human greed, the other key element in the play of events is time. It takes several years for the new offices to come onto the market. In the meantime, office rents continue to rise, fueled in part by the need for all the new lawyers, appraisers, and real estate agents involved in the local property boom. There is plenty of time for new deals to be proposed and approved on evidence of booming market conditions and rising rents. Extrapolations of existing conditions during this phase often imply rents' rising at double-digit rates into the foreseeable future. Loans to finance new construction under those circumstances look as secure as loans to finance a cure for cancer.

Gradually, the new office space comes on the market. Rents stop rising. Then, they start to fall as prospective tenants take a look around at all the cranes putting up still more structures. Some of those buildings turn into "see through" structures with no tenants. An excess supply of offices drives rents down to levels well below where they started in the cycle. Many of the developers are wiped out completely. Some of the banks are forced to take big losses. Some of the auto dealers who sold the luxury cars to those who spent their prospective profits are forced to repossess them, and the downward phase of the cycle gets underway.

Back to the Fed

By now a supply shock should have a familiar ring to it. Enhanced economic uncertainty in some sectors, with dead-end jobs and falling prices, afflicts some industries. Other areas boom. The real cost of capital often rises—greater demand by new industry coupled with falling inflation enhances the spread given to savers. The spread is defined as the difference between the market rate of interest and the decline in the purchasing power of their money by inflation. Investors, and particularly banks, get attracted to new industries (the high-tech sector) and into real estate in new areas (East Asia). Trouble then begins to afflict those sectors, and a banking crisis begins.

If that is such a familiar story, what does the Fed do? Consider, first, the "cost of capital" question.

A new technology has been developed that everyone wants to apply. All that takes money, so the demand for capital rises, forcing up the real rate of interest. At the same time, the supply shock exhibits all the signs of a cost-saving venture. As with other such shocks, the underlying rate of inflation falls as price pressures are reduced because of falling costs. The real interest rate rises.

One natural reaction is for the Federal Reserve to accommodate the supply shock, that is, to provide a stimulus to demand to buy the new output by cutting market interest rates. The effect of this is that output and employment will expand rapidly while the cost-cutting effect of the new technology holds inflation in check. It is worth repeating Greenspan's observation about the current economy: "The domestic economy is expanding at a very strong pace. But what we need to pay attention to is internal imbalances developing in the economy with inflation being a symptom." In effect, Greenspan is saying that he is willing to provide the funds the supply shock needs as long as inflation doesn't develop. The resulting accommodative monetary conditions also provide access to the capital that investors want. The Fed does that by money creation. It buys some of the existing debt on the market, purchasing government bonds from the government bond market. It issues its writ, "money" to pay for that debt. The banking system and private market participants use that money to invest in the firms that are offering the new technology.

The result of that may well be a boom in domestic asset prices. Why? Assets are suddenly a lot more attractive. Recall that the supply shock increases the level of employment and output. That means that there are a lot more goods to go around. Society immediately finds itself wealthier, and if the supply shock is permanent, society is permanently wealthier. The stock market is there to set the price on claims of flows of future wealth. If society is permanently wealthier, the value of those claims on future output should also rise. In short, the stock market should boom.

When the monetary authority does *not* accommodate the increase in output, society is also permanently wealthier, but the higher real interest rate means that markets must attach a higher discount factor to all of that future wealth. Investors must give up more current consumption to get a claim on those future values. When the monetary authority accommodates and there is no rise in interest rates, it is creating the means to buy those claims on future output by printing money. It is expanding its liabilities to buy the existing assets of others, who, in turn, buy the new assets that are being created.

At some level, that creation of new assets comes to be known as a "bubble" or more appropriately as an "asset bubble." Such an asset bubble need not be accompanied by a rise in the general price level, although that might be a long-run consequence. The money creation by the monetary authority goes into buying claims on future output, not on buying current output, so the existing price level, as measured by the consumer price index, need not rise.

Isn't that the situation in which we now find ourselves: stable retail prices but rapidly expanding output and a booming asset market? For Greenspan, it's yes and no:

> That's the question I raised back in my December 1996 speech [in which Greenspan warned of "irrational exuberance."][13] I don't know anything more than I knew back then. Stock prices do seem to be headed skyward. I don't think you see it yet in overall property prices. You see some unquestionable acceleration in the prices of some properties and in certain areas of speculative activity reminiscent of the 1980s, but overall we fall well short of that.

This question of a "bubble" is the real limitation on the ability of the monetary authority to act. As Greenspan noted in the last chapter, the monetary authority acts under a set of laws, most notably the Federal Reserve Act. That legislation and subsequent legislation such as the Humphrey-Hawkins Act set many objectives for the Fed involving output, economic growth, prices, and employment. Nowhere is the level of equity prices mentioned as a legally assigned objective of Federal Reserve policy. So, in a legal sense, the political mandate for the Fed to act against a developing asset bubble is limited.

The same might be said of the more common-sense idea of a political mandate. It is hard to imagine the Fed's self-consciously announcing that it is raising interest rates to reduce the wealth of the 40 percent of American households that own stock. Indeed, the public at large widely perceives that the Fed would never do such a thing. Greenspan seems to agree:

> There is a fundamental problem with market intervention to prick a bubble. It presumes that you know more than the market. There is also a problem of timing. You might prick it too soon, in which case it comes back, and you may just make it larger the next time. There is also the very interesting question as to whether the central bank is intervening appropriately in the market. This raises some fascinating questions about what our authority is and who makes the judgment that there actually is a bubble.

What's wrong with a bubble? Don't people just get richer? What's wrong with that? At one level, it seems harmless enough, even sensible. But it may not be the right thing to do. To see this, consider that one of the key tests of the efficacy of a certain policy action is whether it is reversible. Let us say that we had a negative supply shock. A classic example is the oil price shock of the 1970s. For reasons outside society's immediate control, it becomes *more* expensive, not less expensive, to produce a given amount of output.

If the Fed were to follow symmetric logic, it would respond to that negative supply shock by trying to cut demand as well—raising interest rates. After all, if the positive supply shock was met with an increase in demand, shouldn't a reduction in supply be met with a reduction in demand? Under that logic, the rate of inflation is maintained, and the adjustment by the economy to the new conditions is conducted purely on the side of employment and output.

To many, that would be described as a procyclical action, that is, not acting like a contrarian but acting like the crowd's "animal spirits." It would be taking conditions that caused an increase in unemployment and making them worse by making business conditions even tougher. But, if that were the case, then isn't the Fed also running a procyclical policy when it takes the "good" news of a favorable supply shock and makes conditions even better by accommodating them with an increase in demand? The only real difference between those two cases is the political one. Making a good situation better is unlikely to evoke screams from Congress. Making unemployment rise in the face of an adverse supply shock is certain to provoke numerous congressional hearings.

But the economics may be worse than the politics, for if the Fed raises rates, not only do goods cost more because of the supply shock but the fall in the stock market makes people poorer at the same time. Remember that one of the problems of the depression was that the collapse in stock prices made everyone poorer, reducing their purchasing power. With less money to spend, demand collapsed. Less demand for goods meant that people were laid off, making them poorer still. The economy cycled downward.

That takes us back to the point at which we started this chapter. Did the boom of the 1920s lead to the crash of the 1930s? Greenspan's answer was that "if actions taken in 1930 and 1931 were taken differently," we wouldn't have had the Great Depression. But we still might have had "a fairly significant recession," according to Greenspan. Why? Why can't the bubble go on forever?

Let's go back to the point about "symmetry." If the fall in stock prices in 1929 made people poorer so they spent less, it stands to reason that a rise in stock prices makes people richer so they will spend more. There is no question that in the late 1990s people spent more than they otherwise would because of the booming market. If the market continues to boom and demand continues to rise, at some point the higher demand will swamp the efficiency gains from the supply shock, and prices will start to rise. Higher prices—rising inflation—is exactly the signal that Greenspan said he was looking for to indicate the need to raise rates.

If the Fed raised rates, the bubble would quickly explode. Higher rates mean *lower* valuations on claims on future output like stocks. Higher rates also mean lower amounts of economic activity, falling profits, and hence still lower equity prices. That was the root of Greenspan's other observation that "the effect of wealth destruction on economic conditions is . . . complex."

We have one other very important consideration. The bigger the bubble in asset prices, the more dependent the economy is on the wealth-generated spending caused by the bubble. The economy will get a dose of "the higher they rise, the harder they fall." Greenspan acknowledges as much, "Of course there are dangers, and to be sure, *we don't want to get ourselves hung up on a very expensive bubble*" (emphasis mine). Greenspan is well aware that this is the dilemma he faces:

> If you had a gold standard, there wouldn't be the choice. No matter what we do, we're creating potential trouble. Absent a gold standard, open market policy should endeavor to create monetary conditions in the least worst manner.

So Greenspan sits on the horns of a dilemma. On the one hand, if he tightens monetary policy, he risks disturbing both the political consensus that supports the Fed's independence and the economic conditions that underpin having society make the most of a supply shock. On the other hand, if Greenspan does not act to tighten policy, the bubble simply gets bigger and bigger until the Fed has no choice.[14]

During our conversation, I raise the point in chapter 1 about the Fed's easing monetary policy in late 1927. Like the superlative retainer of facts he is, he recalls the incident well: "You mean the agreement between Montague Norman and Benjamin Strong?" Recall that Norman was the governor of the Bank of England and Strong the president of the New York Federal Reserve. Mr. Norman's caricature was in the *Chi-*

cago Tribune cartoon at the Bank of England. That agreement motivated the Fed to act as it did in the late 1920s, expanding the U.S. asset bubble and ultimately producing a crash.

Greenspan is optimistic that history will not repeat itself. He answers that historic analogy with another one:

> Remember the big one-day decline we had back in October 1987? Its impact on the economy was not all that great. Then, there was the severe decline in stock prices in Japan early in this decade. True, it took growth out of the system, but most of what they have experienced since is the result of an increasingly corrosive nonperforming loan problem. There's no guarantee that even if you get a 1929, you'll end up with a 1932.

And, if the problems of an asset bubble were not enough, Greenspan mentioned the other dilemma he faces: Asia. It is certainly true that tightening the domestic economy might be justified, given the problem of exceptionally tight labor markets and the prospect of incipient inflation. But in so doing he risks causing further problems on the other side of the Pacific. One of the limitations facing economic management in America is that conditions here affect conditions elsewhere. What might be appropriate for the domestic economy might not be appropriate for the international economy. It is one thing to be a contrarian, but your actions should be contrary to what? Lean against the domestic wind and the world falls deeper into recession. Lean against the international economy and the domestic economy tightens further and the putative bubble gets bigger.

But we are getting ahead of ourselves. To understand those international ramifications, we must go to the other side of the Pacific Ocean.

4

The Mandarin

The direction in which education starts a man will determine his future life.

—Plato[1]

Today, the Japanese economy and financial system are widely viewed as dragging down the economies of Asia and potentially the world. A protracted period of slow growth, lasting the better part of the 1990s, has turned into a recession that to all appearances is deepening. The financial system shows signs of severe stress. To meet the crisis the government released a series of packages designed to stimulate the economy, but to no seeming effect. New measures have been coming forward at the average rate of one every six weeks since the fall of 1997.

That is in decided contrast to just ten years ago, when it seemed to many observers that Japan would take over the global economy. "The Cold War is over and Japan won," claimed one author and close follower of Japan.[2] Today, that notion seems a cruel hoax. While the Japanese system of decisionmaking was a major cause of the country's post–World War II success, it is also a major cause of the economy's current difficulties. This chapter considers the institutional reasons why Japan has gone from *ichi-ban* (number one) to *kamikaze* in a free fall, seemingly bent on taking the world economy down with itself.

Deep in the heart of Nagatacho, the section of Tokyo where the government offices are located, sits the Ministry of Finance. It is roughly equidistant from the Diet, the Imperial Palace, and the American Embassy. But cynics would note that of the three, it is closest to the embassy, and that is probably no accident.

Outside, a handful of riot police stand guard while the bulk of their comrades sit discreetly in blue and white riot-control buses parked along the side streets. The passersby look like the least likely rioters on the planet. Two-thirds are men in suits and ties carrying the ubiquitous briefcase; the remainder are women in office attire including shoes that most American women would not consider "practical." Ties, briefcases, and high heels would no doubt have to be discarded before any serious rioting were to take place.

While the Japanese must present identification to gain entrance to the ministry, a well-dressed *gaijin* (foreigner) breezes through. A polite *ohaiyo gozaimasu* (good morning), followed by the name of the senior ministry official you are going to meet "Sakakibara-sama" (something like the Honorable Sakakibara) while doing a motion that implies you are going to see him, is sufficient to gain entry. One does not know why the guards are so easy on foreigners. Maybe they assume we won't riot. Maybe they don't know how to engage us in a long conversation. Most likely, they're just following procedures.

The ministry itself would remind many an American baby boomer of the large high school he attended. Drab tile and faux brick line the bottom half of the walls in the hallways. The upper half of the wall is an equally nondescript painted plaster. Some of the floors are "hardwood" but show living proof that even the hardest of woods succumbs after decades of constant foot traffic and polishing. The rest of the floors lead one to speculate whether they are the same tile as the original kitchens in Levittown, Long Island. Room air conditioners hang from the various subdivided cubicles that line the hallway—all this in a hot and humid climate similar to the eastern Carolinas.

This was General MacArthur's vision of a public building: functional, up to date (in the late 1940s sense of the word), but certainly not extravagant. Why it has stayed that way for fifty years remains an open question. I suspect the reason has something to do with the supposed power centers that are located around it. The Diet, which is the voice of the people, certainly demands, like any parliament, some modesty on the part of its nominal servants. The Imperial Palace, though majestic and covering some prime real estate with some much needed (but inaccessible) green in the middle of Tokyo, conveys through the emperor a similar modesty. Although the emperor has no formal power, the Ministry of Finance's bureaucratic tradition has as much to do with the current emperor's forebears after the Meiji Restoration as it does with the postwar democratic tradition of the Diet.

Finally, and most symbolically, is the nearness of the American Embassy. In conversation, Japanese officials express a reverence for American official opinion that one is hard put to find elsewhere on the planet, especially in Washington. Japanese officials are knowledgeable about the latest statement of some assistant secretary who is so obscure that he wouldn't even be recognized in Washington by a gaggle of reporters. The legacy of MacArthur is strong, and to an American, ironic, given the extent to which many Americans had come to fear Japanese economic superiority in the 1980s. Maybe the best explanation for why the Ministry of Finance is still the way it is is that General MacArthur had not ordered any changes. And the bureaucrats would just as soon keep it that way. But, make no mistake. Drab surroundings aside, that is where the power has been located in Japan for most of the past half century.

On the second floor is the current office of Eisuke Sakakibara, vice minister of finance in Japan's Ministry of Finance, where he and his predecessors have shaped official Japanese international economic policy for decades. He has risen through the various steps of the Japanese career ladder from Tokyo University through most of the key divisions at the Ministry of Finance to sit at the apex of bureaucratic power at the age of fifty-seven. Sakakibara is affable, speaks perfect English, and is exceptionally generous in his willingness to see foreign visitors. In the international financial press he is called Mr. Yen, because every statement he utters strengthens the value of that currency.

Under the Japanese Constitution, Sakakibara is the servant of the minister of finance, who in turn serves at the pleasure of the prime minister. His only power is theoretical—the power to persuade. Today, the popularity of bureaucrats like Sakakibara is at a historic low, and the Ministry of Finance is riddled with investigators from the public prosecutor's office. But one should not assume that the power has completely left the Ministry of Finance. Two vignettes from some of my recent visits suggest just how powerful the bureaucracy still is.

On November 10, 1997, I entered Sakakibara's office to find a dispirited man. Usually effervescent, he sits with his head in the palm of his hand, his elbow resting on an armrest of the chair. He explains that he has just returned from a schedule of round-the-world meetings and is fatigued. But one can deduce the real reason for his depression by following his line of vision. On the wall opposite his seat is a giant tote board that carries the current market data. The Nikkei index for the Tokyo stock market is trading around 15,700 and has been dropping sharply for a couple of weeks. At that price level, many of the largest Japanese banks are technically undercapitalized or worse, bankrupt. The market would continue to drop, hitting a low of 14,664 on January 12, 1998.[3]

In Japan, direct ownership by banks of shares of stock in Japanese companies constitutes a significant fraction of bank capital. Although that is illegal in the United States, the Japanese feel that bank ownership of some of the shares of the companies to which they lend facilitates a long-term business relationship. When the international bank capital standards, known as the Basle Standards, were negotiated, the Japanese demanded a special recognition of that practice. A portion of the unrealized capital gains on shares held by banks was counted as part of the capital of the bank, even though the book value or purchase price of those shares might be substantially lower. But by counting those gains, banks were able to possess a larger capital base and therefore sustain a bigger volume of loans. The downside of that arrangement was quite clear on November 10, 1997. When the prices of those shares fall, the value of the bank's capital is diminished, and the banks do not have enough capital to sustain the volume of loans outstanding.

It certainly seemed in November 1997 that Japan had reached the limits of management by the economy's puppetmasters. This most bureaucratically directed of all the Western economies was on the brink of financial collapse. Long confident of the superiority of its organizational structure, official Japan had been in a protracted period of denial that anything was amiss.

In fact, my meeting with Sakakibara on November 10 was the first time that I had ever heard a senior Japanese policymaker say that significant action was needed. The particular "significant actions" had been fairly clear to foreign observers for quite some time. For starters, Japan needed to put public money into its banking system to shore up its capital position, and it needed a fiscal stimulus package to get the economy going again. Sakakibara had changed his mind about public policy and was signaling that in our meeting.

The trouble was, on November 10, both those actions were considered politically impossible. The ruling Liberal Democratic Party had just introduced a fiscal consolidation bill that was designed to reduce budget deficits and put strict limits on government stimulus programs. The party officials had made clear that a government bailout of the banks was absolutely unthinkable. When some Japanese banks had difficulty, the government closed them, protecting their depositors. Injecting capital into the banks to give them a new lease on life was politically untenable.

Within two months of my meeting with Sakakibara, the Japanese had announced both a massive bank bailout and a fiscal stimulus package. The former, worth ¥30 trillion (about $235 billion at the time), would involve direct purchase by the government of preferred stock and subordinated debt issued by banks.[4] The fiscal stimulus package was for the first quarter of 1998—the last quarter of the Japanese fiscal year, which ends on March 31. The package combined an income tax rebate worth about ¥65,000 per household with ¥2 trillion in construction spending.[5] More fiscal stimulus packages were to come later, as the need to buy time for the economy became more and more evident. But, no doubt, the whole process started on November 10.

Earlier in this book, we considered the problems with Keynesian fiscal stimulus in the American context, and we noted three specific lags in the process: recognition, decision, and implementation. Granted the recognition lag in Japan was long in coming—it took Sakakibara's watching the Nikkei plunge for the recognition of trouble to take place. But, once recognition occurred at the senior ranks of the bureaucracy, the rest was like a hot knife going through butter. The decision to make changes occurred startlingly quickly. Not only did the elected government have to decide to act, it actually had to decide to do a complete about-face in policy, reversing a contractionary fiscal policy and taking the highly unpopular step of appropriating public funds for a major bank bailout.

On January 14, 1998, the *Financial Times* reported Sakakibara as saying, "I think we have solved Japan's problems now."[6] When I next met with him, on January 20, his head was out of his hand; the confident Sakakibara had returned. The Nikkei was rising, and he confidently told me, "We will take whatever measures are necessary" to make sure that the Nikkei was at an adequate level when the banks closed their books and valued their capital on March 31.

Of course, Sakakibara was suitably modest that January day about what he had accomplished. Like a good public servant, he commended the elected officials for their wise and decisive action. But we both knew who was orchestrating events and pulling the strings to power, convincing the officials that change was desperately needed, and who designed the program that was adopted.

The capacity for a government to take bold and decisive action is most often thought of as an advantage. American admirers of Japan and many advocates of adopting Japanese practices such as "industrial policy" have certainly stressed that. But the capacity to take such action requires that decisionmaking power be quite concentrated. The larger the group that must make its assent, the more delays will be involved. Japan had finely honed its decisionmaking process and so had the capacity to be decisive. But even such decisive decisionmaking systems have their disadvantages as well, as we shall discover.

Decisive action, if wrongheaded, can lead to disastrous results. That became clear the week I next saw Sakakibara on March 30, 1998, near the end of the Japanese fiscal year. True to his promise, Sakakibara and his colleagues had coaxed (and purchased enough shares) to push the market up over 17,000. A key part of the program was the price-keeping operations by which the government purchased shares to keep values up. The key moment for market valuation was to be the close of business on March 31.

Midday on March 30, the spokesman for the Ministry of Posts and Telecommunciation, which controls the vast postal saving system in Japan, went before the press. He announced that the ministry had "finished its allocation" for the price-keeping operations and regular stock purchases for the postal saving system. Everyone in the market knew that buying by postal savings was a key part of the effort to manipulate the market as high as possible.[7]

But if the government had stopped buying, who was going to drive the market higher? An avalanche of sell orders promptly followed the announcement. Instead of being up 271 points, the market closed down 476, a net swing on the announcement of roughly 5 percent.[8] For the end of the fiscal year, the bureaucracy's hoped-for approach to 18,000 in the market had collapsed at year-end—ending almost 10 percent short of its mark. A single bureaucratic snafu had led to a loss of $86 billion in market capitalization at a critical juncture.[9]

The months that followed saw nothing but further market weakness and a continuing slide in the yen. The Japanese currency had fallen from a high of 80 to the dollar in 1995 to 148 by mid-June 1998. In other words, it took 80 percent more yen to buy one dollar in 1998 than four years earlier.

Mr. Yen, Eisuke Sakakibara, had used his enormous persuasive energies to stem the fall at critical junctures. He had even provoked a few market rallies for the currency. But, in the end, they were what Wall Street calls "bear market rallies." The fundamental direction of the yen was still down.

In the field of economic management, the difference between the Japanese system's mandarin and the American contrarian is vast. The chairman of the Federal Reserve and his colleagues, after all, have the capacity to take bold and decisive action as well. But their mission statement is altogether different. While the Fed has a mission of being a shock absorber by moderating the effects of change, the individuals who head the mandarinate, at least in its most recent incarnations, have the mission of effecting change. Their collective role is that of the initiator, not the reactor—of being the leader and decisionmaker, not the legal executor of decisions made by others.

Why the difference in mission? In my view, the fundamental economic principle of scarcity is the best way to explain the evolution of the Japanese system. When human capital is relatively scarce, those who possess it have an even more enhanced advantage. The entire Confucian system of a vaguely meritocratic mandarinate in charge of affairs of state maximized the skill level of the state while still conserving on human capital and the resources needed to develop it. Checks and balances are the luxury of a society where human capital is relatively abundant and widespread among the population.

One could make the same scarcity argument about the fundamental mission of the Japanese mandarins: the mobilization of financial capital. Japan was a desperately poor society after World War II that industrialized rapidly. When capital is scarce, the commitment of savings necessary to sustain a market model with numerous competitors might seem wasteful. How much more logical it might seem to rely on a few well-educated elite to make "wise" choices about the appropriate uses of society's hard-earned savings. The rapid industrialization of Japan is in no small part due to the fact that much of the Japanese bureaucratic system is linked to the mission of capital mobilization and allocation.

The reason for Japan to adopt the mandarinate model of decisionmaking can also be said to have deep historical roots. Sakakibara and his colleagues at the Ministry of Finance and throughout the Japanese bureaucracy can also be thought of as the modern embodiment of a natural set of social arrangements that evolved over centuries. Two great shocks cemented that system in place: the Meiji Restoration and the American occupation. Scarcity of both savings and human capital at those critical junctures, coupled with roots in Asian traditions ranging from Confucianism to Buddhism to Japan's unique Shinto past, can help explain the choice of model. But all that cannot answer the fundamental puzzle about modern Japan: *Why is a society that is today among the richest and most educated on the planet still relying on a system whose roots are those of a scarcity of human and financial capital?* It may be that those roots run so deep that they are not easily changed. If that is the case, Japan is in serious trouble because it may be unable to shed itself of the mind-set that has led it to its present predicament. Let us consider those roots.

Education and the Bureaucracy: Meiji, MacArthur, and the Modern Day

Yukichi Fukuzawa, dressed in a traditional kimono, stares out from the front of the ¥10,000 note (roughly the equivalent of the U.S. $100 bill). One could mistake his solemn expression for that of any of his Victorian contemporaries. He had a serious purpose: designing an educational system for the new Japan of the late nineteenth century. In 1868 the last shogun abdicated, and two powerful clans from southwestern Japan, Satsuma and Choshu, restored the emperor to power.

Technically, the feudal age ended, and the era of modernization began. Education was central to that task of modernization. In 1871 a Ministry of Education *(Mombusho)* was established. Its continued centrality of importance may be best indicated by its location: directly next door to the Ministry of Finance, where Dr. Sakakibara sits.

Fukuzawa, and the rest of the newly emerged leadership class, faced a massive task of building a sense of nation and national purpose that centuries of feudalism had destroyed. In 1873 Fukuzawa wrote, "Many millions of people throughout Japan were sealed up in many millions of separate boxes, or separated by many millions of walls."[10] He and his contemporaries sought to develop a sense of *kokutai*, of nationality or national essence. In his autobiography he wrote, "[T]he purpose of my entire work has not only been to gather young men together and give them the benefit of foreign books, but to open this 'closed' country of ours and bring it wholly into the light of Western civilization. For only thus may Japan become strong in both the arts of war and peace."[11]

Fukuzawa's many works in this regard were formidable, including the founding of Keio University, which even today ranks as one of the top universities in the country. He and his associates, in an early version of a "think tank" known as Meiji Six (named after the year of its founding by the imperial calendar), were instrumental in establishing the postfeudal educational system. The founder of Meiji Six, Arinori Mori, was minister of education from 1885 to 1889 and was key to organizing the system of universal education. Mori's schools were clearly devoted to nation building, created to produce graduates suitable for the new task. In one book he defined the appropriate role for the nation's children: "They will be imperial subjects who completely fulfill their duties, which means that when called upon to do so they will willingly give their lives to the state."[12]

In a somewhat different but even more critical fashion, the top of the educational system was devoted to serving the process of nation building. Fukuzawa and Mori instinctively gravitated toward creating a governing mandarin class. That mandarin class was elitist by nature, for it derived its legitimacy not from democratic elections but from the fact that its members passed through an examination system that certified them as the best and the brightest. Such superiority was only modestly camouflaged, if at all. In the Meiji period a slogan emerged to encourage students to study hard and obey the rules: "Exalt the Officials, Despise the People."[13]

At the apex of that system was Tokyo Imperial University, founded in 1886. In 1887 the university's law graduates were granted the exclusive right to move directly into the upper ranks of the bureaucracy by imperial decree. Things have changed little since 1887. Ezra Vogel, writing in *Japan As Number One: Lessons for America,* notes that the educational system's function of supplying top bureaucrats has changed little since early Meiji days:

> Leading bureaucrats invariably have attended the best universities. . . . Tokyo University students are acknowledged to be at the apex of the two million students in Japanese universities. Within Tokyo University, the ablest students enter the Law Faculty, which in fact provides broad training for public administration. . . . The top graduates of the Law Faculty enter the most prestigious ministries. Of the twenty-odd students entering a key ministry in the elite track each year, perhaps fifteen come from the Tokyo University Law Faculty.[14]

So, in a century, the law faculty's market share has fallen from 100 percent to 75 percent.

Some Americans who have come to admire and respect (and fear) the Japanese system have placed a great deal of importance on this link between the educational system and the staffing of the bureaucracy. William S. Dietrich, in his book *In the Shadow of the Rising Sun,* writes of the Japanese emphasis on serving the needs of the state: "These needs, from early Meiji Japan to the present, have involved the training of a self-conscious elite to staff the upper levels of the state bureaucracy."[15]

Vogel stresses the role of Japanese bureaucrats as permanent students or information managers:

> Japan's elite officials from the various ministries have the preeminent responsibility for guiding the acquisition of knowledge. They themselves are constantly analyzing information and deciding what further information needs to be gathered. . . . They are expected not only to keep track of developments in general but to search for examples that Japan could usefully emulate.[16]

But their power goes much further than mere providers of information. The bureaucrats of today really are the decisionmakers. Vogel says:

> The politicians make many important political decisions, but compared to the American government the top politicians have little leverage over the bureaucracy. The key decisions in the ministry are made by the permanent bureaucrats rather than by the politicians of the Diet and the cabinet.[17]

A division of labor emerged between the politicians and the bureaucracy that came to benefit both. The politicians focused on electoral issues, the bureaucrats on policy. Members of parliament lack their own policy staffs. The typical member of the Diet has just two people in his office, while a member of the U.S. House of Representatives typically has seventeen. Thus, the politician usually turns to the bureaucracy to write the legislation to be introduced in parliament. Sometimes the bureaucracy writes the script for the entire floor debate, including, ironically enough, both the questions asked by the opposition and the answers given by the ruling party.[18]

A career arrangement also cemented such a cooperative division of labor. Many Japanese politicians got their start and training in the bureaucracy. There they learned what buttons to push to deliver the goods back home. That continued superiority of an unelected bureaucracy may seem, at the very least, unusual to Americans and their system rooted in the balance of power. After all, today Japan is a modern democratic nation with a highly educated work force and electorate and demonstrable skills in many areas of technical endeavor. Most striking is that such a system of undemocratic accountability survived the postwar occupation.

Following World War II, Douglas MacArthur was de facto dictator of Japan for more than six years. As occupations by conquering military powers go, his was among the most benign on record. He arrived at the end of August 1945, just weeks after the surrender of the Japanese government and declared that he would "sever for all time the shackles of feudalism and in its place raise the dignity of man under protection of the people's sovereignty."[19] MacArthur wrote a new constitution for Japan that made the legislature, the Diet, the supreme organ of government.

At the center of his attempts to make Japan into a democratic state was a purge of more than 200,000 government and business leaders on the grounds of their responsibility for the war. But the purge left the civilian bureaucracy largely in place and actually had the net effect of augmenting its power. Of the roughly 40,000 bureaucrats who were investigated, just 830 lost their jobs.[20] Sakakibara himself notes in his book, *Beyond Capitalism,* that only nine officials in the Ministry of Finance were subject to the purge. Of the early occupation period he notes:

> The basic structure of the public sector that was formed between the late 1920s and the early 1930s was in fact strengthened at this time. Although professional managers in the private sector were filling the vacuum left behind by the *zaibatsu* break-up, the economic bureaucracy was consolidating both its pre- and post-war public sector foundations, and putting the finishing touches on its framework for "mutual understanding" with the private sector.[21]

As things developed, MacArthur came to find that he *needed* the bureaucracy to run the affairs of the country. After all, his occupying army had to govern a country of some 75 million people. Among the occupying forces were few individuals with any knowledge of Japanese history or culture, few who even spoke Japanese. More, but not many, had some knowledge and experience of civilian administration. So, while other areas of public life, including the large corporations, saw many of their leaders barred from high-level employment, the bureaucracy went on just about as before.

Thus, an elite bureaucracy, rooted in a Confucian tradition of education, nurtured in pursuit of nation building, and sanctioned by a conquering military power, holds substantial sway. Sakakibara was just four years old when Douglas MacArthur landed near Yokohama. Sakakibara's career is instructive, both because it is quite typical of Japanese bureaucratic success and because he is something new, a bit of a rebel, with enough deviations in his career to make him very much the kind of man who will lead in a transition.

Sakakibara graduated from Tokyo University (where else?), but with a degree in economics, not law. After a brief stint in the Ministry of Finance, he went abroad to get a Ph.D. at the University of Michigan. He rotated through the various divisions of the Ministry of Finance: banking, finance, and most important to his career—international finance. His assignments also included two positions abroad, at the International Monetary Fund and as a visiting professor at Harvard University. Those foreign rotations are considered a key part of the "information gathering" function of the government bureaucracy. But his education as an economist and his choice of the international finance bureau as his base were most fortuitous.

At the time he joined the ministry in 1965, Japan was still a very minor player on the world financial scene. Its GDP was growing rapidly, but in world per capita income tables, Japan still ranked twentieth with a per capita GDP one-third that of the United States. The yen was still a minor currency, under tight controls, and pegged at a grossly overvalued rate of 360 to the dollar.[22] One story has it that MacArthur selected the exchange rate while staring at the Japanese flag—a red circle depicting the rising sun with the exchange rate representing the number of degrees in the circle.[23] MacArthur's trigonometry may have been flawless, but the choice of 360 gave Japan a decidedly undervalued currency. Still, even by 1970, well into Dr. Sakakibara's career, Japan's foreign reserves including gold were just $4 billion.[24] To imagine a career at that time that would end up with the market-given title "Mr. Yen" and to have that title be one of reverence and awe must have seemed quite a long reach—or maybe not for a clever young man.

In 1960, when he entered Tokyo University, the Japanese-American mutual defense treaty (known as AMPO in Japan) was up for renewal. Protests led by university students broke out in the streets. President Eisenhower was due to visit Japan that June, and the ruling party, led by Prime Minister Kishi, wanted the treaty ratified. In the Diet, opposition Socialist politicians and progovernment members engaged in angry physical confrontations. In the event, Kishi ordered police to carry opposition politicians from the Diet and then ratified the treaty in their absence. Protests then broke out throughout the country, and several hundred thousand people surrounded the parliament. The Eisenhower visit was canceled.

Kishi resigned and was replaced by Hayato Ikeda, who immediately began a program known as the income-doubling plan. The plan was to increase the incomes of the Japanese people by 100 percent within a decade.[25] Clearly, that was a political move intended both to distract voters from the less than savory circumstances that surrounded the passage of AMPO and to unify the nation around an objective that would prove tangible to the average voter and beneficial to the ruling party. The move also signified an end to an ideologically based political process. Japanese politics ceased to be a miniature version of the cold war battle between a pro-American Liberal Democratic Party and the pro-Soviet Socialists. Outwardly, Japan sided with America in the sense that it became sheltered under the American military umbrella. Japan could thus turn inward to attend to its own needs. The public roundly endorsed the plan. In the elections of November 1960, Ikeda's Liberal Democratic Party won an overwhelming 296 seats of 467.[26]

One of the key reasons that the Liberal Democratic Party has so dominated postwar politics in Japan is that the income-doubling plan proved successful. Japan made Ikeda's income target three years early. Rather than the 7 percent compound growth in per capita incomes required for a decade-long doubling, the Japanese managed 10 percent annual growth rates.[27] But by any historical measure to that time, this was an ambitious program. For example, it took America twenty-nine years—from 1959 to 1988—to double its per capita disposable personal income level.[28] To do so in Japan required an enormous concentration of talent and energy into such a single-minded project.

The Foundations of Rapid Japanese Economic Development

Today, that rapid growth period is known as the "Japan model" and has been copied (with suitable deviations for national differences) throughout East Asia. But the logic of it stems right from Keynesian economics and was inscribed by the Keynesian New Dealers who came ashore with MacArthur in 1945. George Kennan, architect of the Marshall Plan, also wrote the guidance for the economic management of Japan in National Security Council directive 13/2. His prescription: "High exports through hard work."[29]

The "hard work" part was self-evident. Japan was in ruins, without its prewar capital stock. The "high exports" was a demand-side-driven necessity. The impoverished population could not sustain a high level of consumption. Investment demand needed both a source of capital and a market for the final products produced by the investment that the domestic market could not provide. Exports fit the bill nicely. Foreigners would be the final consumers and would, in return, remit their currency to Japan, which would allow the purchase of capital goods.

By 1960 and the launch of the income-doubling plan, things were a bit less desperate, but Japan was still a relatively poor country, with a GDP per capita less than one-fifth that of the United States. With capital still scarce and funds desperately needed for industrialization and rapid growth, the bureaucracy was in no position to let the market have free reign in deciding where capital should go. A political promise of rapid GDP growth had to be kept, and the mandarinate was more than willing to accommodate. The bureaucracy designed a series of policies to keep capital in the industrialization process. Or, as Japan expert Chalmers Johnson put it, "[F]or the bureaucracy to have mobilized resources and committed them to a heavy industrial structure as it did in postwar Japan, the claims of interest groups and individual citizens had to be held in check."[30]

One of the keys was to provide strong support for certain industries while letting others wither—a practice that came to be known by the catch-all phrase "industrial policy." A 1963 study by the *Economist* reported that Japan followed a conscious policy of promoting certain industries key to what the bureaucracy considered Japan's stage of modernization and industrialization and chose to "throw away" other industries.[31] That, however, is probably an overly harsh description of the actual practice. Instead, a close and continuous consultation goes on between the senior bureaucracy and the management of key companies. That can include private afterhours conversations in restaurants during which both sides can feel free to discuss their particular needs. In downsizing an industry, the bureaucracy might take an instrumental role in arranging mergers, for example.

But the array of instruments at the bureaucracy's disposal to achieve its desired end is impressive. The bureaucrats at the Ministry of International Trade and Industry (MITI) might work closely with their counterparts at the Ministry of Finance to determine a company's allowable tax deductions or the amount of depreciation of equipment they might deduct. They also might work with the Ministry of Finance to encourage or discourage bank lending to particular firms. That is in addition to the direct levers of authority over licenses, zoning, and regulatory waivers that are more typical instruments of bureaucratic control.[32] The bureaucracy groups all that informal power under the euphemism "administrative guidance."

Stretching Financing to the Limit

All that bureaucratic power may imply more formal "public sector" dominance than is actually the case. Today, many Japan scholars are arguing that the bureaucracy's actual intervention in corporate decisionmaking was relatively circumscribed. Consider, instead, an analysis that American scholars would recognize as the "capture theory": Government regulators tend to adopt the same viewpoints as the industries they are regulating; that is, they become captured by the industries. As we shall see later, the senior bureaucracy and senior corporate management had a lot in common, thus making a common viewpoint a likely approach.

The second key to the Japanese development strategy was to make maximum use of scarce capital by encouraging a corporate debt-to-equity ratio that American corporations would consider imprudent. During the rapid development period, debt-to-equity ratios in large Japanese companies were three and four to one and higher. Typically, U.S. companies would use debt to leverage their equity at a one-to-one ratio.[33] Even the equity positions in Japanese companies might be a disguised form of debt. Japanese banks owned substantial portions of the shares of their corporate customers. Estimates of that practice suggest that Japanese financial institutions may hold as much as 45 percent of the value of Japanese equity on their own books.[34] As we noted earlier, when the market was rising, that caused no problems. In the current environment, it is turning a stock market decline into a devastating banking and financial crisis.

Such a system also allows for both the rapid creation of capital and its direction to the use the bureaucracy desires. As Chalmers Johnson summed up the process, "Large enterprises obtain their capital through loans from the city banks, which are in turn over loaned and therefore utterly dependent on the guarantees of the Bank of Japan, which is itself . . . essentially an operating arm of the Ministry of Finance."[35]

This is such a powerful system for the rapid accumulation of capital because it harnesses the entire financial system of the country to the industrial process, from the creation of money to every nook and cranny of the balance sheet and regulatory check on the banking system. Start with money creation. The central bank, in this case, the Bank of Japan, issues currency (or its equivalent) in return for a government bond. That currency is, in effect, an interest-free loan from the holder to the Bank of Japan. For a variety of reasons, most deliberate, currency holdings in Japan (at roughly 8 percent of GDP) are many times what they are elsewhere. (In the United States, for example, currency represents about 5 percent of GDP, but roughly 70 percent of U.S. currency circulates outside the United States, lowering the effective ratio to just 1.5 percent of GDP).[36] Thus, a system with a high reliance on currency generates a substantial interest-free loan to the central bank, which in turn lends to the government through the purchase of government bonds.

When the government spends money for a project, the proceeds are deposited in the banking system. Of that amount, most is re-lent. Through a process known as the "money multiplier," in which the re-lent money is itself redeposited in the banking system, an initial deposit in the bank can ultimately expand the balance sheet of the banking system—and its lending capacity—by many times. The size of the money multiplier depends on the fraction of each deposit that is re-lent. The more that is re-lent, the bigger the multiplier.[37] A system that relends 80 percent of all deposits has a money multiplier of five. One that relends 90 percent has a money multiplier of ten. One that relends 95 percent has a money multiplier of twenty.

Obviously, the more money a bank can relend, the bigger the fraction of each deposit on which it can earn interest. For the system as a whole, the higher the fraction that can be re-lent, the greater the lending capacity of the system. If you are trying to rebuild the industrial infrastructure of a society, a highly geared banking system, one that relends a big fraction of all deposits, is certainly a great way to operate.

One has three things to worry about when it comes to lending "too much" that keep this explosive growth of the banking system in check. The first is the fear that your depositors will want to withdraw their money and that you will not have enough money in the bank to let them withdraw their funds. One can minimize that concern in two ways. First, if your bank is part of a rapidly growing economy, on net, the amount of money on deposit in the system is growing quite rapidly as well. So the chances are that if one depositor wants to make a withdrawal, someone else is making an equally large or larger deposit. Second, the central bank can lend you, the bank, the cash to cover your temporary shortfall. That happens in all major economies today, and it certainly happens in Japan. The Bank of Japan will gladly extend temporary credit to a bank if it runs short of cash.

In most of Japan's postwar history that was not a cause for concern, chiefly because the economy grew rapidly. Today, that practice is causing a real problem. In late fall 1997, depositors began a "run" on their banks.[38] That is, they began to withdraw their deposits and demand cash. That put enormous strains on the system. First, the commercial banks found that they had to stop lending and even began to call in loans because they needed the money to pay back their depositors. That put enormous strains on the commercial economy, which needs bank loans to survive. Second, it put enormous strains on the Bank of Japan, which had to expand the currency it issued at the rate of 1 percent per day. By way of comparison, most monetary authorities expand their currencies by a few percent per year. That money was transported to the banks and paid out to depositors. It was said that one could not obtain either a safe-deposit box or even a home safe in Tokyo during December. They were all purchased to hold the resulting cash hoard.

The second concern you should have as a banker is that your bank has some capital, or net worth, to absorb some losses. After all, not all of the loans you make will prove profitable. The economy might have an economic downturn that might cause a whole group of your borrowers to have to renege on their debts at the same time. Capital requirements in Japanese banks were lower than those of almost all their international competitors. As a result, Japanese banks were expanding at a rate that far exceeded that of other countries, and in the late 1980s that lending was becoming international in its scope. So dramatic was the effect that in 1988 the large industrial nations got together to create international capital standards. One important ulterior motive was to restrain the rapid growth of Japanese institutions.

Those were the "good old days." Fear by the competition has now been replaced by terror on the part of the Japanese banks. Those institutions are now finding their capital positions in jeopardy. As I mentioned earlier, the situation is so bad that the government has proposed that it directly purchase ¥30 trillion (U.S. $235 billion) of bank preferred stock and subordinated debt to maintain the banks' capital positions.

The final concern a banker should have is the profitability of his loans. Even if he has no worries about depositor withdrawals or about capital adequacy, too aggressive a lending pattern might lead to a surplus of loans that cannot be repaid. Under normal bureaucratic behavior, no one wants to admit that he made a bad loan. The incentive is to assume that the borrower's circumstances will change and that he will be able to repay at a later date. That fiction is most easy to maintain if the borrower is at least paying interest; those loans are known as "evergreen" loans.

The role of bank regulators is to "blow the whistle" on that kind of covering up of bad loans. Standards of regulatory supervision certainly vary among countries and, over time, within particular countries. It is fair to say that the Japanese authorities have been known to be extremely permissive by most standards in that regard. As Charles Calomiris noted in his international comparison of bank lending standards, "The Japanese banking system has hidden its losses behind a veil of regulatory forbearance for several years, hoping that improvement in economic performance will pay for bank loan losses."[39]

Thus, undercapitalized companies borrowing from undercapitalized banks became a key producer of capital for industrialization in Japan. Readers might make the analogy that the Japanese system was set up to create as many of those Cancer Cure plants as possible that we discussed in chapter 3. As the current problems in Japan suggest, the analogy hangs together. That said, the system worked quite well for many years. William Dietrich, who as the head of an American steel processing company had to compete with the Japanese, wrote approvingly of that system in 1991:

> The strengths of the Japanese financial system go well beyond providing low-cost capital. Given the overborrowed position of industrial companies and the overloaned condition of the city banks, the government, as the lender of last resort, is able to direct investment toward areas that will yield maximum benefits to the economy. . . . The Japanese financial system is so structured and operated that it is a powerful and effective instrument of state policy.[40]

That may have been the case when all was going well. Today, that house of cards is crashing down. The unrecognized bad loans are cluttering up the banks' balance sheets. While a bank can hide a small amount of bad loans, a bank full of them cannot lend. Why? While "good loans" are repaid, allowing the bank to relend the money to new customers, bad loans never repay their principal. So no new lending can take place. No new lending means that new economic activity is hard to finance. Eventually, the entire bank balance sheet comes to represent loans that financed economic activity that occurred years before. Recession sets in.

Lifetime Employment

The final key for building capital for rapid industrialization was the lifetime employment system. That system has received a lot of praise from foreign observers, particularly on the political left, but it was the real basis of Chalmers Johnson's notion that "the claims of individual citizens had to be held in check." The system had three elements: lifetime employment with virtually no mobility between firms, promotion with the firm by seniority, and compulsory retirement at age fifty-five. In essence, a school leaver makes a lifetime commitment to a firm and has very little freedom of choice after making that decision.

While the individual gives up freedom, an economic system that has just been ravaged by war and is desperately short on capital gains a lot from such a permanent employment system. The most obvious benefit is that the working-life compensation of such a system is "backloaded," that is, it occurs late in the worker's life. The firm can begin with an age pyramid dominated by younger workers and, at first, "underpay" them relative to the average compensation the worker expects over his working-life. That shortfall in wages can go directly into profits and therefore capital formation. A second boost to capital formation comes in the form of the early retirement age. While firms promise pensions, few pensions are sufficiently high to maintain an adequate lifestyle. In a society that has as high a life expectancy as anywhere on the planet, retirement at fifty-five or sixty requires significant saving during one's working life to provide for a long and idle period after retirement.

Those two boosts to capital formation are rather explicit in such a labor market arrangement. But two, more subtle, supports exist. The first is that a lifetime employment arrangement makes the cost structure of the firm more variable, reducing the risk of lending to the firm. Labor becomes a variable cost tied to profitability as firms more easily obtain wage concessions from workers who have nowhere else to go. That lower risk environment helps sustain the high debt-to-equity ratio described above, in which capital, paid for with interest, not dividends, is a fixed cost.

The other subtle support comes from a lack of options for the highly skilled and highly competent worker. In the U.S. market, particularly in a high-tech area like the computer industry, a dissatisfied group of top-ranking workers might think nothing of leaving the company and starting their own firm. That gives them enormous leverage over management, which must either pay them more (diverting capital) or face a severe disruption. The potential for such types of mutinies also makes lenders much more cautious and makes high-debt finance impossible. Most high-tech firms rely heavily on equity financing. In constrast, in Japan, with a financial market dominated by bank debt and no room for employment except through a lifetime system, these "malcontents" have no options, and the existing firm is a "safer" place.

Of course, all those arrangements carry side benefits to a society. Many Western admirers of Japan have noted the lower disparities of income, particularly lifetime income, in Japan relative to the United States. Of course, in a society where a single lifetime employment choice is made available, pay is set bureaucratically, and promotions are based solely on seniority, disparity of income can be sharply reduced. Most important, the high income outliers in the American income distribution, often entrepreneurs who left the corporate culture to start out on their own, are a much greater rarity in Japan. It is also obvious to the Western visitor that Japanese society manifests its inequalities not through income but through interpersonal relations. Hierarchy and status are continuously reinforced in every interpersonal encounter—from bowing as a form of address to where one walks in relation to one's boss.

The Bureaucracy as Ruling Class

In such an environment, little doubt exists about who really is boss. When a MITI official meets with the head of a company to discuss affairs informally, the MITI official is typically ten or fifteen years younger than the corporate chief. In a hierarchical society dominated by seniority-based promotion, that would be similar to a junior vice president in one company being the counterpart of the chief executive officer in another. Albert Craig quotes a young bureaucrat, Masuda Yoneji, in a most candid comment regarding his treatment by businessmen much his senior. His treatment was "with such a combination of respect and deference that for the first time in his life he felt the 'indescribable pleasure' of embodying in himself the 'power of the state.'"[41]

Why does the rest of Japanese society, in particular, the business community, tolerate such a concentration of power? Of course, the most obvious reason is that the bureaucracy holds enormous power. The development model described above gives the bureaucracy a substantial amount of control over the success and failure of an individual company. But that is somewhat circular: the bureaucracy has power because it has power. First among the reasons is a factor that all students of bureaucracy, dating at least from Max Weber, would recognize: the bureaucracy is cohesive in asserting its power.

Furthermore, the background, training, and recruitment of the bureaucracy serve to create a degree of homogeneity of perspective that allows the bureaucracy to maintain that cohesiveness of purpose. But, for practical reasons, the "bureaucracy" as a class is much larger than the upper reaches of public-sector employment. The informal ties between senior civil servants and their private-sector counterparts are vast. History goes a long way in explaining that development, and Sakakibara himself tends to give substantial credit to the U.S. occupation, at least indirectly. As noted earlier, the economic bureaucracy was left intact after the war's purges. The current structure of the Ministry of Finance remains virtually unchanged from that of 1937.[42] But the bureaucracy may also have had an easier time because its compatriots were taking over the corporate sector as well, thanks to MacArthur. Many of the individuals who provided the intellectual basis of the occupation were, naturally enough, American New Dealers. They argued that the owners of the prewar companies were largely responsible for Japanese aggression. The head offices of the major private firms were all purged. In contrast to the untouched government bureaucrats, even the minor children of major industrial families were subject to the purge. In the case of Mitsui and Mitsubishi, any two former employees of either of the firms were prohibited from ever going into business together.[43]

When the entrepreneurial founding families of the industrial concerns were eliminated from the scene, professional managers took over. In effect, the governing structure of the corporate sector of Japan also became bureaucratized. Or, as Sakakibara says, "GHQ's [General Headquarters'] extremely tough antimonopoly-anticapitalist policies, however, firmly established professional management power, which eventually was to act as a sturdy foundation for large Japanese corporations."[44] Interestingly, financial institutions were not subject to the general breakup of prewar industrial concerns. That allowed a shift to the bank-based capital lending described earlier that was not intrinsic to Japan. Before the war, direct financial markets, particularly the bond market, were flourishing. After the war, they were replaced almost entirely by the banks and their more bureaucratic and regulatory practices.

Thus, the occupation cemented bureaucratic control of the corporate sector as well as the government and put in place a system of corporate finance that reaffirmed the arrangement. That change meant that the system also concentrated power in a very small and cohesive group. In 1963, for example, roughly 65 percent of the top bureaucrats at the economic ministries were graduates of Tokyo University. The same was true for 40 percent of the top business executives in the country.[45] Of course, individuals enter those exalted ranks solely on the basis of a meritocratic examination system. While that may mean that the family backgrounds among this ruling group vary, their skill sets and socialization have been ruthlessly homogenized by the process of gaining admission.

William Dietrich, who by and large is an admirer of the Japanese system, summarizes that homogeneity well:

> In the United States the social-selection process may extend over a lifetime, allowing for several variables: "late bloomers," inheritance, class, family connections, the exercise of skill and cunning in lieu of formal education, and even a fair role for Lady Luck. In the much tighter Japanese social system, the importance of these factors is greatly diminished. The educational system, for better or for worse, carries the bulk of the burden of assigning each member of society a function and status, and thus his or her "proper place."[46]

Thus, a business leader questioning the legitimacy of the bureaucrat in making a decision, as is often the case in the United States because of a lack of experience in the "real world," would mean that leader's questioning the legitimacy of his own position.

As the bureaucrat and the business executive in Japan share a similar past and outlook on life, they also share a similar future. The Japanese have a special name for the signal that it is time to leave, "*katatataki,*" or patting on the shoulder. But early retirement in the bureaucracy means that the business community ends up attracting a large number of former bureaucrats into high positions of authority. In fact, the Japanese have a most telling name for retired bureaucrats moving into top positions in private corporations—*amakudari*—literally, descent from heaven. In a system in which knowledge of the bureaucratic decisionmaking process is financial life or death, recruitment of those individuals is a most sensible policy for the company.

Bureaucracy and Politicians

What is more remarkable than the acceptance of the bureaucracy by the corporate sector is the acceptance of the bureaucracy by the political sector. Again, though, the bureaucracy finds itself in a peculiarly influential position and thus is, by and large, able to influence the political process for much the same reasons as it influences corporate decisionmaking. This extent of power and influence makes it largely invulnerable from attack.

Members of the Diet have no independent policy staff and so are required to rely on the bureaucracy for all phases of their work. But the most important adage for any bureaucracy is that information is power. A recalcitrant politician who may seek independence from his nominal subordinates will soon be punished by them. An "inadvertent" but still critical omission during a briefing might leave the official unprepared for parliamentary debate. That form of discipline helps keep the individual politician in line.

But, as with the corporations, it is history and particularly the occupation by MacArthur that really cemented the dominance of the bureaucracy. That resulted from MacArthur's following a very natural path of least resistance in seeking talented men, relatively untainted by the war, to hold senior positions. Who else in 1946 had both the talents to govern and the absence of disqualifying military involvement in the war but the upper echelons of the civilian bureaucracy? Step one in bureaucratic ascendancy in politics was the bureaucrats' becoming the top politicians.

The first man MacArthur picked to be prime minister, Shigeru Yoshida, exemplified that. Yoshida had graduated from Tokyo University (of course) and pursued a successful career in the prewar Foreign Ministry. He was an acceptable prime minister because during the war he took an early and forceful position in seeking peace with the United States, for which the Tojo government had imprisoned him. Although he held office for seven years, Yoshida was still a Tokyo University–educated bureaucrat turned politician, hardly a "man of the people." Where else would he turn to staff the top political jobs in his administration but to men with similar backgrounds?

After he was forced from office, Japan had a brief interlude of professional politicians' holding the office of prime minister. But in 1957 Nobusuke Kishi took power. Just like Yoshida, Kishi was a former bureaucrat. Indeed, he had been a key member of the cabinet for economic mobilization during the war. So important was his bureaucratic role that the occupation declared him a class A war criminal. It was probably his bureaucratic arrogance that caused him to push the AMPO through the Diet in 1960. But, during his regime, former bureaucrats continued to hold most of the top political posts. He was followed by Hayato Ikeda (of income-doubling fame). Ikeda had been a top official in the Yoshida administration and had become famous for noting that "bankruptcies [of medium and small companies] were inevitable" and that poor Japanese families unable to afford rice should "eat barley." His bureaucratic arrogance had gone too far in 1952, when as minister of industry he was quoted as saying that it "cannot be helped" if some bankrupt business owners were "driven to suicide."[47] Next in line came Eisaku Sato, who, like the others, was a graduate of Tokyo University and a career civil servant. To show how tightly knit the fabric of the top classes was, Sato actually was the younger brother of Prime Minister Kishi. Thus, from 1946 until 1972 the political establishment was in no position to challenge bureaucratic rule. Indeed, a virtually seamless web existed between the upper echelons of the bureaucracy and the top elected officials in the land. The close alliance between the bureaucracy and the ruling Liberal Democratic Party continues to exist to the present.

In 1972 the first cracks began to emerge in that system, and they are cracks that are part of the undermining of the system to which we now turn. But even today, if we look to the mandarin to reform the system, we are looking in the wrong place, because, in Japan, the mandarin *is* the system.

5

Mandate of Heaven Withdrawn

Hell hath no fury like a bureaucrat scorned.

—*Milton Friedman*[1]

Today, with the Japanese economy and financial system in the midst of severe crisis, we can easily criticize the mandarin system. But we should first acknowledge its successes. Not only did Prime Minister Ikeda's income-doubling plan succeed, but Japanese GDP continued to expand at an extremely rapid rate. Today, Japanese per capita GDP is roughly equivalent to that of America or Europe.[2] Furthermore, if that sincerest form of flattery, imitation, is any guide, the Japanese created a model that has been imitated throughout East Asia. When America's leaders lecture Japan, as they did at the G-7 summit in 1997 and, as they regularly do when they visit Tokyo, they should bear in mind that before taking office, some of them were recommending that the United States imitate Japan in areas ranging from labor markets to industrial policy to fiscal affairs.[3]

Nor should any criticisms of Japan reflect negatively on the hard work and sacrifice of the Japanese people, for it is they, not the bureaucrats, who really rebuilt Japan. There is absolutely no reason why Japan, with a hard-working, highly educated, and talented population, cannot again be the envy of the world. But to do so, Japan must recognize its weaknesses. Furthermore, as the current financial crisis unfolds, we on the outside must understand why Japan has trouble acting the way we think it should to minimize the crisis. As we saw in our examination of America, the contrarian may have been successful, but he has limitations on his freedom of action. So, too, does the mandarin.

So we turn not to the programmatic changes that the Japanese government and bureaucracy might implement, but to the structural features of the Japanese paradigm that keep it performing the way it does. Those structural features grow from the choices Japan (and the occupation) made after the war, although some have even deeper roots. Until the political economy of Japan changes, and with it the assumptions that underpin its governing structure, Japan will continue to make the same types of choices that have characterized its postwar history. Understanding that structure of choices is key to determining the boldness of the Japanese response and evaluating whether the system will continue to be paralyzed in the face of the financial crisis in which it is now mired.

Structural Feature #1: Pork vs. Policy in Politics

One of the supposed strengths of the Japanese paradigm had been that highly trained and educated bureaucrats made policy. William Dietrich and others have contrasted that professional management of policy with the narrow "political" focus of American decisionmaking. In essence, "nonpolitical" means "beyond debate." While Americans may argue whether a government is "probusiness" or "proconsumer," or whether government should help business or be laissez-faire, the Japanese have settled those issues, especially with regard to trade and industrial development. In Japan, the bureaucracy is the guiding hand of business, and those issues are beyond debate.

But politics must be based on something. Politicians do not go before their constituents and ask them to toss a coin. Nor is it credible for a politician to go before the electorate and say, "Vote for me and I'll leave the bureaucrats alone to do the great job they've been doing." Suffice it to say that, as in other countries, politicians must justify their existence or they will be turned out of office.

The bureaucratic emphasis on policy setting meant, effectively, that national policies were not the realm of the politicians. That left an undue emphasis on what all politicians everywhere try to deliver: pork. No one imagines that pork-barrel projects are unique to Japan. They exist everywhere, and all politicians try to produce projects back home paid for by the central government. We have no more a concrete (literally) symbol of what a politician did for his voters than cutting the ribbon on a new highway or a new building paid for by the government.

In America, former Speaker of the House Tip O'Neill was famous for his saying, "All politics is local,"[4] by which he meant that delivering the goods and services to the constituents back home was crucial to electoral success. But that did not stop O'Neill and his colleagues from playing an active role in national policymaking and in using those policy issues to sway voters back home. In America and in most other democracies, we expect the politicians to take stands on "the issues." Nor do Japanese politicians completely ignore "the issues." A Japanese electoral campaign has some ideological content. What is different is the emphasis. When the bureaucracy makes all the key decisions, the emphasis on issues is misplaced. If a typical American campaign is five parts pork and five parts policy, one in Japan is nine parts pork and one part policy.

The constitution that General MacArthur bequeathed to the Japanese contributed to that deemphasis of policy. MacArthur had as his principal objective prohibiting the rise of a strong militarist leader and so designed a representation system to make that difficult. Instead of the single-member system of seats in which the largest vote getter is elected, MacArthur created multiseat districts in which the top three, four, five, or six vote getters enter Parliament. A national party with 55 percent of the votes might sweep Parliament in a single-member system. In the multimember system, the party would have to fight hard and carefully control its supporters to hold three of the five seats in a multimember district.

That system worked well at MacArthur's objective. But it also meant that members of the same political party were effectively competing against one another at election time. It is hard to run an issues-driven campaign when one or more of your competitors have endorsed exactly the same political manifesto as you have. The "marginal voters" to whom each politician naturally appeals are likely in such a system to be those of the politician's own party who may be tempted to vote for another candidate of that party. So the incentive to appeal on ideological grounds is replaced by the question, Who in my party has done the most for me?

The rise of one of the most successful mavericks in Japanese postwar history—Kakuei Tanaka—drove that point home to the Japanese political system. In 1972 the bureaucracy got the biggest surprise of its postwar stint in power when Tanaka bested Liberal Democratic Party rival Takeo Fukuda to succeed Sato as prime minister. Fukuda was clearly the favorite of the establishment, not only a graduate of Tokyo University, but first in his class at the law school. Tanaka, by contrast, never graduated from college. Fukuda rose on the fast track as a bureaucrat at the Ministry of Finance. Tanaka was a self-made man with a background in construction. In short, Fukuda was a mandarin, Tanaka was a man of the people.[5]

To pull off a coup like that against the policy-driven bureaucracy, Tanaka had to succeed famously at building a career on that other leg of politics: pork. Tanaka represented Niigata, the western Honshu prefecture where he grew up. It is on the "wrong" side of the spine of mountains that runs down Japan and thus is dominated in winter by blizzards, originating in Siberia, that gain moisture as they blow off the Sea of Japan. Tanaka, who learned the construction business from the ground up in his youth, founded the *Etsuzankai,* "the Association for Crossing the Mountains," which became the core of his political machine. He made sure that every village in his prefecture got the road, or the bridge, or the snow plow that it needed.

That tendency to deliver the goods persisted throughout his career. In his stint as postal minister he controlled licensing of new television stations. Before his ascendancy, the bureaucracy had granted only a handful of licenses. In a single weekend Tanaka overruled the bureaucrats in the ministry and gave out forty-three new permits, saying, "This is the time to make history in Japan's electronic waves."[6] In 1965 a crack in the stock market threatened a collapse in the securities sector. Tanaka, then finance minister, arranged a direct loan from the Bank of Japan to one of the four large brokerage firms of the country. It is a historical footnote that the firm in the most trouble during the Tanaka bailout was Yamaichi, which finally collapsed in 1997, during the current economic crisis.

It should surprise no one that this process creates a close tie between money and politics. Tanaka, a businessman and not a bureaucrat, had few compunctions about making the role of money more explicit in his new-found business. He is alleged to have told supporters that he got his cabinet job in 1958 by giving Prime Minister Kishi ¥3 million in cash. In his 1972 election as prime minister over Fukuda, he was rumored to have spent some ¥5 billion—the equivalent of U.S. $16 million at the time. At another juncture, Tanaka is reported to have taken a television announcer to his home to persuade him to be a candidate. There, a pile of cardboard boxes sat next to a safe. He opened a box, filled with yen, and handed it to the prospective candidate saying, "You can't be a politician if this amount of money makes you nervous."[7]

Money and favors created a powerful political machine. They inevitably undermined the bureaucracy as well. When Tanaka was succeeded as finance minister, his successor was reportedly told about the need to distribute midyear and year-end presents ranging from cosmetics for telephone operators and neckties for clerks to wads of cash for those of higher rank. The typical semiannual gift to the top 200 officials was ¥500,000 (about $3,500 today).[8]

Of course, one of the problems with delivering such money is the need to raise it. What ultimately brought Tanaka down was the so-called Lockheed bribery scandal. Tanaka urged All Nippon Airways, a private firm, to buy Lockheed planes for its fleet. In return, Lockheed paid Tanaka a ¥500 million commission. Of course, that was all part of the same system that began with his formation of the *Etsuzankai.* As was once attributed to him in another "deal," he said, "I don't want a bribe, I just want to receive political donations from the contractor who wins the bid."[9]

The scale of corruption only grew after Tanaka left office and perhaps reached its peak in the 1993 arrest of Shin Kanemaru, a great political fixer of the 1980s. When his homes and offices were raided, police found more than $30 million in cash and bearer bonds and more than 200 pounds of gold bars.[10]

Sakakibara notes that tendency as well:

> The role of politicians in this process is to tend to the funding needs of their local "enterprises" and to lobby the central government on their behalf. In this sense, Japanese politicians have a much stronger "entrepreneurial" side than their European or U.S. counterparts. This trait owes largely to the nature of the Japanese public sector, which is dominated by public works and financial operations.[11]

Some commentators, particularly Japanese critics of the system, identify such corruption and money politics as the problem. While unsavory, the Japanese economy and political system could well survive side payments between politicians and bureaucrats and winning contractors and politicians. No, the root of the problem is that politics has been reduced to the delivery of pork—or, as Sakakibara so delicately put it, that the "entrepreneurial" side of Japanese politicians stems from the public works nature of the Japanese public sector. Those side payments are just a natural outgrowth and supporting pillar of a system in which too much money is simply wasted on pork barrel projects.

Japan is world-renowned for having a high savings and investment rate. But a substantial portion of that investment is devoted to public works and private-sector projects related to those public expenditures. In 1985, for example, Japan spent 4.8 percent of its GDP on infrastructure projects, three times the share of GDP spent in the United States and roughly twice the share spent in Europe. Fixed-capital formation comprised 28 percent of total GDP compared with about 18 percent in the United States and Europe.[12]

Those two facts are related since the government spending is often only a portion of the "development" that happens when a new infrastructure project is laid. Sakakibara summed that point up nicely:

> In the process of implementing public works, the state plays an overseeing role as fund supplier rather than acting as the direct instigator. Even in the area of roads, where the share of the state and public corporations is comparatively large, it still only accounts for 30 percent. This state role is extremely important when subsidies and other direct funding are combined with the previously mentioned indirect fund supply of investments and loans.[13]

In short, much of the extra 10 percent of GDP that Japan spends on fixed investment is infrastructure-related. Japan has reached the situation where it has one construction company for every 200 people, where 10 percent of all jobs are in construction. Today, that extra 10 percent of GDP spent on infrastructure amounts to roughly $450 billion per year.[14] The real question is, What do the Japanese get for all that extra money spent on infrastructure? The answer is far from clear.

Despite Japan's vast financial wealth, typical Japanese workers live in small apartments and are forced to commute standing up, packed like sardines, for sixty to ninety minutes each way to get to work. Surely those extra infrastructure funds have not bought better housing or better rail service. To get to a golf course on a weekend (assuming one has the $200 green fee and can get a reservation), the golfer must set out extra early for the two- to three-hour drive. Surely those extra infrastructure funds have not gone into parks and recreation.

Thus, one of the most fundamental problems caused by the political emphasis on "pork" is a low return on public-sector investments. The key issues—adequate rail service, particularly at rush hour, better housing, and better recreation facilities—have managed to get pushed to the back of the agenda. Furthermore, because government infrastructure spending attracts private spending, much of the investment by Japanese companies gets tied into similar low-return projects. The politicians and the bureaucrats who control those funds benefit from this system—so the system is resistant to change. The people and economy of Japan pay the price.

Of course, everyone realizes that the political system is dysfunctional and corrupt. So everyone regards investigations of money politics and corruption as the "problem," much as they are viewed in the United States. Scapegoating, as we noted before, is an inevitable part of a system trying to save itself. But American political reformers should take note. Despite all the money floating around in Japanese politics, the government bans political advertising on television and strictly limits individual and corporate contributions. The problem is not the corruption but rather the issueless nature of the Japanese political scene. As long as the bureaucracy makes policy, the politicians have only one job to do: bring home the pork.

Structural Feature #2: Excessive Debt Finance

As we discussed in the last chapter, the highly leveraged approach to Japanese finance was one of the keys to its success. By relying on debt finance and a highly leveraged banking sector, an impoverished Japan was able to take full advantage of the scarce capital that was available to it. Unfortunately, that important part of the postwar growth paradigm was left unchanged, even though Japan became one of the richest societies on the planet. The result was a hyperabundance of capital that created a frenetic asset boom followed by a financial collapse.

Consider again the process described in chapter 3 by which an asset bubble gets going. An initial shortage of land or buildings leads to a variety of new investment projects. Land prices and existing space get bid up in price. People feel richer, borrow against the higher value of their land, homes, and offices, and invest the proceeds. Some of the investment is in still more capacity; some simply results in ever higher prices for existing real estate. At some point, the process comes to a halt when too much real estate is on the market and prices collapse.

The Japanese experience of the late 1980s—the "bubble"—developed along the same psychological lines that exist everywhere. What was different about Japan was the extent to which the banking system force-fed capital into the bubble to make it one of the most explosive in history. At one point during 1989, analysts estimated that the land of the Imperial Palace grounds in the middle of Tokyo had a theoretical value more than the entire state of California.[15] Typically, the rate of growth of land valuations fairly closely tracked the rate of growth of nominal GDP in Japan. Beginning in 1984, the trend began to diverge. At the peak of the trend, commercial land prices in Japan traded at a level over three times what would have been their normal level. Residential land prices were at two times the "normal" level.[16]

The Japanese economy has languished ever since the bubble burst. That too is an outgrowth of the highly leveraged bank-debt-driven financial system that was key to the postwar Japanese economic miracle. To understand that process, imagine yourself as the typical bank officer. You have just followed standard procedure and approved a loan of ¥95 million to match the ¥5 million a developer has put up to build an office building. You assumed that real estate prices would continue their historic trend upward and therefore had no trouble with the high debt-to-equity ratio in that loan.

Now imagine that instead of rising, real estate prices fall by 20 percent. The ¥100 million property in question is now worth ¥80 million. The borrower comes in and says, "I am so sorry, but I am unable to repay the loan as the property is now worth less than what I owe." What should you, the banker, do? Consider your options.

The first option is to foreclose on the property. A number of reasons unique to Japan, including its bankruptcy procedures, make that an unlikely option. But that option looks unattractive for another reason that has little to do with the details of Japanese law. Remember, not only was the borrower highly leveraged, but so was your bank. The bank would have to take a ¥15 million loss if it foreclosed on the property and would reduce the value of its capital by that amount. Following the highly leveraged procedures of Japanese banking, the bank had extended its loan-to-capital ratio at a twenty-to-one ratio. Taking a ¥15 million reduction in capital would eliminate not only the capital standing behind that ¥95 million loan, but behind loans totaling ¥300 million! In effect, the bank would have to start calling in more of its outstanding loan portfolio to keep up its capital-to-loan ratio. The trouble with calling in all those other loans is that most of the other borrowers are in similar difficulties and would require further write-downs of capital. So foreclosure is not an attractive option.

The second option is to offer the borrower a deal. As a lending officer, you have long valued this customer's business, you explain. It is, after all, a Japanese tradition to believe in long-term business relationships and not short-term profit. So the bank will not foreclose on the loan. All it asks is that the borrower continue to pay interest on the loan. That way, with interest coming in, the bank could continue to classify the loan as "performing." It would not have to write down a loss on the loan, reduce its capital, or call in other loans. Oh, and by the way, if the old interest rate should prove unaffordable, we can be flexible on terms as well. As long as the interest rate covers the cost of funds, the loan will still generate a cushion. Over time, the bank can use that cushion to build up a loan-loss reserve to cover the eventuality of foreclosure.

Japanese banks went for that second option, arguably a very sensible call in a difficult situation when considered on a case-by-case basis. But remember the famous lesson of Keynes—the fallacy of composition. The balance sheets of the Japanese banking system began to fill up with loans like the one described above. They continued to pay interest and so were never counted as "bad" loans, but the bank was in no position to get rid of them and free up either the money or the bank capital it had committed to the loan. To do so would require the bank to take a loss and mark down the value of its capital.

Consider, for example, what happened to the portfolios of the eleven city banks, what in the United States we would call commercial banks. In 1985 they had outstanding real estate loans worth some ¥6.9 trillion. Ten years later, their real estate loans totaled ¥26.7 trillion.[17] The trouble was, the value of Japanese commercial real estate in 1995 was actually a bit lower than it was in 1985.[18] Virtually the entire ¥20 trillion increase in the banks' real estate exposure probably represented loan commitments not unlike the one described above.

On top of that, banks also lent to construction companies and other financial conduits. The latter were part of the financial pyramid scheme that helped the Japanese system gain access to cheap capital. The former were naturally good customers during the boom period. But, after the bubble burst, all those industries were in trouble. Of the twenty-one big banks in the country, including the commercial, trust, and long-term credit banks, total loans to those three industries expanded threefold between 1985 and 1995, from ¥32 trillion to ¥103 trillion, an increase worth $680 billion. Roughly one-third of the balance sheet of the twenty-one largest Japanese banks comprised loans to those three sectors in 1995, up from just one-fifth ten years earlier.[19]

What is the harm in this? Not foreclosing on someone whose investment just happened to go bad seems like the kind of bank with which many readers might like to do business. As long as the original borrower still promises to repay the loan sometime, is there any harm in this practice? After all, this resembles somewhat the way many Americans treat their credit cards, just paying the interest and letting the principal sit.

Not foreclosing on such loans has two problems. The first is that those funds are essentially "dead" when it comes to funding new economic activity. Imagine a small businessman walking into one of these banks to fund his expanding enterprise. "Sorry," he would be told, "but all of our funds are lent out and our capital committed." For an economy nurtured by bank capital, that is slow strangulation. All the economic activity that the banking sector finances had already taken place years ago when the bad-loan office buildings were constructed; the banks have no room to finance new activity.

The second problem has to do with the property market itself, for it too is dead in this circumstance. None of the owners of any of the property purchased during the bubble years can sell. The proceeds from the sale would not cover the bank loan on the property. Buyers also recognize the problems in the market. When everyone knows that all those bad loans are underwriting property that has to be liquidated *sometime,* why would anyone want to buy *now*? The overhang on the market is quite substantial, and its eventual elimination would keep prices depressed for a long time to come. No one should want to buy in such a structurally depressed market.

So Japan sits and languishes, drowning in bad debt, with its banks paralyzed. A highly leveraged capital market driven by bank debt works fine when an economy is booming along at record rates of growth. Maximum use is made of scarce capital. The other key advantage of bank debt over bond debt is that it is more easily subject to regulation. Just as the political system is set up to give mandarins, not politicians, control over policy, so the capital markets are set up to favor bureaucrats, not capitalists.

Structural Feature #3: The Revenge of Lifetime Employment

Just like bureaucratic control and a highly leveraged banking sector, the third pillar of the Japanese success story—its labor market—has also turned into an economic ball and chain. Much of this was eminently predictable. Recall that one of the key advantages of lifetime employment to firms rebuilding after the Second World War was that an employee's lifetime compensation (the only issue that mattered when you have lifetime employment) was back-loaded. That allowed firms to load up on a relatively young work force at an artificially low labor cost. But time passes, and the age structure of the Japanese work force is decidedly unfavorable to the traditional age-based wage structure.

Demography has also been punishing. Like many countries, Japan enjoyed a baby boom just after the war. But the baby boom collapsed much sooner than in other countries. For example, 46.5 percent more babies were born in the five-year period centered on 1950 than in the five-year period centered on 1960. Today, the Japanese birth rate is well below the replacement level.[20] In such a demographic structure a seniority-based system of wage compensation produces a high-cost, not a low-cost, system. Indeed, in one important respect, the labor market system is quite like the bank debt system. Once the period of rapid economic growth stops, the institution is left with a large stock of older loans and workers that produces subpar returns but cannot be replaced. As a result, the institution has no room for the new and the profitable.

But a lifetime employment system also creates an inefficiency for an economy in transition. Today, the market is changing very rapidly and demands nimble firms that are able to redeploy their productive assets—capital and labor—very quickly. The contrast with America is quite striking. There, every week roughly 325,000 people apply for unemployment benefits, even as total employment grows at the rate of 50,000 per week. Total new job creation therefore amounts to some 20 million per year, more than making up for some 17 million jobs that disappeared.[21] On net, roughly one job in six in America is "new" every year.

Also missing from the Japanese lifetime employment system is a vibrant entrepreneurial system. A Bill Gates (cofounder of Microsoft) has very little chance in a society that favors meritocratic advancement. After all, Gates dropped out of Harvard. In Japan he would have had no access to capital. Yet the Bill Gateses of the world are key to a dynamic economy. In the first quarter of 1998, for example, the rise in the market capitalization of Gates's company equaled roughly half the growth of American GDP.[22] Granted, that may say more about irrational exuberance in the stock market, but the virtual absence of such firms in Japan is a real problem. Cultural biases certainly do not help. It is hard to imagine a Bill Gates succeeding in a society where a popular expression is, "The protruding nail gets hammered down."

If one had to select a word to describe the Japanese labor market, like so much else in Japan, it would be *bureaucratic.* How else would one assess a system that places its newcomers on a career path dictated exclusively by their performance on a written test? Or in which that test examined factual knowledge rather than aptitude? Where but in a bureaucracy does one find promotion and compensation based solely on seniority?

Interestingly, like the political system and the capital market, such a labor market helps maintain the bureaucratic status quo in the decisionmaking process. The key to bureaucratic domination is that it be clear to all that the governmental apparatus attracts the best and the brightest. That would tend to produce a higher quality of decisionmaking, of course. But, probably more important, that is the key to the bureaucracy's legitimacy as well. If high fliers were to go elsewhere, one might tend to think that they could make decisions at least as well as individuals in the government. By making the entire private labor market universally unattractive to those high fliers, the attractions offered by a career in the elite civil service suffer no competitors.

It probably also helps in this regard that the Japanese tax system is particularly punishing on high earners. The top tax rate is 65 percent. It is very difficult to become independently wealthy as an entrepreneur when the Ministry of Finance is a two-thirds partner in any success you might have. Making money is therefore diminished as an alternative. It is much more sensible to be the bureaucrat in the Ministry of Finance who collects the 65 percent while letting others do the work and take the risks.

But now the Japanese lifetime employment system faces another challenge that no one dreamed of after the war—emigration. Today, nearly three-quarters of a million Japanese citizens live abroad, a figure that has risen 50 percent in a decade.[23] Many corporations make sure that they rotate some of their most promising managers through foreign assignments. Exposure to the world outside Japan gives individuals exposure to an alternative their parents and grandparents never dreamed of. It is not simply a choice of lifetime employment by one large corporation or another—but of an entirely different working life.

Exposure to an alternative lifestyle is particularly corrosive for one key element of the population—educated women. Employment prospects in Japan for professional women exist, but only if the individual is prepared to make extraordinary sacrifices. The great majority of Japanese women face truly dismal prospects in the work force and therefore stay home, focusing on the children's education and managing the family finances. But, when their husbands are stationed abroad, they are exposed to American or European upper-middle-class living standards, especially housing, that would be considered palatial in Tokyo. Nearly all the younger Japanese who have been exposed to life abroad have a common goal—returning to live abroad. They also share a common motivation: pressure from their wives.

The potential threat this poses to the Japanese economy should not be underestimated, for Japan now faces the possibility of a brain drain. Educated women and men are both likely to find their immediate postgraduation prospects brighter abroad than at home, particularly if they are already fluent in a foreign language. Freshly minted MBAs can well earn more in New York or London than they could expect to earn on the traditional career ladder in Tokyo until they were well into their thirties, or perhaps later. And, if those MBAs are female, their lifetime earnings, lifestyle, and professional prospects are much higher abroad. While that threat to the system is still limited, its menace will grow in the years ahead, siphoning off the very workers a revitalized Japan will need the most, unless the Japanese substantially modify the traditions established in the postwar labor market.

Structural Feature #4: Bureaucratic Attitudes

The labor and capital markets are foundering because they were established along lines that are no longer the best suited to a thriving modern economy. The political system prevents a rapid change in policy because the politicians have essentially been eliminated from the process, leaving most matters to unelected mandarins in the bureaucracy. All this means that if one is going to find the key to the challenges facing Japan, he must return to examining bureaucratic behavior and attitudes. Given the entrenched position of the bureaucracy in Japanese politics and the Japanese economy, it is quite reasonable to argue that if change is to be made, it will be made by the mandarins.

Sakakibara, our quintessential mandarin, is quite confident: "As we have done for the 130 years since the Meiji Restoration, we will quickly absorb what needs to be absorbed and become fully competitive with the Anglo-Saxon and other systems."[24] The term *we* can be subject to two somewhat different interpretations, *we* the Japanese and *we* the elite bureaucracy. After all, the elite bureaucracy did the absorption after the Meiji Restoration. Suffice it to say that Sakakibara believes in reform from the top down. In ruminating on Japan's immediate prospects, he states:

> [T]he history of reform is surprising: it has often been tough conservatives who have implemented genuine reforms. Edmund Burke spoke of radical reform to preserve nationhood, and it is exactly that type of reform that the Hashimoto government has set about implementing. I, for one, have long defended the Japanese-style market economy, and my position remains unchanged.[25]

What exactly is the "Japanese-style market economy" that Sakakibara is defending? It may be quite different from what we now think of as a market economy. Certainly, different countries will adopt political and economic systems that are suited to their histories and particular circumstances. (This book in fact is an effort to explain the distinct political and economic paradigms of the United States, Japan, and continental Europe.) Sakakibara goes further:

> However, a more fundamental issue is whether or not democracy and neoclassical capitalism are the only or ultimate goals, or even whether any goal needs to be established. China has set its sights on establishing a socialist market economy, and relative to Russia . . . (which experimented in shock therapy aimed at swiftly establishing democracy and neoclassical capitalism) . . . has so far succeeded in introducing many facets of market mechanisms without major economic or political upheaval.[26]

Sakakibara tends to agree with Samuel Huntington's argument that the cold war was largely a Western civil war between the conflicting ideologies of socialism and neoclassical economics. Those ideologies, in Sakakibara's view, were different versions of progressivism, which sought "a rapid increase and fair distribution of material welfare." Today, Sakakibara says, "Progressivism, which has been the dominant ideology for the past 200-odd years and particularly the past 50 years, has to be and is, in fact, ending."[27]

The first threat to progressivism is the rise of the multinational corporation whose interests "and those of workers and consumers start to diverge and the cohesion of the nation-state as an economic unit disintegrates."[28] Sakakibara concurs with former U.S. Labor Secretary Robert Reich's view that the relatively free movement of financial capital and the globalization of markets lead to strategic trade rather than free trade, undermining the progressivist global trading order.

The second threat to progressivism is the environment, and in this regard he also departs from advocates of economic progress:

> Optimists argue that the causality between greater human activity and environmental destruction is not well established, and that environmentally friendly technological innovation will eventually solve these problems. This is a typically arrogant progressivist view. . . . The progressivists' confidence in human competence and technology could properly be termed a myth because there is no logical reason to believe such path-breaking technological change will occur.[29]

Sakakibara sees this collapse of Western progressivist ideology as leading to a new nationalist impulse, away from the dominance of the West and its alleged universality:

> The reemergence of civilization consciousness is directly related to deep disillusionment with the ideology of progressivism. . . . Not universality but domination has produced the ascendance of the West. The clash of civilizations is not the unavoidable result of coexisting civilizations, but rather the result of contact with Western progressivism.[30]

It would, of course, be a mistake to ascribe the views of Sakakibara to that of the entire Japanese bureaucracy. Nor are his views uniquely Japanese. His views of the shortcomings of neoclassical economics might well be echoed in the upper ranks of American academia and bureaucracy, for example. But it is striking that this man is not likely to turn Japan over to unbridled markets. Nor is his view questioning democracy as an ultimate goal and praise for "market socialism" in China a particularly ringing endorsement of government by the common man.

Someone seeking a single word to describe that view might well choose "Confucian." His views are nationalistic, anticapitalistic, and bureaucratic. He emphasizes that "premodern philosophies and religions, particularly Eastern ones, respect nature and the environment. In Japanese Shintoism there is no clear-cut demarcation between nature and human beings."[31] He takes pride in what has been achieved in Japan and in particular, "that there are virtually no capitalists, that an extremely egalitarian pattern of income distribution has been realized, and that competition via an efficient market system exists in Japan."[32]

Japan, he argues, is a system of "true equality and participation." The question is whether it "can be maintained as the system becomes more open and transparent in response to the trend toward deregulation and internationalization."[33] The skeptic can wonder about the term *true equality*, which has a regrettably Orwellian ring, and about whether the office ladies and late bloomers stuck in dead-end jobs—bowing from the waist—fully appreciate just how extremely egalitarian Japan really is. But that is arguably a cultural difference.

Sakakibara is willing to make reforms, but no one should doubt that his objective is really to defend the status quo. Those wondering what path Japan is likely to take in the future take the following words by Sakakibara quite seriously:

> It is precisely in order to uphold the basic tenets of the system and to maintain the prototype that its antiquated parts should undergo an extensive overhaul. . . . Instead of trying to turn Japan into some cheap, capitalist society in the name of deregulation and internationalization,

> for example, bold, structural reform is required to maintain the impartiality of the public sector and the democratic features of the Japanese firm.[34]

The question for Japan, Asia, and the world is whether this type of conservative reform, led by the bureaucracy and instituted from the top down, is really the solution or whether instead it will perpetuate the problem. At the moment, we wait for the answer. But one thing is certain: the bureaucracy is unlikely to reform fundamentally a system of which it is the central part. The Ministry of Finance will not voluntarily go out of business. Either those Burkian reforms succeed or Japan may risk a political upheaval that will place more than its economy at risk. Neither eventuality is likely to be painless.

6

The Dictates of History

Whosoever desires constant success must change his conduct with the times.
—Attributed to Niccolo Machiavelli[1]

So far we have seen how the American system of political economy sought out a contrarian to play the role of economic stabilizer. The system appears to have found him in Alan Greenspan, carefully monitoring the dials and levers of the U.S. economy. In Japan, a Confucian bureaucracy, inadvertently entrenched in power by the American occupation half a century ago, wrestles with a major economic crisis. Both systems are products of historical development, the depression and Second World War having pruned and shaped the institutions of political economy. But, in both cases, history has left its mark and then has been left behind. That is not the case in Germany, where historical memories not only influence policy through the shaping of institutions but live on as the driving thoughts of today's decisionmakers.

The city of Bonn sits on the west bank of the Rhine River far from the center of Germany in any sense of the word: geographic, demographic, or economic. As capital cities go, it is far from impressive, with just 295,000 people; it ranks as Germany's twentieth largest city. But, for nearly half a century, Bonn has been the capital of Germany not because of its size or centrality, but because of historical dictates. Two historical facts converged to tell how Bonn happened to become the capital. First, in the final competition between Frankfurt and Bonn, Bonn won owing to the fact that Konrad Adenauer, Germany's first chancellor, had his home in Rhöndorf, a cozy twenty minutes away by car. Frankfurt, being a bankers' place, got the Bundesbank, the central bank of Germany, and the Bundesverfassungsgericht, the Supreme Court, was located in Karlsruhe. The Allies were obsessed with preventing a concentration of power; hence, the three principal pillars of political power were neatly decentralized, one in the British zone and two in the American zone, and each in what today we would call a different "media market."[2]

The second, and most pragmatic, historical fact was that Bonn was as far away from the Red Army as possible, putting the Rhine, the only significant natural barrier in Northern Germany, between the capital and the most likely would-be invader. As late as the 1970s, that was a serious issue, as described in the best-selling book *The Third World War*, by the British NATO General Sir John Hackett.

For the forty-four years before 1989, the prospect of invasion from the east was a central fact of German life. NATO planning indicated that Russian tanks could cross most of Germany in a matter of a few days, before support from across the Atlantic was possible. Universal conscription was therefore a fact of life for German teenagers. But casualties would likely go far beyond males of military age. Tactical nuclear weapons, as well as biological and chemical agents, were all potentially in play in the event war broke out. That a war could leave much German territory essentially uninhabitable was not impossible.

That deep-rooted fear expressed itself in the emergence of Europe's largest peace movement in the 1970s. Ultimately, the peace movement and the environmentalists merged to form the Green Party. Today, the German Green Party is the largest of its kind in the world and has become a coalition partner in the national government.[3]

These sobering facts would focus the mind of any leader. Helmut Kohl, Germany's chancellor from 1982 until October 1998, also shared most of that history from personal experience. His home, the chancellery, sits in Bonn, just a short drive from the parliament building. But the prospective war that Kohl successfully avoided during his tenure—and on terms of which he (and Germany) should be justly proud—was not just an isolated prospect of the future. It was a logical extension of the past. Germany had been through three major wars in the century before Kohl became its leader.

The first, against France, whose frontier sits roughly 150 miles southwest of Bonn, was successful and led to the creation of a modern, unified Germany. (Bonn is just sixty miles from the Belgian frontier, which the German armies used as a crossing point into France.) The second, against France and Britain to the west and Imperial Russia to the east, led to the collapse of Russia and the rise of the Communists. That war also led ultimately to a German defeat at the hands of the Western powers. The third war, again on both fronts, ended with Germany effectively partitioned among four victorious powers: America, Russia, Britain, and France. The blessedly avoided fourth war would most likely have resulted from Russian attempts to push its zone of occupation further west.

Kohl's vision of how to prevent a fourth war involved change on both the eastern and western fronts. In the west, it involved linking a reunified Germany inextricably into a unified European framework. In the east, it involved a reunified Germany, linking the eastern zone under Russian occupation to the rest of Germany. That paradox is highlighted by the fact that Kohl would have vetoed unification if the price had been German neutrality. All Soviet pressures to trade unification for Germany's NATO membership were fruitless. Thus, surrendering a measure of German sovereignty to a (Western) pan-European decision process was a logical consequence. Given the shared border with nine neighbors, a nonintegrated, unified Germany would become unbearable for the continent.[4]

That geopolitical reality had long shaped the views of West Germany's leaders. Former Chancellor Konrad Adenauer, recognizing the dictates of history, dubbed "Westintegration" as the cornerstone of his philosophy. When the Federal Republic was fully integrated in the West as NATO member and cofounder of the European Economic Community, former Chancellor Willy Brandt opened a second front known as "Ostpolitik."[5] Former Chancellor Kohl took the Western victory in the cold war—triumph on the eastern front—to establish a deeper integration with the West. Reunification had only made the integration of Germany into something larger all the more imperative.

An important piece of that merger of sovereignty—the establishment of a single European currency—plays an important role in our story of global economic developments and the development now taking place in the international economy. That is what brings us to Bonn.

Personal History and Monetary Union

One of the greatest monetary experiments in history is being undertaken today in Europe. Chancellor Kohl was the key economic puppetmaster who pulled the strings on this one. But, as we shall see, historic necessity pulled the psychological strings on Kohl. What is most difficult for a non-European to understand is German motives in such a process. After all, it would appear that Germany is dealing from strength and yet sacrificing so much. Its currency, the deutsche mark, is the envy of Europe and, along with the Bundesbank, the pride of Germany. In effect, Germany's monetary policy dictates the monetary policies of its European neighbors. Under the arrangements that Kohl worked out with his compatriots, the deutsche mark would disappear and be subsumed by a pan-European currency: the Euro. On the board that will determine European monetary policy, German nationals will have just two of seventeen votes. That does not, at first blush, seem an attractive tradeoff.

The answer to understanding German (and Kohl's) motivation lies not in the parliamentary buildings of Bonn, but in a modern building near the Rhine about a half mile from the chancellery. It is the Haus der Geschichte der Bundesrepublik Deutschland—the History Museum of the German Federal Republic, also known as the Bonn Republic, that Kohl played an instrumental role in building. On display are the artifacts of everyday life through the past half century, from 1945 to 1995, artfully used to tell the story of the country from a viewpoint seldom seen by the Western world. Chancellor Kohl, who led his party for roughly half that period, of course figures prominently, but the displays are decidedly nonpartisan in their presentation.

Here you can see the dictates of history as they bear down on a modern Germany. But when you hear members of the Kohl family speak, you realize that the story told in this museum is also the story of their own lives. And among the most important parts is the German history *before* Helmut Kohl became chancellor. That early piece explains *why*

Kohl became chancellor and why he acted the way he did once in office. The history in this museum is not some abstraction gleaned from textbooks. Some of its most moving moments were lived by many of the same people who are making Germany's choices today and offer an experience that extends across all political parties and social groups.

Since the museum depicts the history of the Federal Republic of Germany, the story in the museum begins with the Allied armies' occupying German soil in 1945. The details of the war are left behind. So the most dramatic impression one encounters in the museum is just how miserable an experience it is to be on the losing side of a war. To older readers, that may sound trite. But to Americans and to the vast majority of Germans who are under age fifty, defeat in war is something that they have never personally experienced. Granted, the Western occupation of Germany was far less draconian than that which Germany had earlier inflicted on Europe. But that is batting in a weak league. Even in the best of circumstances, defeat necessarily entails destruction, which in Germany was vast. It also means the end of many of the most cherished relationships in one's life. Further, despite the Western occupation's relatively benign character, it still had its decidedly punitive aspects.

At first, the Western occupation seemed to be governed by the Morgenthau Plan, named for its creator, U.S. Treasury Secretary Henry Morgenthau. That plan was designed to turn Germany into a harmless pastoral demilitarized zone in the heart of Europe. The population was put on rations of 900 calories per day. Those rations are exhibited in the museum along with a comment on them at the time: "Too little to live on, too much to die on." Even British Field Marshal Lord Montgomery noted that the average rations given to the Germans in the British zone were the same as had been given to the inmates of the Belsen concentration camp during the war.[6]

The population was put to work cleaning up the devastation from the war. A leading occupation was scraping the dried mortar off bricks in the rubble, so the bricks could be reused. And there was a lot of rubble to clean up, mostly from the civilian infrastructure. An analysis by the noted Harvard economist John Kenneth Galbraith examined the effects of Allied bombing. He concluded that virtually all the destruction had been meted out to the civilian sector, while the German war machine had been virtually untouched by the relentless Allied carpet bombing. The study points out that German military production peaked in December 1944, right at the height of the strategic bombing offensive.[7]

Though the bombing did little to win the war for the Allies, it did ruin the German civilian economy. And with wartime production without a market, the country was broke and starving. That experience also had an important psychological effect. Though Germany was flattened, its economy came back quickly once the economy was freed from wartime controls. The Germans who lived through that subsumed an important lesson: They understand the difference between physical destruction and an economic problem. In the 1920s they had experienced the latter without the former; now it was the reverse.

One is also reminded, walking through the museum, that the political hatreds of Europe are deeply embedded. Konrad Adenauer, who eventually became the first chancellor of West Germany, had to flee his temporary refuge in a Benedictine monastery in the French zone of occupation and move to the British zone to escape arrest—and possibly worse.[8] Despite his later policies at rapprochement with France, the postwar French government clearly viewed him as an enemy.

If life in the zone of Western occupation was bleak, the behavior of the Russians was truly ghastly. As the Soviet army advanced, native Germans were displaced and forced to flee westward. Some fled on the ice of the frozen shores of the Baltic. Black and white file footage of that exodus across the ice is played on a screen at the museum, along with scenes of Soviet aircraft strafing those fleeing unarmed civilians and dropping bombs around the group in an effort to break up the ice and drown them.[9] In total, more than 12 million people, roughly one German in every five, were displaced wanderers, forced to flee their homes on foot.[10]

One of those 12 million was Hannelore Kohl, the former chancellor's wife. An attractive and petite woman who looks far younger than her sixty-five years, she and her family fled from their home in Saxony to escape the advancing Red Army. When she arrived in the West, emaciated and exhausted, the Red Cross officially classified her as "unsavable." She recounts how an American GI, the first black man she had ever seen in her life, gave her a large container of strawberry jam as she and her family lay exhausted on the side of the road. She repackaged the jam and proceeded to sell it on the black market, earning enough for the family to buy the food they needed to live.[11]

Also striking to an American listener is the absence of a sense of "victimhood." These stories are told matter-of-factly. One also gets a strong sense of Germany's having been in the wrong, particularly in the case of the Second World War. Kohl, despite his position, but perhaps because of his sense of history, does not fully trust Germany on its own. As one walks through time in the museum, one sees pictures of Adenauer and other early German leaders attempting to make amends to the State of Israel through contributions to Jewish refugees who settled there. That sense of having been historically in the wrong, accompanied by a continuing sense of guilt, is the reason Kohl feels that Germany must be inextricably linked to Europe—that it cannot be on its own. That thus explains the twin purposes of German policy—a reassertion of sovereignty in the East through the reunification of Germany coupled with a partial surrender of sovereignty in the West as Germany becomes inextricably linked to Europe.

To the outsider this seems a paradox, a puzzle. But the answer to the puzzle about what motivated Chancellor Kohl to make the deals he made is here in the "history" museum, which was built at his instigation. For to Kohl, and to his family, this is not history; it is the story of their lives. It is also the story of the lives of the generation of voters who returned Kohl to power—against the odds—in four successive elections.

Generational Shift

Born in 1930, Kohl represents the generation that was just a bit too young to serve during the war, but old enough to have had the war and its aftermath shape their lives. He lost his older brother in the war. His father, who had seen service in the First World War, was called up in the reserves and returned to his family in 1943 after having seen service in Poland.[12] Making sure that the suffering that marked their youth is not experienced by their children and grandchildren is a powerful and highly personal motivation.

On September 27, 1998, Chancellor Kohl was defeated after sixteen years in office. The election appeared to hinge on economics. German unemployment, although it has fallen somewhat since, began in the spring of 1998 at a postwar record. Dissatisfaction, even angst, has been the dominant mood for several years. Once again, Germany has an economic problem, but no destruction. Doubts about the economic deal Kohl made in 1990 to merge the former Soviet sector into western Germany are frequently voiced. Much quiet opposition still exists to Kohl's plan to bind Germany to Europe so tightly economically through monetary union and to sacrifice the deutsche mark in the process. The view is widespread that the unemployment and economic difficulties of modern Germany are in large part the result of these two mergers: of the two Germanies and of Germany into Europe.

So, on the surface, the election may well have hinged on economics. But much deeper down, it hinged on history. Mr. Kohl's opponent, now chancellor, was the fifty-three-year-old leader of Lower Saxony, Gerhard Schröder. He has no memories of the war or its immediate aftermath. Although his father was killed in the war the year of his birth, in his memory Germany has always been a prosperous economic power. And, for the first time in Mr. Kohl's political career, the majority of German voters also shared no memories of the war or the occupation. What the typical voter had was a sense that the German economic miracle had come to a halt. And the story of that miracle takes us back, once again, to the history museum.

Roots of German Postwar Success: Free Markets and Hard Money

The Germany that the Allied armies occupied in the spring of 1945 was a land of bombed-out buildings and a subsistence level of economic activity. With the production and transportation systems largely destroyed, the prospect of widespread starvation loomed for Germans in the winter of 1945–1946. But genuinely severe economic deprivation continued for three long and seemingly endless years after the Allied armies entered Germany. Why? In large measure, the occupying forces did not know what to do, so inertia took its course. Wartime price controls were continued and rationing provided the skeleton of the distribution system for what little there was. Commerce existed only on the "black" market, at prices and under terms that the occupation rules technically prohibited.

Then, on Sunday June 20, 1948, one of the most amazing policy coups in economic history took place. Ludwig Erhard, the occupation-appointed minister of economics, issued an order that immediately abolished nearly all controls on wages and prices. Erhard was fond of telling visitors that he acted on Sunday because the offices of the occupation armies were closed. Given their predilection for wanting to control everything, he felt sure that they would have countermanded his order. The next week, when he was called before the military authorities to explain on whose authority he had issued his price-liberalizing decree, he answered, "My own."[13]

Within days the shops were full of goods, and within months the German economic miracle was underway. The success of the Erhard reform was so obvious that the American occupation authorities decided to let the process proceed. By 1950 production reached its prewar high, and by 1958 West Germany passed Britain to become the world's second largest exporter. Three years later, Germany became a fully employed economy with an unemployment rate under 1 percent.[14] Thus, on one Sunday in June, one of the key cornerstones of the German economic miracle—a market-based economy—was firmly implanted.

But, though Erhard was in many ways a radical reformer, he and his fellow citizens had learned another lesson of history that is distinctly conservative: the need for a stable currency. In Erhard's view, monetary stability deserved a place among the "basic human rights."[15] By 1948 the German population had endured two hyperinflations that had wiped out the savings of the middle class. The first, in 1923, was the result of the postwar problems of meeting the reparations payments dictated by the settlement terms of the First World War. The government issued debt, which the central bank purchased with freshly minted banknotes. The purchasing power of the currency naturally declined, leading to the necessity of printing still more currency. By August 1923 the central bank was printing 60 trillion marks per day, the equivalent of 500 times the total money supply of just two years earlier. On November 23 the bank stopped the presses and issued a new mark worth 1 trillion of the old. It was backed by a mortgage on the property in the country.[16] Things stopped getting worse. But an entire generation had been wiped out, among them Helmut Kohl's father.[17]

Today, history leaves little doubt that this crisis contributed to Hitler's rise to power. It undermined respect for the Weimar government and created a desperate situation for millions of Germans who sought strong leadership. A political commitment to not making the same mistake again was clear-cut. The vice president of the Reichsbank, the Nazi central bank, wrote to Heinrich Himmler in 1939, "We embody the iron commitment not to defraud the German people through inflation."[18] But the dictates of war and the mistakes of the individuals in charge did not permit them to carry out that pledge. Through a system known as "noiseless financing," the central bank could extend short-term loans to the banking system collateralized by short-term government debt. By using the banking system as an intermediary, the central bank left no large stock of long-term government bonds in the public's hands. But the system still led to a sixfold increase in the money supply during the Second World War.[19]

Making the inflation situation worse was a collapse in the amount of goods available for purchase. One report indicated that per capita industrial output during the winter of 1946–1947 had been reduced to the level established in 1865, a sharp drop even from levels attained late in the war under around-the-clock bombing.[20] For all intents and purposes, the German middle class had been wiped out for the second time. That economic destruction through inflation, having happened to two generations in a row, has left an important mark on German economic psychology.

In addition to the lifting of controls by Erhard on June 20, 1948, a dramatic currency reform was put in place. Assets denominated in the old money supply were written down drastically. For example, savings accounts were written down by a factor of roughly sixteen to one. In addition, each West German was given DM 40, with an additional DM 20 to be paid out later that summer.[21] That meant a massive redistribution of wealth as well as the reestablishment of a strong currency. But Erhard summed up the necessity for change very well: "We heard already during the time of the Nazis that monetary stability was based on the work of the nation. But, this was only a half truth, and therefore a lie."[22] In money, as in government, Germany got a new start. This time it was determined not to make the same mistakes as before.

A Stable Currency in a Continent of Instability

Thus, one must add a third dictate of history. The first is reunification of Germany. The second is German integration into Europe. Third, Germany must have a stable currency. The monetary history of Germany taught a number of lessons about how inflations get started. It begins when the politicians seek to use the central bank for their own ends. That clearly happened during the Nazi years when wartime finance used the central bank's controls over the commercial banking system. It also happened in 1923 when the government relied on the central bank's money creation to cover a host of sins. So rule number one became ensuring the independence of the central bank.

The 1948 law setting up the Bank of German States (forerunner to the Bundesbank) was quite explicit. The new bank "shall not be subject to the instructions of any political body or public nonjudicial agency."[23] The result was an institution that was far more independent of political forces than America's contrarian or even the bureaucracy in the Japanese Ministry of Finance. As early as 1950, Wilhelm Vocke, president of the directorate of the bank, said: "The central bank is forced, depending on circumstances, to take unpopular measures. It must be better for the government, from a political point of view, that these measures do not have to depend on the outcome of parliamentary debates." He added that "[t]he cardinal question determining the fate of the currency is the independence of the central bank."[24]

The politicians had a somewhat more restrained enthusiasm for that independence. Adenauer said in 1956: "The central bank is fully sovereign in its relationship with the government; it is responsible only to itself. We have a body which is responsible to no one, neither to a parliament, nor to a government." At times, the relationship bordered on jealousy, as one finance minister told the Bundesbank council, "You see, we live in the realm of politics, we do not have it as easy as you." That jealousy also bordered on frustration, as when former Chancellor Helmut Schmidt derided the job of some of the more hawkish regional presidents: "What is his job? He has to discount one bill and travel to Frankfurt every other week and raise his finger and say no."[25]

The second lesson of these twin inflations had to do with the state of public finance. To the great majority of Germans it seemed that, in both the Weimar and Nazi inflations, deficit spending by the state was the cause of central bank monetization of the debt. That dislike of excessive deficits explains German attitudes toward the behavior of some of its neighbors.

Nonetheless, whatever the reasons, nothing succeeds like success. The German mark quickly became the stable monetary anchor of Europe. When the Bundesbank was founded in 1957, the German mark had already been pegged at 4.2 to the U.S. dollar. Today it trades at more than twice that rate of exchange—roughly 1.8 to the dollar and has traded below 1.5 to the dollar. By contrast, the French franc was forced into a major currency reform when the Fourth Republic collapsed in 1958. The franc that emerged was pegged at about five to the dollar and now trades around six to the dollar. Stated differently, in the past thirty years the franc has fallen 63 percent against the mark, even though the two countries are closely linked economically and politically. In the case of Italy, the next largest economy on the continent, the change has been even greater. Thirty years ago, a deutsche mark would have bought you 156 Italian lire. Today it will buy 990 Italian lire, a decline in the lira of 84 percent relative to the mark. In the case of the British pound, the decline has also been dramatic. The pound was forced to devalue by 30 percent shortly after the war. After that devaluation the mark traded at roughly eleven to the pound. In the past thirty years the pound has weakened still further, and today a pound will buy you only three German marks, or 73 percent less.[26]

Such massive devaluation does not instill confidence in the average German citizen about the resolve of Germany's neighbors. So when former Chancellor Kohl announced that he wanted to integrate Germany more closely into Europe and use money to do it, he made a lot of Germans nervous. What we have seen is essentially a conflict between two of the important dictates of history: a need to be integrated into the rest of Europe to avoid war and a desperate political need to provide a currency in which the typical German citizen can have confidence.

In December 1991 the European heads of state met in the Dutch town of Maastricht to see whether they could bridge that chasm. Their approach was to make the other European nations more like Germany with regard to their monetary and fiscal regimes. A prerequisite for joining the single currency regime was to have a central bank that was independent of the government. To meet the fiscal concerns that dominated the German experience of 1923 and 1945, strict limits on the size of government budgets deficits were agreed to—3 percent of GDP and overall government debt not to exceed 60 percent of GDP. In addition, the inflation rate and long-term interest rates of prospective members had to be brought down to Germanic levels.

The assembled heads of state provided one other key concession to the Germans: the new European Central Bank was to resemble the Bundesbank in its structure and particularly in its independence from political pressure. Each country would establish an independent national bank that would have one seat at the European Central Bank. Those heads of independent central banks would then select six other members that would be the members of the central directorate. Furthermore, the statutory aim of the new European Central Bank was to be price stability, just as the statutory objective of the Bundesbank is to "safeguard the currency."

Europe Becomes Preoccupied

The mandate of Maastricht was clear. The nations of Europe were to embark on a historic mission—uniting their currencies, and in so doing, uniting their economies. But, as a prerequisite, each member state had a lot of work to do to get its own fiscal health in order. One is reminded a bit of a wedding in which both the bride and the groom decide they like the other just fine, with a few minor problems. But each expects that marriage will change these bad points into good ones. In addition, the partners are trying to make themselves as attractive as possible for that "big day" when all the families will assemble to bless the union.

Maybe it was just bad luck, but the economic fates threw a curve ball at the would-be wedding partners. In much of Europe 1991 turned out to be a business cycle peak. By 1993 the level of industrial production throughout the European Union had fallen more than 4 percent from its 1991 level. The decline in the core of Europe was most pronounced—5 percent in France and 10.5 percent in Germany. It took until 1997 for Germany to reestablish its 1991 level of industrial production.[27] Unemployment soared into double digits, with roughly one worker in eight unemployed in both France and Germany.[28]

As a result of those economic misfortunes, the fiscal situation in just about every European country began to deteriorate. By 1994, the fiscal deficit in France was 6.0 percent of GDP; in Italy it was 9.0 percent. The same was true for the smaller countries of Europe, including Belgium at 5.3 percent and Spain at 6.6 percent.[29] To adhere to the

Maastricht Treaty's guidelines, those countries had to shrink their deficits to 3 percent of GDP by the end of 1997.

It was here that the lessons of John Maynard Keynes began to come into play. To shrink those deficits to meet a prescribed target, the governments were forced to raise taxes and cut spending. But those fiscally contractionary measures had the effect of slowing the rate of growth of the economy. With less economic activity, tax revenues fell below their expected levels, and with more unemployed, social welfare benefits rose. The net effect was only extremely slow progress on deficit reduction. That "demand-side" feedback of fiscal contraction on the budget was particularly pronounced in Europe because of the high tax rates and generous social welfare programs. Typically in Europe, the government claims between 40 percent and 50 percent of GDP,[30] and social welfare spending often replaces 70 percent of a laid-off worker's pay. A fiscal contraction worth 2 percent of GDP might push unemployment up one percentage point. Therefore, on net, the government might lose as much as half the "deficit saving" in the form of lower tax revenues and the majority of the other half owing to higher social welfare spending. Europe has been in that fiscal trap for most of the 1990s as it has tried to pursue the Maastricht Treaty's deficit criteria.

If fiscal policy was of little help, monetary policy also had to be contractionary. The Maastricht Treaty required consumer price inflation to converge toward the lower end of European inflation rates. In effect, by 1997, that meant a consumer price inflation rate of less than 3 percent. Many European governments were modestly above that target in the 1990s. Some, particularly Italy and Spain, were significantly above that target.[31] That required major monetary contractions in those countries and the process of forgoing monetary stimulus in the rest of Europe. Thus, for much of the 1990s, Europe was experiencing a Maastricht-mandated backward shift in its aggregate demand curve.

Europe: Free Trader or Economic Fortress?

Europe was turning inward to deal with its historical problems. In many ways former Chancellor Kohl and other students of history should be satisfied with the results. A free trade zone had been established within Europe, and intra-European trade now dominates trading patterns across the continent. In Germany, for example, exports comprise 29.5 percent of GDP, and in France the figure is 22.5 percent.[32] But a closer look at that trade shows that the apparent openness of individual countries within Europe merely reflects trade to other European countries, not an exposure of Europe to the outside world. For example, roughly two-thirds of total German exports were destined for other European countries. In this case, roughly 8 percent of German GDP was actually traded with "the outside world," roughly the same percentage as in the United States.[33]

Part of Europe's problem is that its companies are also focused on history. According to the Organization for Economic Cooperation and Development, expenditure on research and development as a percentage of GDP in Europe is consistently running below levels in both America and Japan. According to the *Economist,* Europe's comparative advantage in exports seems to be in medium- and low-tech export sectors, in marked contrast to America and Japan. In 1995 America had one computer for every three people. Germany had one for every six.[34]

It is certainly not the case that Europe is incapable of high-tech development. For example, Germany has a reputation for being on the cutting edge in design and engineering. But an overly rigid set of labor relationships that seem to date from another age limits that advantage. Recently, on a visit to Munich, I was taken to a German automaker's state-of-the-art design facility. It was midafternoon, around 3:30 P.M., and virtually no workers could be seen. Those that were visible were running for the time clock. Labor rules mandate that those individuals can work only seven and a half hours a day. Violating the rules might mean that the union fines the worker for breaking union rules. So if those high-tech engineers are right in the middle of a hot idea, they must lay down their calculators and run for the exits. The flexibility of work arrangements that so dominates the high-tech sector in America is a world away.

But history has left its mark elsewhere as well. Consider shopping. Recently Germany "liberalized" its store hours. Instead of having to close at 6:30 P.M., stores can now stay open until 8:00 P.M. But you still have to forget about shopping on Sundays, and Saturday hours are still somewhat curtailed.[35] An American visitor might wonder when Germans are able to do their shopping, particularly two-career couples. Why have such rules? The answer is to protect the small shopkeeper who is not able to hire the help to stay open for extended hours, again a bow to the historical shape of the business world. During the past election campaign in France, President Chirac denounced supermarkets as a major threat to the French way of life.[36] Recently, the Italian government decided to increase store hours (not, of course, on most Sundays), but in return promised not to give licenses to any new "hypermarkets," or large-sized supermarkets. Italy, a country with 57 million people, has 230 of those supermarkets.[37] Shoppers in Europe, like so many others, have their lives run by the dictates of history. They have short hours because they have always had them—probably since the time of Napoleon.

Thus, while Europe clearly has demand-side problems imposed by Maastricht, it also has serious supply-side problems. By American standards, the notion of Reaganite solutions—supply-side improvements—is philosophically abhorrent. Consider, for example, the action taken by the French National Assembly on February 10, 1998. Faced with double-digit unemployment, the French decided to cut the legal workweek from thirty-nine hours to thirty-five. The government is using rather mechanical reasoning: if you cut working hours by 11 percent, you create 11 percent more jobs. But one opponent of the plan in the French National Assembly, Alain Madelin, noted, "[W]hen you are in trouble, it is not by working less that you get out of it."[38] Even without this reform in place, the typical French worker works about 300 hours per year less than his American counterpart—1,650 versus 1,950.[39]

It would seem that ideologically Europe is out of step with the changes that have shaken Anglo-Saxon economies. Madelin is a rare exception in his advocacy of free-market principles in the French National Assembly. Many continentals look longingly across the channel at the United Kingdom and particularly with favor on the type of politics practiced by Prime Minister Blair. But, as *Le Figaro* noted shortly after Blair's election, "la gauche française n'aura son Blair que si la droite française a d'abord sa Thatcher [The French left will have its [Tony] Blair only if the French right first has its [Margaret] Thatcher]."[40]

With rigid rules in place throughout so much of business and industry, and a political process seemingly hostile to change, one might wonder whether a supply-side revolution is possible at all in Europe. Stated differently, is Europe so wedded to its past that it is incapable of moving forward? An analysis by CS First Boston provides one measure of the cost of European inefficiency. The firm estimates that European companies have consistently failed to earn enough to cover the true cost of their capital. The total market value of large European firms' capital position is roughly 13 percent less than the money invested in their business.[41] If true, that speaks of a capital market that is also backward looking, not one that is interested in correctly accounting for costs or one that is interested in maximizing shareholder value.

The prospect of a Europe that continues to look backward—a continent that still produces 30 percent of world GDP—is an unpleasant one.[42] But there is also a bright side. It could be that the decision to move to a continental system and a continental currency is just what Europe needs to get its supply side in order. If that is the case, the possibility of very steep gains in European productivity may lie before us. We shall turn to this experiment with Maastricht and the possible gains and possible problems with a single currency. But it is important to keep in mind that supply-side reforms have their impact over an extended period of time. The transition to a more robust economy usually involves pain before the gain.

The net result is not a pleasant one. From a growth perspective, for example, Klaus Friedrich, chief economist of Dresdner Bank, told *Business Week*, "I don't see Europe or Germany being any kind of growth engine for the world economy." *Business Week* concludes, "The most probable scenario is that Europe—which had a $100 billion current account surplus with the rest of the world last year—will continue to count heavily on exports for growth. As will Asia. The jackpot question: Who's going to do the buying?"[43] So, even if it turns to solving its problems, Europe will continue to be inwardly focused. That likely scenario puts even more strain on the decisionmaking structures in Japan and the United States to meet world crises.

It is probably inevitable that Europe would turn inward at this time, for that is where the dictates of history compel attention. A generation is dying off that, because it is the last one with memories of the war, also feels that it is the last to remind its successors that the past century is not one that should be repeated. And that is not just a German view, but more broadly, a European one. Dominique Moisi, editor of *Politique Étrangère* and deputy director of the Institut Français des Relations Internationales, expressed a French concern about Germany without Kohl:

> Deep down, a Germany without Mr. Kohl will be a Germany led for the first time in its recent history by someone with no significant personal or emotional links with the second world war. Here the loss of Mr. Kohl would be felt. For it would mean that *a country with too much history* would be led by a man with too short a memory, a man without enough of a past. Mr. Kohl has been a great chancellor because he provided a bridge between Germany's past and its future. It is because he had living memories of the sufferings and destruction of the war that his commitment to Europe's cause has been a matter of personal faith, not simple political dogma.[44]

7

Europe's Great Experiment

A nation's monetary system mirrors everything that that nation wants, does, and suffers.

—Attributed to Joseph Schumpeter[1]

As we learned in the last chapter, Europe is in a hurry to deal with its past. Historical necessity is driving it to cement together a much tighter political and economic union before the last generation with memories of World War II passes from the scene. But cynics would note that Europe is really in a hurry to go nowhere. At the very least, its efforts are inwardly focused and are being driven as much by the fears of the past as by hopes for the future.

But even a Europe in a hurry to deal with its past can have a profound effect on the economy of the rest of the planet. For example, the Bank for International Settlements estimates that European banks have $180 billion loaned out to troubled Asian countries.[2] If that money were suddenly to come back into Europe by regulatory fiat, undoubtedly there would be trouble in Asia. Or, if Europe sought to move its aggregate demand curve by stimulating exports to the rest of the world, say doubling its current account surplus to $200 billion, who would be the buyers and what countries would see their current account deficits rise because they couldn't sell as much in the world market?

But the most direct question with which the Europeans confront the rest of the world is the introduction of their new currency. The political and historical motivations that underpin this move are clear. But, as is so often the case, the devil is in the details. Those details have been scrutinized and negotiated in a thirty-six-story skyscraper about eighty miles up the Rhine River from the Haus der Geschichte der Bundesrepublik Deutschland—the History Museum of the German Federal Republic. While Bonn is a quiet town, Frankfurt, headquarters of the new European Central Bank (ECB), formerly the European Monetary Institute, is a booming city of 655,000 and the financial center of Germany.

The ECB draws the best and the brightest from all the central banks of Europe, especially from across town at the Bundesbank. The politics of the institution are intense, as they are in any international bureaucracy. To get around some of the most obvious of those problems, the first head of the European Monetary Institute was Alexandre Lamfalussy, an émigré from his native Hungary who fled the communists just after the war. Now, Wim Duisenberg, former head of the Dutch central bank, presides. He will head the bank once currency union takes place, but intense competition from the French has caused him to agree to resign before his term is over.

The view from the ECB is definitely inspirational. The rather low, fortresslike buildings of the Bundesbank can be seen in the distance across the river. They seem to belong to the age of a divided Europe. The ECB high-rise is symbolic of the modern, hopefully soon-to-be-united Europe. But analogies can be painful as well. Although this is the center of town, with the very traditional Frankfurter Hof just a block away, some of the vacant storefronts that are seemingly endemic in recession-torn Germany are also in evidence around the ECB.

A ride down in the elevator from the top of the building just after close of business is also instructive in highlighting the challenges facing the new central bank. Most of the bureaucrats converse in one common tongue—English. That is, everyone but the French, who hold to their lingua franca, resisting this obvious assault on French culture by the seeming universality of English in the field of banking and commerce. On this day, the men in the elevator are happy. They speak of just having ironed out all the details on a key protocol. It is one of hundreds that they must conclude before the monetary union can get started. Talk of champagne on the twenty-third floor elicits universal interest from the glassy-eyed who are carrying their stacks of briefs from what must have been an extended afternoon meeting.

Is the Euro a Strategic Threat?

The endless sets of details that form the reality of launching a new currency seem far from the high-minded thoughts of those who will launch it. Certainly, the new currency will be a proud moment for those European federalists who, for half a century, have been trying to steer the continent toward a United States of Europe. Some of these federalists already display signs of a new nationalism, although in some cases, it is merely a transformed anti-Americanism. Among them are some European policymakers, who, to some extent, see the Euro as a strategic weapon that could potentially pose a threat to the current dominance of the dollar as a global reserve currency. In late fall 1997, the Europeans floated the rumor that the central bank of the People's Republic of China would sell some of its dollars and move toward holding the Euro as their reserve currency.[3] That was ultimately denied. But it does indicate at least a potentially disruptive force for the world financial scene in the years ahead. Is this a challenge that the rest of the world should take seriously?

Probably not. In the foreseeable future, the most likely scenario for the relative importance of the dollar and the Euro is that the dollar will continue with its current relative position and the Euro will assume the cumulative relative importance of the currencies that the Euro replaces. At present, the dollar constitutes about 62 percent of world currency reserves, the deutsche mark 15 percent, and other European currencies 5 percent.[4] Thus, the dollar should remain about three times as important as the Euro after it becomes an official currency on January 1, 1999.

Two potential reasons for deviations from that ratio deserve comment. First, aggregation of currencies into a larger zone is most likely to reduce the demand for the new Euro relative to the currencies it is replacing. This is so because the precautionary balances held by central banks, clearing houses, and others involved in transactions in a number of European currencies will no longer be necessary.

The second reason for a change from the status quo is that the Euro will come to perform a store-of-value function that will make it a desirable asset to hold. Yet a European currency that plays that role currently exists—the deutsche mark. We would have to assume that the Euro will be an even better store-of-value than the deutsche mark for it to rise above current world demand for the latter. While many may argue that the Euro will be as good as the deutsche mark, few argue that it will be better.

But we have another reason why we would be quite surprised if the Euro were suddenly to increase its importance as a global currency: it would require a major change in European exchange rate policy. Consider for a moment how you, a citizen of the planet, get to hold a currency. Someone had to give you that currency in exchange either for some of your own currency or in return for some goods that you sold him. Now, if all we witness is the exchange of one currency for another, then the relative importance of one currency over another doesn't change. But, if a currency is to increase its circulation around the planet relative to others, then the issuing country must buy more goods from others than it sells to them. In this case, Europeans must buy more goods from non-Europeans than they sell to them. In other words, Europeans must start to run a current account deficit.

The problem with this scenario is that Europeans are now running a current account surplus—they are selling more goods abroad than they are buying—and few observers expect that to change much. Consider the effect of any change on aggregate demand. A country's exports have a positive effect on aggregate demand because someone is buying the goods that the country produces. Imports have the opposite effect. This means that to turn their currency into a reserve currency, the Europeans would have to see yet another adverse factor in their demand equation—a reduction in exports or a surge in imports. That would only keep Europe in recession longer, certainly not an attractive policy prospect for any economic puppetmaster.

Lessons for Europe from American History

Thus, the most likely challenge that the new Euro will impose is on Europe, not on the rest of the world. Europe is imposing on itself the discipline of a one-size-fits-all monetary policy. That is an extraordinary challenge both economically and politically. By and large, Europeans have been underestimating the challenge they face by pointing to the United States as a successful experiment in a continent-wide single currency. But the so-called success of America masks a host of problems. The first of those is historical. The surprising fact is that a single discretionary monetary policy in the United States is a fairly recent development and has created enormous political and economic problems along the way.

One of the key issues faced by America's founding fathers was that of a single currency, and they made a key decision in Article VI of the U.S. Constitution: "All Debts contracted and Engagements entered into, before the Adoption of this Constitution, shall be as valid against the United States under this Constitution, as under the Confederation." In short, the new government promised to pay the debts of the old government, and Alexander Hamilton, the secretary of the Treasury, set up the Bank of the United States to facilitate that process. Hamilton's action, in fact, helped cement the credit of the new government, but it was perceived as a transfer of wealth from the citizens of the largely rural parts of the country to the monied interests of the cities. The unpopularity of that plan was a major cause of the collapse of Hamilton's party—the Federalists. The political side effect was to give the concept of a central monetary authority a bad name.

After the bill to renew its charter was defeated and Hamilton's bank went out of business, the commercial interests of the East agitated again for a central bank. The Second Bank of the United States was chartered in 1816. But the political process was repeated in the 1830s when a new bill was introduced to recharter the bank. The Senate supported the measure. President Jackson opposed it. So intense was the feeling over that issue that Jackson commanded that the Treasury Department be built in the middle of Pennsylvania Avenue to block his view of the Senate, so he wouldn't have to see "that damn place." Jackson won. Except for a brief interlude of wartime finance by the Treasury's minting of greenbacks, the United States lacked both a central bank and a monetary policy until 1913. And even then, that central bank did not really have the authority to run a truly discretionary monetary policy, since the country was on the gold standard until 1934.

But the economic ramifications of a single currency zone for a continental economy still exist. In any dynamic modern economy the size of the United States or the European Union, significant regional differences in economic performance are bound to exist. Economic policy tries to assuage such differences and set up automatic stabilizing mechanisms by which they become self-correcting. At present, movements in exchange rates can act as such an automatic stabilizer in Europe. A country's exchange rate varies with the business cycle. A recession depresses a country's real interest rate, lowering the attractiveness of its currency and thus making its exports more attractive. In a boom, the higher real interest rates raise the currency's value, cooling off the domestic economy by reducing exports and encouraging imports.

Under a single currency, an alternative mechanism is needed. If a particular region becomes depressed, then one way of attracting new economic vigor is for the price of factories and homes in that region to fall. When prices get low enough, workers and businesses relocate to the depressed area. The United States experienced such difficulties throughout the 1980s and 1990s. When oil prices collapsed in the mid-1980s, so did the price of real estate and other assets in Texas. The same was true after the collapse of the so-called Massachusetts miracle of the late 1980s. In the early 1990s a similar collapse occurred in California's real estate prices.

Had the United States had a Texas dollar, a California dollar, and a New England dollar, those particular currencies would have declined, absorbing much of the shock. The effective price of homes and factories in those regions would have fallen because of the decline in the exchange value of the currency operating in those regions. Instead, the U.S. dollar price of homes, factories, and commercial property had to absorb the entire decline. The result was a collapse in real estate prices and the consequent stress on the banks that had done the lending to underpin the regional real estate markets. In Texas virtually the entire state banking system was wiped out. Somewhat smaller, but still significant declines in the New England and California banking sectors also occurred.

The Start of a Monetary Party

Although the currencies of Europe have just recently been locked together, parts of Europe are already entering the "boom" phase of the monetary cycle. For example, in the year ending in December 1997, the

German money supply had increased 4.5 percent while the Italian money supply had increased nearly 10 percent.[5] Growth during early 1998 accelerated even more. The result has been an explosion in Italian equity and land prices, as well as in land prices in other parts of Europe far from the central Franco-German core, such as Ireland. The reasons for this are very similar to those discussed earlier in the book when we considered financing creative destruction.

The supply shock now hitting Italy and other parts of the periphery of Europe stems directly from monetary union. Since the end of World War II, Italians faced the constant specter of politically mandated inflation finance. The result, as noted in the last chapter, was an 84 percent depreciation of the lira relative to the mark over that period. Capital markets in Italy were forced to compensate for that risk in the only way they can—lenders charged borrowers a higher price for their money. In 1991, the year the Maastricht agreement was signed, the German government could borrow at 8.6 percent for ten years while the Italian government had to pay 12.9 percent to borrow for the same time period.[6]

Monetary union essentially does away with that risk. Interest rates in Italy must fall toward their German level. Consider what happens to real estate prices and all other asset prices (like stocks) whose pricing mechanism is much like that of the real estate market. Let's say you're a prospective homeowner in Italy who can pay only a certain amount per month for a mortgage, and the mortgage rate is 12.9 percent. Suddenly, the interest rate on a mortgage drops to 8.6 percent. For the same amount of monthly payment, you're now able to take on a mortgage that is 41 percent greater. If you and all those in the market are in a similar situation, it is fairly easy to see how a rise in real estate prices can get going. (By the way, stock valuations are usually computed on a similar basis in which the flow of future profits or dividends is discounted by the prevailing ten-year interest rate. When interest rates decline by that magnitude, the present discounted value of a given stream of profits or dividends rises by 50 percent.)

Now consider what happens when foreign investors hear that Italian real estate prices are on the move. They do the kind of calculation that we have just performed and see the prospect of a large capital gain. So the amount of increased demand for Italian real estate (and stocks) is not just the additional ability to pay for existing units by Italians, but by foreign investors hearing about a boom taking place as well. So money begins to pour into the market, which causes the ultimate price to rise by much more than what is justified simply by the "ability to cover a mortgage" calculation done above. The result is (and will be in much of Europe in the next few years) a real estate bubble.

Then the next phase of the real estate–banking cycle gets under way. Prices of assets are bid up to levels that are "too high" by domestic market conditions. By "too high," we mean that the homeowner who used to be able to pay 100 million lire for his apartment and could then pay 141 million lire owing to lower interest rates now faces a price of 180 million lire because of the "bubble conditions." The fact that prices are so high will choke off demand by new home buyers, eventually stopping the market from rising and beginning a decline in prices to more affordable levels. Once such a reverse cycle gets underway, however, not only does domestic demand decline, but as soon as prices start to fall, they will fall below the equilibrium level of 141 million lire as foreigners rush to get out of a falling market.

That will pose a particularly difficult situation for the central bank. Commercial banks will have financed many of the home purchases (and other investments) during the boom that the borrowers can no longer afford. If monetary policy was made exclusively for Italy (or any other bubble region), the authorities could have taken action to stop the bubble from growing. But, in the case of a large continental currency, a "regional" problem—limited to Italy, Spain, or Ireland—is not of sufficient import to cause the entire continent's monetary policy to be affected. So both the local commercial banking system and the local real estate and investment market will suffer, without any help being available from the monetary authorities.

The Importance of Labor Mobility and Fiscal Transfers

The banking and real estate cycle is only one of the areas in which monetary union creates a potential economic problem. More politically sensitive is the question of unemployment. As already noted, exchange rate variations often tend to smooth the business cycle as economies in decline tend to see their currencies weaken, thus providing an external stimulus. But, if that stimulus does not occur, something else must take its place. In addition to changes in real estate prices, one would usually expect either migration or fiscal transfers from the central government to play such a role.

The United States, for example, has a constant migration of people, much of which is economically related. In any given year, roughly one American in six changes his residence, and 3 percent, or 7.7 million Americans, change the state in which they live. During the California recession in the early 1990s, for example, an estimated 1.2 million people left the state. Many of those people went to the rapidly growing Rocky Mountain states. Utah saw its labor force grow 24 percent in just four years, for example.[7] In Europe, cross-national migrations occur but are largely secular in nature, not cyclical. While we see a constant flow from poorer regions to richer ones, we rarely see individuals depart a rich part of Europe for another rich part simply because of swings in the business cycle.

America also has an important automatic stabilizer in its national tax system. For example, during the boom and bust in California in the late 1980s and early 1990s, the state's marginal contributions to federal receipts fell from 17 percent in the boom to just 8 percent during the bust. In the case of California, that difference meant a net fiscal injection of roughly $11 billion in 1994 alone, or more than $350 per resident of the state. The effect of that automatic stabilization process was even greater in the case of Massachusetts, which saw a $550 swing in per capita tax payments from peak to trough, or roughly 2 percent of personal income.[8]

Europe now has neither an automatic stabilizer such as the federal income tax nor a tradition of widespread migration. The tax system in Europe is still based on a nation-state level. Although contributions to Brussels are somewhat sensitive to economic activity, being tied to value-added tax receipts, that sensitivity is much lower than in the United States. Furthermore, linguistic and cultural differences present much greater impediments to migration between member states than in America. Thus, the forces that tend to cushion the effects of regional recessions in the United States are far less present in Europe.

In addition to those economic problems, Europe faces two critical political problems with the creation of the central monetary authority.

The first involves the nature of decisionmaking within the European Currency Union; the second involves democratic accountability.

Institutional Challenges

On its surface, the European Central Bank, which will make monetary policy decisions for the new European Currency Union, resembles the structure of the U.S. Federal Reserve's Federal Open Market Committee (FOMC). Both the ECB and the FOMC have roughly the same balance between the center and the regions. On the FOMC are seven "national" members, members of the Board of Governors, who are appointed by the president of the United States and confirmed by the Senate. In addition, there are twelve regional bank presidents, one from each of the Federal Reserve districts.[9] In the ECB there will be six officers at the center joined by the heads of the national central banks whose governments have joined the European Monetary Union, which at present number eleven. Thus, on paper, it would appear that the balance between the center and the regions is almost identical.

But consider how the various individuals are picked. In the United States, the presidents of the Reserve Banks are jointly selected by a board of directors in their region and by the Board of Governors in Washington. In addition, three of the nine members of the regional board of directors are selected by the Board of Governors, including the regional board's chairman and deputy chairman and a majority of the "search" committee for the president. It would not be too much of an exaggeration to say that the regional bank presidents are effectively selected by the Board of Governors.

It is also important to stress that in the U.S. model, local political authorities have absolutely no say over the selection of those regional bank presidents. The regions do not conform to any of the political subdivisions of the United States, as all twelve regions include parts of several states. The state governors and their legislatures have no input into the selection of the board of directors. In addition to the three that are chosen by the Board of Governors, the rest are elected by member banks in the region. That process produces individuals who tend to be strongly apolitical and interested in the national, as opposed to the regional, economy.

By contrast, the ECB is built up from the regions. What are now the national banks of the members of the currency union will each send their heads to Frankfurt to sit on the ECB governing council. Those individuals will then be crucial to the question of who will be selected as central bank officers. The six center-based candidates are therefore responsible to the individuals from the regions, while at the Federal Reserve, the regional representatives are responsible to the individuals at the center. In addition, and in contrast to the United States, in Europe member governments select the regional representatives. While the central banks are technically independent of those governments, they are selected by and accountable to the elected governments of their countries. It is only natural that they will reflect the political views of the governments that select them.

Therefore, an important operational difference between the Federal Reserve's Open Market Committee and the European Central Bank will exist. While the Fed tends to act like a collective CEO or corporate board of directors, the ECB is designed to work more like a legislature. This point was brought home in 1997 at a summit including Prime Minister Tony Blair of the United Kingdom and President Chirac and Prime Minister Jospin of France. The French leaders assured Blair that if the United Kingdom chose to join the European Monetary Union, the United Kingdom would get one of the six seats at the center in addition to its seat as a member state.[10] The press conference following the summit was not even subtle on that arrangement.

Such a deal simply reinforces the legislative functioning of the ECB. First, this summit showed that the political leaders of France and the United Kingdom thought that it was in their purview to decide who would be on the ECB board. Needless to say, that was not the arrangement specified in the Maastricht Treaty. Second, it showed that those leaders felt that what mattered was how many seats each country would have, not the qualities of the individual who would fill the seat. If the ECB were really to function as a board of directors, the political leadership of the member states would have to care more about whether such a member was a "hawk" or a "dove," or whether he was from an academic or business background. Where the individual came from would be of minor import if policymaking were really going to be European in its scope.

Accountability and Independence

The second problem that the new European Central Bank will have is political. It will lack democratic legitimacy or accountability. The members of the Federal Reserve Board of Governors derive their power from the elected leadership of the country. As noted, members are appointed by the president and confirmed by the Senate. Their independence derives from the fact that their terms are quite long—fourteen years—and thus the board is not subject to the current electoral environment. But that independence from the electoral cycle is different from accountability to the electorate that sustains and supports all political institutions. Failure to be accountable to the long-term desires of the electorate will ultimately undermine any monetary policy body.

No mechanism for accountability to elected European institutions exists. While the head of the ECB may, from time to time, appear before the European Parliament, his job tenure is not dependent on its pleasure. Governors of the Federal Reserve are continuously asked to testify before Congress on a variety of subjects. Not only is their job tenure dependent upon the national legislature, but the existence of the Federal Reserve can be changed by legislative action at any time. By contrast, the European Central Bank is created by treaty among the member states and has no "escape clause" or process for amendment except by amending the treaty itself, which would require ratification by every EU country.

What conclusions can we draw about the likely behavior of the new European Central Bank and its effect on the European economy and political decisionmaking in coming years? The first is, as already mentioned, that Europe and its economic policies are likely to be inwardly focused. Establishing an entirely new currency is not an easy task. The Europeans have decided on a three-year phase-in period for the introduction of the currency. At first, domestic currency will continue to circulate, and the Euro will be used only for the largest of payment settlements and for the issuance of new government bonds. Then, during a short transition and no later than January 1, 2002, the economies of Europe will switch over to the new Euro-denominated notes and coins. The technical details of that transition, particularly the establishment of a new Euro settlement system, are likely to consume a major portion of decisionmakers' time.

The second likely behavior is that the new central bank, once it is fully in charge, will stress that the Euro be viewed as a "hard" currency, not a "soft" one. The key challenge will be to establish credibility in the new regime. A failure to do that at the inception would be catastrophic for the new currency because credibility, once lost, is virtually impossible to regain. This should mean that, within a certain band of discretion, monetary policy will tend to be restrictive. But until the ECB is fully in charge, a window of monetary irresponsibility exists. National central banks will be in charge of money creation but will not be around to take responsibility for its consequences. In the short term that should mean easy monetary conditions.

One of the difficulties in that regard is determining the correct standard for judging the effectiveness of monetary policy. Under the Maastricht agreement, the objective of the new European central bank is to maintain price stability. Unfortunately, at present, Europe has not a single market basket whose price can be stabilized. Instead, the monetary authorities will have to deal with a variety of different national market baskets, each collected under different methodologies. Decisionmakers might set out to target the price level of each market basket, which would create a very difficult situation, inasmuch as they have one policy instrument to control eleven or more policy targets. Or they might seek to stabilize a weighted average of all the market baskets. But, in either event, what does one do if some of the member states are enjoying inflationary booms with full employment while others are in recession?

Furthermore, the markets will be inexperienced in reading the policymakers' response to whatever price level target might be chosen. In that event, markets might misjudge the actions of the European Central Bank. The way to avoid that confusion would be to rely on a yardstick with which the markets have substantial experience: the exchange rate. An exchange rate of one Euro for one dollar corresponds roughly to an exchange rate of two deutsche marks for one dollar. Recently, the deutsche mark has fluctuated in a band of roughly 1.6 to 1.9 to the dollar, suggesting a Euro-dollar exchange rate of one Euro to U.S. $1.20. Even if the European Central Bank were formally to choose not to target the exchange rate, it would have to pay some attention to the exchange rate. If the rate were to approach a one-to-one parity with the dollar, it is virtually certain that the markets would assume that European monetary policy is too loose and the Euro was becoming soft. Thus, a significant amount of attention is likely to be paid to maintaining the exchange value of the Euro in the $1.10 to $1.30 range.

A third probable challenge for the new European monetary arrangements involves the health of the European banking system. The Asian crisis is not coming at an auspicious time for the start of the new system. The estimated exposure to Asian economies in distress of some of the European national banking systems, particularly those of Belgium and the Netherlands, may prove to be considerable. In addition, as we've already mentioned, Europe seems to be developing a prospective banking crisis itself due to the sudden run up in real estate and equity prices in the peripheral sections of Europe. While this particular banking cycle is still in its early boom stage, the history of such cycles, coupled with the transition in currency and monetary authority going on in the affected region, is not a cause for optimism. The combination of losses both in Asia and in peripheral Europe showing up on the books of the European banking system in the next few years would create a genuinely rocky start for the new currency.

One of the most confusing aspects of the currency union is that it creates a split in the role of the supervisory function in the banking system. Under the Maastricht rules, national bank supervisors will continue to oversee the books of the banks. But the European Central Bank would have to be the lender of last resort in the event of a liquidity breakdown. Of course, it is not impossible for that division of labor to exist, but it would require an enormous degree of acceptance by the ECB of the judgment of the national banking supervisory agencies. One of the basic rules of central banks acting as lenders of last resort is that the affected banks be illiquid but not insolvent. That is a judgment that only the supervisory agency can make. So one can expect still more introspection within the European monetary regime as the natural tension between supplier of liquidity and bank supervisor comes to the fore.

Monetary Marriage and Divorce

The final point to watch for in Europe is a closer political union. Many of the supporters of monetary union do so in the expectation that a single currency will make a single government for Europe inevitable.

We have already noted that the fiscal transfer mechanism is a key substitute for variable exchange rates when it comes to stabilizing regional recessions. In terms of political economy, those fiscal transfers represent a form of "log rolling." The richer area makes a payment to the poorer area to make up for the costs of staying in the monetary union, which presumably benefits both.

History has not been kind to monetary unions that do not include the prospect of political union or at least the subsidies they involve. Of course, the most common time for a monetary union to take place is at the time of political union. In European history two instances of that were the unification of Germany under Bismarck and the unification of Italy by Victor Emanuel in the latter half of the nineteenth century. It also occurred when Scotland and England were joined in 1707. Hamilton pulled off a monetary union at the time of the Constitution, but the politics that followed indicate that there were not enough side payments in the fiscal equation to appease the "losers" on the frontier, and so they outvoted the commercial class and got rid of the Bank of the United States. By contrast, the Federal Reserve has survived as a monetary union for eighty-five years, but in an era of enormous side payments through a very active fiscal transfer mechanism.

In an extensive search of monetary unions, Gerard Lyons of DKB International found two that have survived despite the absence of political union. The first is in Africa, where the West African currency zone (CFA Zone) was established in 1948 for French colonies in that region. It has survived intact, including a major devaluation in 1994. But here is a case of subsidies' taking care to smooth over any economic difficulties. The French government subsidizes the members and keeps the CFA zone on a close peg to the French franc, largely for reasons of national pride. The only other example of a surviving currency union sans political union is the one between Belgium and Luxembourg, established in 1923.[11] While no formal fiscal transfers occur between the two, the 400,000 people of Luxembourg were spared the cost of maintaining an independent central bank. One might call this an "economies of scale" monetary arrangement. Besides which, if monetary union in Europe succeeds, the union between Belgium and Luxembourg will be subsumed in the wider union. Or perhaps some of the more proud locals in those two countries could claim that their monetary union has been expanded to cover the whole continent.

In any event, the most likely scenario is a greatly increased interest in deepening the political bonds among the members of the single currency area. That will tend to maximize the chances for their collective success, as well as work to smooth out any political difficulties caused by having a single monetary policy. That move toward tighter political union is not without its potential difficulties. Indeed, some commentators have been concerned about monetary union because of the political risks involved. Whether political integration is successful or not, the rest of the world is likely to be on the sidelines, as an entire continent wrestles with the dictates of its history.

8

On a Clear Day You Can See Forever

At present, the peace of the world has been preserved, not by statesmen, but by capitalists.

—*Benjamin Disraeli*[1]

Our tour of the corridors of power has left us with a sense of three major economic powers, each confronting its own limitations. In America, the successful integration of Keynesianism and Reaganomics has produced a remarkable economic performance, but at the same time it may be producing an equity asset bubble. The contrarian in charge lacks a clear mandate to prevent the bubble from expanding. In Japan, bureaucratic management is on its last legs. Desperate attempts to buy enough time to reform confront a well-entrenched system that finds change difficult. In Germany and most of Europe, the ghosts of the past drive contemporary policymakers to institutionalize solutions before a new generation takes charge.

But how do all these pieces fit together? Can you go to any single place to sort out what all this means for the world economy and financial markets? We shall make two stops—one with a leading market player to get his perspective, the second, a return to academia to look at a more formal explanation of why things are the way they are.

If there's any place on the planet where you can get a good global view of markets, it would have to be on the thirty-third floor of 888 Seventh Avenue in New York. That is the headquarters of Soros Fund

Management, investment advisers to one of the largest and best-known hedge funds anywhere in the world, the Quantum Fund. George Soros and the Quantum Fund became globally famous in 1992 when they forced an embarrassed British government out of the European exchange rate system. That move marked the beginning of a new era of market dominance over political considerations. It also netted Quantum quite a profit. It takes money to make money, but it also takes brains, information, and in this case guts. Someone like this can "round out our view" of the corridors of power.

The view from here is spectacular in every sense. The urban pioneers who developed the New York skyline set out to impress, and even now, more than half a century after their heyday, the effect is still the same. Today, probably only Hong Kong exhibits a more audacious display of man's efforts to reach skyward in an effort to again touch the hand of his Creator. But the global boom of the 1990s has created many would-be competitors, as the combination of financial wherewithal and the unrestrained ego that boom creates became more widely dispersed on the globe.

At Soros, the best vista is from the north side of the office suite, where one views a spectacular and unobstructed panorama of Central Park. In the days before Rudolph Giuliani became mayor, a quirky but patient spectator with binoculars could observe the muggings for which the park was infamous. Today, it overflows with pedestrian traffic as the midtown financial community and their families go about their daily lives. To the west, one can see the Hudson River and New Jersey, though in this case, somewhat obstructed by the competing skyscrapers going up on the Upper West Side. In the northwest corner sits the office of George Soros, creator of the Quantum Fund. When I mention the view, Soros modestly nods and says, "That's one of the nice things about working here."[2]

But the view that really matters here is not of Manhattan but of the world. Soros, and his colleague Stan Druckenmiller, chief investment strategist of the Soros Fund empire, are responsible for managing some $20 billion in assets. To do so successfully, they maintain one of the best global intelligence networks anywhere. Information flows in from a wide variety of contacts and analysts all around the world, including the companies in which the fund invests. Unlike the CIA, the foreign service bureaucracy, or even the staffs of central banks, this information network is subject to a test of profitability. If the fund doesn't make money, the information network gets pruned.

Just as for Greenspan, Sakakibara, and Kohl, the offices here are designed for the information age, with computer screens dominating the executives' desks and intermittent interruptions from a "squawk box" in the background. Of course, these people live and breathe the developments of the market, and so their focus on market-breaking news is both intense and immediate. But the world is certainly full of information sources. Financial publications are proliferating. Global broadcast networks are being added that cover just financial news. What makes the information network here so much better, or to continue the analogy, why is the view from the thirty-third floor reputed to be better than anywhere else in the world?

The Value of Information

Finance is an information-based industry, and Soros and top-ranking professional investors like him have three advantages that most ordinary investors do not and for which ordinary investors pay a premium to have Soros do their investing. The first is global reach. Much of the information flow is in the public domain but may not be universally known. Many investors in the United States feel that if they read the *Wall Street Journal,* they're up on events. A more rarefied group also reads the *Financial Times.* Few read *Corriere della Sera, Le Figaro,* and the *Asahi Shimbun* or have people who report to them who do. When you have a global network, the valuable tidbits from each of these make their way into the hands of someone who can use them.

The second advantage is context. The phrase, "All the news that's fit to print," means that some news is not fit to print. Who decides? Often it's the reporter himself. To write intelligently about a story, a writer must know much more than what he conveys to his reader. Sometimes, the editor is the information arbiter. Each column inch must justify itself. Today, one can make both ideological and financial justifications. As a result, anyone who talks to a reporter will learn far more than he can possibly learn from reading a story. Just because there is news that's not fit to print does not mean that it isn't valuable. At Soros, not only does all the news flow in, but the consumer of the information knows the biases of the reporter and can place the information provided in the proper perspective.

The third big advantage is process. At Soros, there isn't any. The news flows directly to the top. No fancy reports to impress the clients. No bureaucratic staff and no committees to review and approve the information flow. No bureaucracy to justify its existence. The ultimate consumer of information decides its value.

How do Soros and other hedge fund investors make their money? Essentially, a hedge fund is very much like a mutual fund. Investors buy shares in the fund, and the firm's managers invest those pooled funds. One important difference is the level of risk. While most mutual funds simply buy stocks dollar-for-dollar with investors' funds, hedge funds use "leverage." That is, they take a position several times that of the amount of funds invested with them. That can lead to spectacular returns—or spectacular losses.

Another key difference is that the hedge fund may go aggressively "long" in one position and aggressively "short" in another. A short position involves borrowing an asset and then selling it. This shorting can also contribute to the leveraging of the portfolio. For example, a fund may borrow yen and pay a very low interest rate, say 1 percent. It may sell those yen and buy dollars, which it in turn uses to buy Treasury bills yielding 5 percent. Now, as long as the exchange rate between the dollar and the yen stays unchanged, the fund does extraordinarily well, making a profit of 4 percent on each yen borrowed. Because the fund is leveraged, this means a big return on investors' capital. For example, a ten-to-one leverage position on that play will mean a 40 percent return to the investor.

Of course, if the yen were to rise in value, it would be more expensive to pay back the borrowed yen, and the total return could fall rapidly. The fund might choose to cover or "hedge" that risk by making an offsetting investment in the foreign exchange market. Or the fund might choose to bet that the dollar would rise and the yen fall, leaving the fund's position unhedged. If the fund is right, it makes money both by "arbitraging" the difference between U.S. and Japanese rates and by making a correct guess on foreign exchange movements.

With billions of dollars of initial investment and a leveraged position on each of those dollars, the hedge fund has a high premium on seeing world events clearly. Hence the premium on information.

But, having said all that, the bottom line is that Soros cannot "buy" any information that others cannot. A central bank or finance ministry can certainly afford the global information network—indeed, most governments maintain extensive networks at a cost several hundred times what Soros expends. Certainly, a central bank governor or finance minister can call up any information source and get the whole story from a reporter as effectively as Soros can. Indeed, the reporter would be flattered. And, at least in theory, decisionmakers should be able to define the process by which they get information.

The Center of Conspiracy Theories

Still, the aura that these men can get something that no one else can is pervasive. Global conspiracy theorists spin tales of all kinds of evil machinations stemming from offices like this one. Indeed, in the recent crisis, Prime Minister Mahathir of Malaysia took on Soros and those like him directly, appealing to age-old prejudices of anti-Semitism and fears of conspiratorial manipulations. Why do these conspiracy theories gain so much ground? Soros himself has a two-part explanation: "First, a lot of people find it difficult to believe that events occur without anybody specifically intending them. So, if something happens, somebody must have done it." Soros goes on to note that in the current crisis, we seem to be having a severe financial disruption from which the West seems to be actually benefiting: "Moreover, the problems in Asia are going to be cured by the disruption of the Asian model and the penetration of the international banks and other multinationals into those markets. So, it stands to reason that those who benefit must have manufactured the crisis."

It is certainly the case that anti-Western and particularly anti-American sentiment is on the rise in countries such as Thailand, Indonesia, and even Korea. Interestingly, efforts to resolve the crisis do involve the Western, particularly American, purchase of indigenous assets. Soros is observing that those forced to sell will naturally feel that they have been "cheated" and look to the West as the cause.

While that all may make some psychological sense, Soros feels the reason that the conspiracy view is particularly popular is that the alternative explanation that the West—and particularly the economics profession—advances is completely implausible:

> The conspiracy theory actually is a much easier explanation than the one we hold in the West—the efficient markets, rational expectations view. If that is the only alternative explanation, then only a conspiracy could have done it. In my opinion, the real explanation is that financial markets are inherently unstable.

The efficient markets hypothesis, particularly in its extreme form, holds that all information about the future is "in" the market at any given time. Supposedly, rational actors take the available information and price assets accordingly. Skeptics like Soros wonder how any supposedly rational process could produce the kinds of price volatility that we have seen recently.

It is more than a little ironic that this master of markets is himself a market skeptic. Soros's view as to why the central banks and finance ministries "didn't see it coming" (to use Mervyn King's phrase) is that they are predisposed to view markets as self-correcting and rational. Economists and economic policymakers tend to rely on economic theories in which systems move toward equilibrium. Soros, by contrast, is always looking to exploit instability profitably because he believes that instability is the inherent condition of markets. Certainly, most economic analysis focuses on the point at which markets reach equilibrium. But the process of getting to equilibrium may be a very unsettling one for markets and thus a potentially profitable one for Soros.

His theory, which he has dubbed "reflexivity," is the economic parallel to the Heisenberg uncertainty principle in physics. Heisenberg held that simply by measuring something you affect it, and therefore it cannot have the same value that you measured. The name of the main Soros fund, "Quantum," comes from that analogy to physics. Soros elaborates on this point:

> You have reflexivity in financial markets because you are always discounting future values. But the future is not something that is out there independent of how you discount it. So the present valuation of a stream of future earnings can vary in the present, not in response to what happens in the future, but simply by the act of discounting it today.

At one level, that is very much like the story of the real estate cycle we told in chapter 3. A speculator shows interest in a lot on which to construct a skyscraper. Immediately, all those around the lot in question revise their net worths upward. That leads to a local consumption boom. All of this is not based on any "reality" but on the perceptions of, or rumors about, one of the players in the market.

As to the reason for his success, Soros says:

> What I know is that the situation is reflexive. I don't know the outcome, because nobody can know the outcome. I'm ahead of the other guy because I know that there is nothing to be discounted; that there is, in fact, something contingent, and therefore my discounting will change what is being discounted.

Again, the focus is not on the objective reality of the situation but on what others are thinking. In this case, the market may be like a card game in which each player must guess how others are assessing the odds to know whether to bluff, to hold, or to fold.

That Soros views others as understanding the world the same way he does certainly helps him play the "game" this way:

> I think that central banks, and certainly Greenspan, understand reflexivity. His statements are exercises in reflexivity. Take "irrational exuberance," for example. What business does a central banker have talking about that stuff if markets weren't reflexive? And the Japanese understand it even better because the Japanese have actually pursued a reflexive policy. They have been exploiting reflexivity as a way of manipulating the economy.

That latter comment no doubt reflects his many experiences being lobbied—or bullied—by Japanese officials. Japanese bureaucrats have been known to call hedge fund operators and threaten them with intervention designed to wipe out their position. The bureaucrats make announcements of policy moves, often ones on which they never ultimately need to follow through, to get markets to move in desired directions. Again, the model is one of the mandarin imposing his will through a well-placed bluff at the card table, not of market forces' producing a reasoned outcome.

The view from 888 Seventh Avenue is therefore not so much the perspective of a rational calculator as that of a game theorist. Each of the players in the game has his own objectives; each will try to influence the outcome by his own behavior. But in this view no "efficient" market outcome—no "true" equilibrium—exists. At the same time, no single player can manipulate the outcome by himself. Consider, for example, the Japanese officials, who, according to Soros, have so efficiently been exploiting reflexivity. They not only are playing by those rules, but they have an enormous stack of "chips" with which they can enforce any bluff. Why are they now in trouble?

Soros acknowledges that they were quite talented and had enormous resources at their disposal but adds:

> Where they made their mistake is that they believed in their own omnipotence. They got very cocky, and they thought that, in fact, you can manipulate the market. But the fact is that actions have unintended consequences. The Japanese exploited the reflexivity of markets but didn't recognize their own fallibility.

This is something less than a statement that an ultimate reality comes back to bite the speculator who bets wrong. It is more the admission that even the smartest poker player can find that his opponents can wise up to his tricks. On the other hand, it is certainly not a recommendation that public policy be run on the basis of game theory.

Here is a major dilemma for policy. Japanese (and other) policymakers who intervene in markets are *not* driven by the profit motive. This can be liberating, as the profit motive requires one ultimately to "buy low and sell high." Thus, whatever reflexive actions may result and whatever side signals or game-theoretic maneuvers might be undertaken, the market player driven to make profits *must* move the market toward equilibrium or lose money.

A policymaker "playing" the market may pursue some other objective: raising or lowering the exchange rate, for example. That behavior may move the market *away from* long-run equilibrium and toward the politically desired target for the market. But such an outcome is not free. It costs the policymaker financial resources to keep a price at some level other than market equilibrium. It also contributes to the "reflexive" behavior that Soros and others contend leads to unstable (and therefore potentially profitable) markets.

What is the right course of action for policymakers faced with markets that they can manipulate and that may be inherently unstable? Soros contends: "You don't want to eliminate instability; you cannot eliminate instability. The only thing you want to do is to prevent excesses." In short, he sees a role for decisionmakers in injecting stability into markets. That certainly carries echoes of a Keynesian need for an economic contrarian. In that regard, he gives policymakers a high grade: "We have effectively avoided a meltdown in the center since 1929, and we've had at least four occasions when, without proper action by the authorities, it could have happened—1982, 1987, 1994, and 1997."

Unfortunately, Soros does not see the 1997 crisis as necessarily having ended completely: "I think that our financial markets have lost their moorings. We are far from an equilibrium now. I think that we're in an asset bubble and every bust is preceded by a boom; now we are in the boom phase." To Soros, the best analogy is what happened after 1987, when the U.S. stock market crashed:

> Then, Japan decided to be banker to the world. I remember a Japanese politician telling me that Wall Street is no longer the center; we will be the center. We are going to provide liquidity to the world. And they were there and they did it and they saved the world. Today, America is going to do the same thing. Asia is in trouble. We will keep liquidity flowing to Asia to be bailed out. I think if it hadn't been for Asia and the resulting liquidity we created, our market would have stopped. So it is because of our reaction to Asia that the current bubble is forming. That is just like 1987, when Japan's reaction to events here caused their bubble to form.

Soros does think that we are improving our ability to handle such crises. In that regard, he not only is complimentary of Greenspan, but sounds like him. Like Greenspan, he sees the potential bubble forming here. But he also thinks that the policy world has learned from past mistakes. Therefore, the kind of megacrisis with disastrous consequences is unlikely, and the current bubble need not end the same way as 1929: "The Japanese bubble was the first bubble in history that was deflated and didn't burst. So it's possible that the same thing would happen here. This bubble can also be deflated, but you might have some sort of ongoing malaise for a decade, just like in Japan."

Greenspan said virtually the same thing. He argued that, while there were plenty of parallels to the 1920s, it did not follow that we were headed to the depths of 1933. Greenspan argued that we had learned something—that the Japanese did much better in the years after their crash in 1989 than we did after our crash in 1929. By way of comparison, both Soros and Greenspan think that the next bubble may well be deflated with even less pain.

Soros has a tremendous amount of respect for the central bankers and their ability to control events. He has particular respect for Greenspan. Greenspan understands the tools of "reflexivity" but seems to be using those tools to help stabilize global conditions, not to impose a politically determined outcome on markets. Soros also has a remarkably clear prediction about how all of this is going to end:

> I think the Asian crisis will be a victory for the global capitalist system. It will cause the demolition of the Asian model, which is still based on national politics with the individual political regimes' effectively controlling the economy. It also means the end of family-based ownership in which families did not want to give up control and so took on enormous amounts of debt. Absent a crisis at the center, the Asian crisis will take a couple of years, maybe even less, to be corrected.

He continues, "The essential characteristic of global capitalism is the free movement of capital. Worldwide, the balance has swung in favor of capital because it can move freely and everybody needs it and has to compete for it."

But this quintessential global capitalist does not necessarily think that the victory of global capitalism is necessarily a good thing: "When it comes to saying there should be absolutely free convertibility of currency, I think that developing countries should not have totally convertible currencies. They should maintain capital controls until they are fully developed." If he feels that way, why does Soros have the job he has? After all, much of the Soros fortune had been made exploiting currency markets: "If I didn't do it, somebody else would."

But perhaps Soros is being too hard on himself and his profession. Soros himself made both money and a good deal of his reputation for his activities in forcing the Bank of England to leave the European exchange rate mechanism in 1992. Largely as a result of that decision, Britain has had the best economic performance of any of the European countries. In fact, Stan Druckenmiller, the fund's chief investment strategist, has an ersatz certificate of knighthood hanging at his country house for his service to the British economy.

Don't hedge funds serve a useful purpose by making errant policymakers behave? Answers Soros:

> Yes. They make their economic position untenable. The hedge funds force discipline on the central bank. Actually, [in that case] the central bank acted irresponsibly by selling futures beyond their capacity. So they actually lost all their reserves. They should have acted much sooner. The crisis turned out to be much bigger because it took them so much longer to react to it than they should have.

The United Kingdom was not the only case of the hedge funds' forcing a country to face up to economic reality. Another good example was Sweden, which had borrowed heavily in deutsche marks, converted those into Swedish krona, and lent the krona domestically. The Swedish banks did that because rates in Sweden were higher than in Germany. The exchange rate between the krona and the mark was fixed. So the banks saw that as a one-way bet—an opportunity to borrow cheap and lend at a much higher rate. The result was an enormous bubble in Sweden. Says Soros:

> The Swedes were very slow to devalue. They had to protect their banks. In the end, they effectively nationalized the mistake that the banks made. They were trying to hang in there to allow their own banks to act with their own favorite people to make a little extra money. That's why they got in such a big hole. So it would be fair to say that the hedge funds keep the central banks honest. They impose the discipline.

Why then aren't hedge funds more popular? After all, as a citizen of a country and not one of the elite in the central bank or in the government, wouldn't I want the hedge funds there to keep my government honest? Maybe it is modesty, and maybe it is realpolitik, but Soros cannot imagine himself or his profession ever being popular, even if they do the right thing:

> I think that as a citizen of a developing country I would be pretty upset if the mistakes of a central bank could be exploited by fund managers. I would find it galling. It is always easier to deflect blame to the foreigners than to accept the blame yourself. Recall the French finance minister who wanted to hang speculators from the lamp posts? So, even in a country like France, there is a very strong prejudice against speculators.

Even in his own mind, Soros is quite ambivalent about the role that hedge funds play in stabilizing the world economy. He acknowledges that on some occasions they provide a valuable service, when the institutions of government default. But, by and large, he is not a fan of the role he plays. He would much prefer an alternative. His ambivalence comes through loud and clear. On the one hand, he says:

> Of course, it would be better if the authorities were responsible to their own citizens. But in many of these countries you don't have a proper democracy. You don't have newspapers that can criticize. What keeps central banks honest is that they have to interact with the market. So, if they ban the market, they have nothing to interact with and they don't know when they are making a mistake. That is the argument for our keeping central banks honest.

On the other hand, Soros continues:

> But the discipline that we impose is a discipline of instability because the markets are inherently unstable. By imposing market discipline, you are actually imposing an instability. Society cannot take instability beyond a certain point, particularly in systems where you do not have social safety nets in place. I mean, what have coolies got to do with decisionmaking? Why should they suffer for the mistakes of the central bank? So you need discipline, but market discipline isn't the right sort because markets are unstable. That's where democracy comes in—free discussion, self-discipline, the search for the truth.

George Soros is not a man one thinks of as a starry-eyed idealist. But in many respects he is. He sees the victory of global capitalism coming out of the current crisis, but it does not cheer him. His sentimentality does not get in the way of his investment decisions. The path ahead to him is clear, if not exactly desirable:

> There is an element of validity in the Asian model. But it cannot withstand the forces of global capitalism. It's like Western civilization coming into America and destroying the Indians. Who is to say that Western civilization is superior to the Indian civilization? They had a very happy relationship with nature but couldn't withstand the intrusion of firewater and firearms. So it is with the global capitalist system. It conquers. It overcomes domestic resistance, and it sweeps it away.

One can almost hear a "cultural relativist" speaking. But unlike many such relativists, Soros does not necessarily condemn capitalism either. Capitalism is part of a process of reflexivity, which by itself will cause other changes:

> That's the way it is. It doesn't make it a horrible force, and it doesn't make it a good force either. In the Asian model, states have considerable authority that's now being swept away. Global capitalism will conquer all, at least for now. But unless we also recognize the flaws in our system, our system will collapse. I think global capitalism could be a viable and continuing system, but it needs to recognize that it is not stable; it is anything but stable. It will expand, it has to expand, but it also has to be controlled and limited, because if it doesn't, it will destroy itself.

Is it in the process of destroying itself now? Maybe. But let us not jump to any hasty conclusions. It is important to separate the *financial markets* in which Soros operates from the underlying *economic trends.* Recall from chapter 3 that creative destruction is a generally positive long-term economic trend. But it can be a disastrous short-term event in financial markets. Soros is focused on the bumpy ride that moves us from one equilibrium to another. But let us not forget the ultimate equilibrium to which we are moving. We explore that distinction in some detail in the next chapter and see how the policymakers we met earlier in the book are influencing both the economic trend and the financial market.

9

An Intellectual Confusion between Supply and Demand

"What is the answer?"
"In that case, what is the question?"

—*Gertrude Stein*[1]

Our tour of the world's three largest economies brings us back to the question we began with: So, this is a global economy? Not much seems to be global about it. America is driven by its contrarian to a near-perfect economic mix but runs the risk of "too much of a good thing" and the creation of an economic bubble. The financial processes that accompany creative destruction lie in the background. In Japan there is very little creative about the economic destruction taking place, at least on the surface. A well-entrenched bureaucracy is trying to hold things together and keep the system in place while market forces demand a major market restructuring. Meanwhile, Europe seems to be moving forward focused squarely on its rear-view mirror. Yet, as a fairly open economy, Europe cannot be isolated from the events in America and Asia.

One of the instances in which this confusion is most apparent is when world leaders give each other advice. For example, the U.S. administration is constantly advising the Japanese to increase their budget deficit, which is already large. Yet at home the same administration is claiming that the reduction of the American budget deficit is the proof of its economic success. The Japanese might have every reason to be suspicious of advice based on the notion, "Do what I say, not what I do."

This chapter explains the basic economics behind such apparently paradoxical advice and the reasons why we really do have a global economy. The chapter provides a way of understanding how sound policy in one country may be disastrous for another. It also helps us understand why certain economies are not performing so well as others in the current environment. At its root, much of the current misunderstanding among world leaders and among investors comes down to knowing the difference between supply and demand. To resolve the confusion, this chapter takes us back to my days as a professor at Harvard University. The lessons we taught our undergraduates there have direct applicability to the variety of economic circumstances around the world.

The previous chapters told us *why each country made the choices it did.* This chapter gives us the means for seeing that *the consequences of those choices are predictable.* That is the role of economics as a discipline. It is not to say, "Do this," or "Do that," but, "If you do this, then such and such will happen."

Just reading the popular press gives an indication of how wedded our society is, intellectually, to a particular world view and a focus on demand. For example, the *New York Times* said on September 18, 1997, that "inflation is almost nonexistent despite steady growth and an unemployment rate hovering near a quarter-century low."[2] The *Times* uses the word *despite* because low inflation and low unemployment seem contrary to much post–World War II economic experience. So profound is that change that some suggest that we may be in a new era in economics. In fact, the "laws" of economics have not been repealed. Actually, all the quotation indicates is that the reporters and their editors have all been schooled in a correct, but limited, view of economics. The focus of their education was on shifts in *demand.*

Ever since the Second World War, the focus of economic policy in most countries has been on the question, Will there be enough buyers for the output of society to ensure that firms will be able to sell what they produce and therefore not have to lay off workers? That is a demand-side question. It assumes that plenty of goods are available to buy. Ask an official forecaster in the United States, Europe, or Japan how fast the economy will grow in the next year, and he will go through a story about each of the major components of demand: how fast consumption spending by households will grow, how fast investment by firms will expand, what will happen to government spending, and what will happen to the net export position of the country. In short, how much more will people demand or choose to buy?

We have two good reasons why that has been the approach most forecasters have taken. First, from an empirical point of view, such demand-side analysis has generally been a good way of making an economic forecast. So it passes a kind of "market test"—it works. Second, the analysis proves especially useful for a very particular kind of market—the economic policymaker. The legacy of economics since the depression and the Second World War has been to convince governments that they can—and *should*—manage demand. If demand is falling short of its policy goals, it is widely believed that government can remedy the problem by changing a policy either to stimulate or to restrict one or more of the components of demand. Too much demand? Raise taxes to cut consumption or cut government spending directly. Too little demand? Why not give firms a special tax credit to stimulate investment? Whether the policy is actually effective, that gives congressmen, parliament, and cabinets *something to do* to appear to make things better.

As a result, such a policymaker approach has really come to dominate public discourse on economic performance. Voters have come to expect that policymakers should act. In turn, policy decisions drive much of the volatility in the business cycle. So, private-sector interest groups developed an incentive to obtain the same kind of information that policymakers use so they could at least guess what policymakers were going to do and, one hopes, influence their actions. A kind of intellectual market monopolization resulted, with virtually all economic discussion and thinking focused on which demand-side levers the policymakers would pull.

The problem with that analysis is that it ignores the "supply side" of the economy. Suppose we guessed exactly right as to how many goods people wanted to buy but then found that a different quantity of goods was produced. If too few goods were produced, shortages would develop, and buyers would bid up the prices of what was available. In macroeconomic terms, we would characterize that as inflation. If too many goods were produced to sell at the existing set of prices, sellers would have to cut their prices to clean out their inventory, and "deflation" might develop.

Chairman Alan Greenspan was one of the first global policymakers to comment officially on the existence of a supply surprise—what economists call a "supply shock." In the mid-1990s, he spoke in congressional testimony about the effect of lags in technological dissemination and cautioned that this might be a major reason why current economic policy was not producing the results most economic models had predicted. By 1997, Greenspan was theorizing that the kind of changes we were witnessing in the economy could be a "phenomenon" one might encounter only "once or twice in a century."[3]

The events that were helping move the supply curve were wide-ranging. In the domestic economy, the development of microprocessor technology led to a rapid decline in information processing and telecommunications costs. Those cost reductions affected not only the office but the assembly line by allowing firms to economize on inventory and in effect letting the bits of information carried on electrons substitute for precautionary stores of intermediary physical product. Globally, the entrance of hundreds of millions of workers into the world's labor market after the collapse of Communism meant that firms could reduce the cost of labor if they diversified production globally. Not only did the collapse of Communism allow workers in Eastern Europe, Russia, and China to compete, but it also discredited the communist approach in third-world countries as well. Economic openings occurred from Latin America to the Indian subcontinent. On top of that, the cost of transportation fell rapidly, allowing globalization of production without the attendant risks. Augmenting that has been the reduction in barriers to trade all around the world.

Each of those events, viewed in isolation, would have to be considered a good thing. Indeed, we would generally view an increase in supply favorably by most normal standards. Aren't more output, lower inflation, and lower unemployment good? Yes, probably. It is important, however, to realize that economic analysis per se is not about "good" and "bad." The actions that policymakers take in response to a supply shock are critical to the outcome and, indeed, will determine whether most people's normative judgments describe the outcome as "good" or "bad." To understand such a policy construct, let's consider how econo-

Figure 9-1
The Phillips Curve: Inflation and Unemployment, 1958–1969

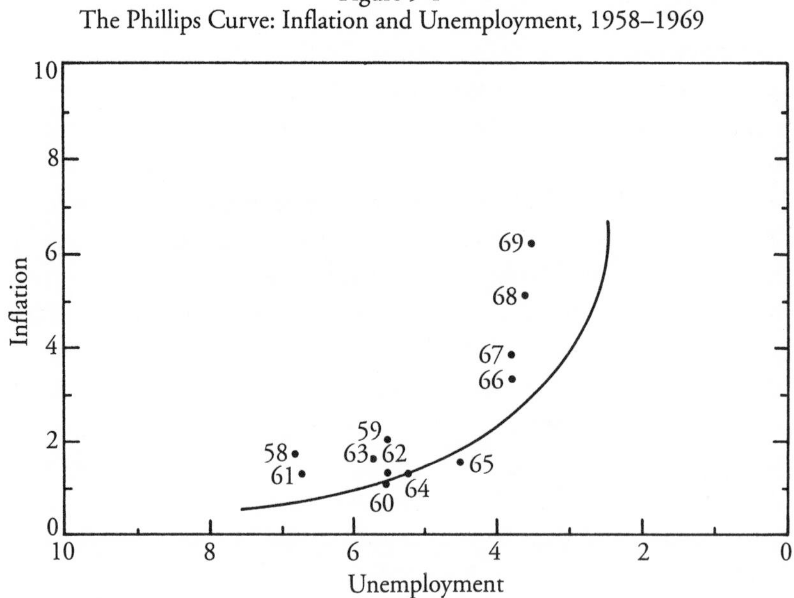

Source: Data are from the *Economic Report of the President* (Washington, D.C.: Government Printing Office, 1997), tables B-40 and B-61.

mists developed a supply and demand context for looking at the economy.

Back in the days when demand-side analysis had a monopoly on policy, the policymaker's view of economics came to be characterized by a useful analytic picture known as the Phillips curve, developed by A. W. Phillips in 1958. The Phillips curve traced out the combinations of unemployment and inflation that prevail at different levels of economywide demand. Figure 9-1 presents the levels of consumer price inflation (vertical axis) and average annual levels of unemployment (decreasing as one moves rightward along the horizontal axis) in the United States from 1958 to 1969. What was most remarkable was how well the Phillips curve seemed to work empirically. The original work of Phillips pertained to the United Kingdom. But his analysis produced the same type of picture as figure 9-1 illustrates for the United States. In social science, when one has a theoretically plausible story that empirical experience validates, the result is as close to "scientific" proof as one can get.

What emerges is something resembling a standard supply curve that one would introduce as a professor in an introductory microeconomics class. But that supply curve is macroeconomic for the economy as a whole.

The logic behind the shape of the Phillips curve is not at all dissimilar from the logic behind the shape of a microeconomic supply curve. For purposes of this discussion, we shall call it an aggregate supply curve because it reflects the supply of *all* goods and services, not that of a single product. In the Phillips curve, a nation can obtain higher levels of employment and output only at the price of higher levels of inflation. In the typical microeconomic supply curve, an industry can produce higher levels of output of a particular product only by charging a higher price for the good in question. Higher prices for a product are not quite the same as higher rates of inflation for the whole economy. But one can imagine that if an economy were experiencing a given level of inflation anyway, bringing more workers into the work force and producing more output could be done only with prices' rising even faster than people thought they would—in other words, under a higher rate of inflation. So the logic is quite similar, if not identical.[4]

It may seem odd that a demand-side-based policy world would put so much faith in what is effectively a supply curve. But remember, what actually matters is not the curve but the point of intersection between supply and demand, which economists call the "equilibrium."[5] Phillips argued that the supply curve (the Phillips curve) was *fixed* in place. Thus, all that mattered was what happened to demand since that would determine the economy's equilibrium. And demand is therefore all that mattered to the policymaker.

One can see the policies of the 1960s traced out in figure 9-2. Note that what is moving is *not* the Phillips curve, not the aggregate supply curve, but the aggregate demand curve. The figure shows two aggregate demand curves—one for 1960 and one for 1969. But one can imagine a similar curve for each year. Those aggregate demand curves depict how much all buyers, consumers, businesses, and government wish to purchase. The period started with the rather cautious policies of the late Eisenhower period. Balanced budgets and a stern monetary policy were the order of the day. Nobel laureate and MIT professor Paul A. Samuelson termed that period "an investment in sadism."[6] Under newly

Figure 9-2
Aggregate Supply and Demand: Inflation and Unemployment, 1958–1969

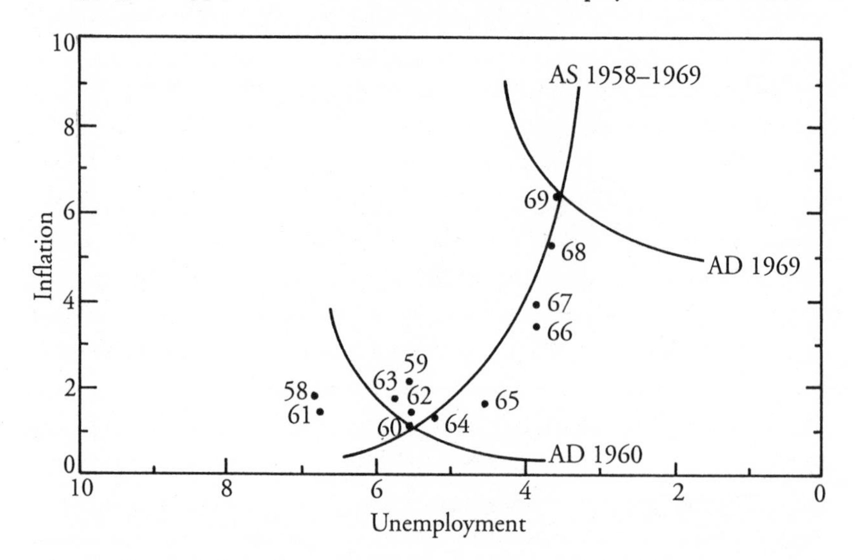

Source: Data are from the *Economic Report of the President* (Washington, D.C.: Government Printing Office, 1997), tables B-40 and B-61.

elected President Kennedy, the new economics of Samuelson and others were tried. A major tax cut that took effect in 1964 during the Johnson administration stimulated demand. Later, Johnson sought to conduct both the war in Vietnam and the War on Poverty simultaneously without a hike in taxes through borrowing and money creation. The result was a very dramatic rightward shift in aggregate demand between the early 1960s and the later 1960s. Viewing that as a policy choice, one could argue that Johnson chose to run a more inflationary policy later in the decade to reduce unemployment and achieve other national objectives.

In the late 1960s and early 1970s, the view of the bulk of the economics profession was that the role of the policymaker was like that of a restaurant customer choosing from a menu, albeit at an establishment with a chef who was very strict about side dishes. The menu was given by the Phillips curve—or aggregate supply curve—and was fixed in place. The policymaker could select the unemployment rate at which he felt the economy should operate, but he would have to put up with the inflation rate that accompanied that level of unemployment. He would implement the choice by manipulating the tools of demand management to move the aggregate demand curve. For example, cut personal taxes to stimulate more consumption, or increase government spending to boost the public sector. He could use investment tax credits or other forms of corporate tax relief to stimulate investment. He could throw each of those policies into reverse if he desired less aggregate demand.

One other very important policy tool came to be added to that mix as the 1970s progressed: interest rates. To understand that link, think of interest rates as the price or rental cost of money. At high interest rates, borrowing costs more, and fewer investment projects are profitable for borrowers to undertake. That is true both of investment in the business sector and of household investment in new housing construction. High interest rates also tend to depress the wealth of consumers by driving down the value of stock and bond holdings. That lowers consumption, particularly the purchase of consumer durables like autos and appliances. The central bank can influence short-term interest rates by controlling the supply of money available to the banking sector. As a practical matter, most central banks in the world choose an interest rate at which they wish overnight transactions to trade and supply enough money to meet the market demand at that interest rate. While we have different economic models to describe how the money supply and interest rates affect the economy, it is sufficient for this analysis to note that monetary policies (affecting money and interest) can also be used as policy tools to move an economy's aggregate demand curve.

Some economists have argued that these government policies could manipulate not only the level of demand but also the composition of demand. If the policymaker thought that consumers were living too well and that more resources should be devoted to public goods like roads and health care, then he could combine higher taxes and higher spending. He could stimulate investment by biasing any tax policy change toward the corporate side.

The mix between monetary policy and fiscal policy could also help influence the composition of demand. A great deal of debate occurred in the United States, for example, about the relative merits of an easy monetary–tight fiscal policy versus a tight monetary–easy fiscal policy stance. Some argued that the former was more conducive to stimulating investment because it produced lower interest rates. Others argued that tax-based incentives were more important and advocated the latter stance.

Thus, it appeared as though a multifaceted policy debate could be undertaken not only about the *level* of aggregate demand in an economy, but also about the *composition* of that demand. In a world in which policymakers (and those who sought to understand or influence them) were the ultimate market for economic modeling, that was an ideal paradigm. Our institutions came to reflect this richness of approach. Budget policies were established with explicit economic forecasts in mind. In the United States, both the executive and the legislative branches developed institutions (the Office of Management and Budget and the Congressional Budget Office, respectively) to link formally fiscal policies with the projected level and composition of demand. The Federal Reserve established a process of monetary policy evaluation that took fiscal policy as a given and then targeted the level and path of demand that met its price level and employment objectives.

But the world turned out not to work this way. We learned that the Phillips curve, our aggregate supply curve, was remarkably unstable, contrary to our expectations. That became increasingly evident during the 1970s, when jobs were hard to get and prices skyrocketed. The underlying inflation-unemployment tradeoff was worsening continuously, as figure 9-3 illustrates. By the early 1980s, the inflation-unemployment tradeoff had reached wholly unacceptable levels. Double-digit inflation (which peaked at 13.3 percent in 1979) was corresponding with levels of unemployment, which a decade earlier would have been considered to be at recession standards.

At this point we must note that demand management would still work. Policymakers could still choose from a menu of unemployment-inflation tradeoffs. But that must have been of little solace. In each successive period, the quality of the menu before the policymaker got worse. In the space of a decade, the menu of choices confronting policymakers had deteriorated from those worthy of a *Michelin Guide* to those of a low-quality, fast-food joint. Instead of inflation at 1 percent and unemployment at 5.5 percent, which was the case in the mid-1960s, by 1980 policymakers would have to tolerate 12 percent inflation just to hold unemployment near 7 percent.

Figure 9-3
The Worsening of Aggregate Supply: Inflation and Unemployment, 1958–1983

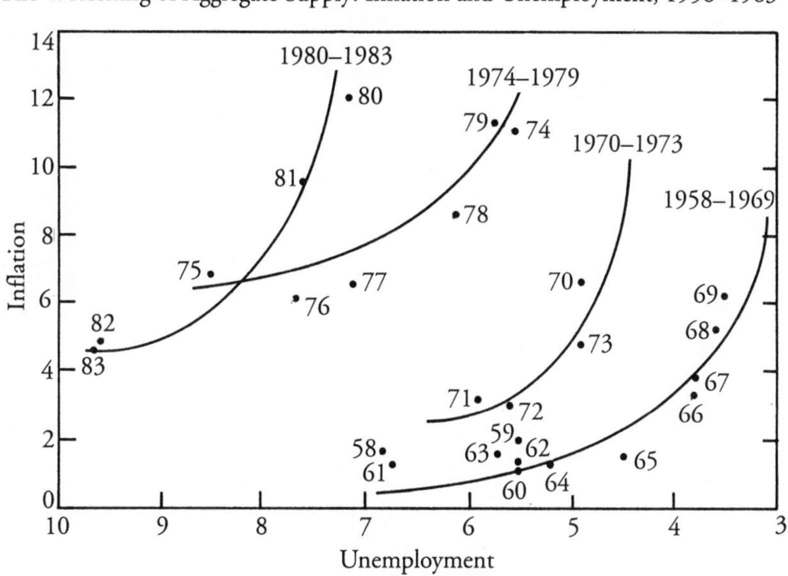

Source: Data are from the *Economic Report of the President* (Washington, D.C.: Government Printing Office, 1997), tables B-40 and B-61.

We shall consider the reasons why this happened and how the process reversed when we examine how the U.S. economy augmented its use of Keynesianism with Reaganomics in the next chapter. We shall also note that these shifts in supply are *reversible* by using the correct policies and that governments therefore need supply-side policies as well as demand-side policies. Analytically, *both the demand curve and the supply curve shift.* As a result, the usual presumption, as evidenced in the *New York Times* quotation earlier in this chapter, that lower unemployment necessarily means higher inflation, is incorrect.

Some commentators have even argued that falling unemployment and inflation mean that the "old laws of economics have been repealed."[7] In practice, what those commentators forgot was that the "laws of economics" or, more precisely, the principles of supply and demand allow for four possibilities, which we set out in figure 9-4: *increased demand* with higher inflation and higher employment; *decreased demand* with lower inflation and lower employment; *increased supply* with lower in-

Figure 9-4
Supply and Demand Possibilities

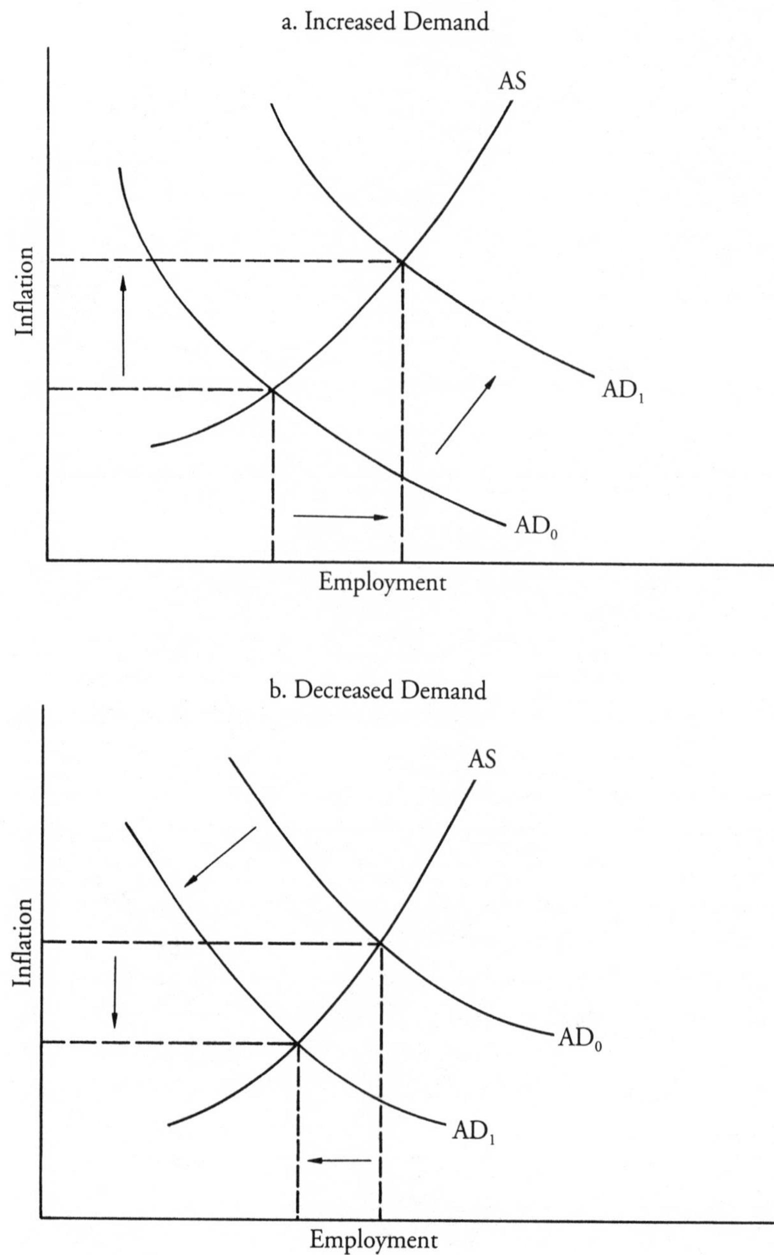

Figure 9-4 (continued)

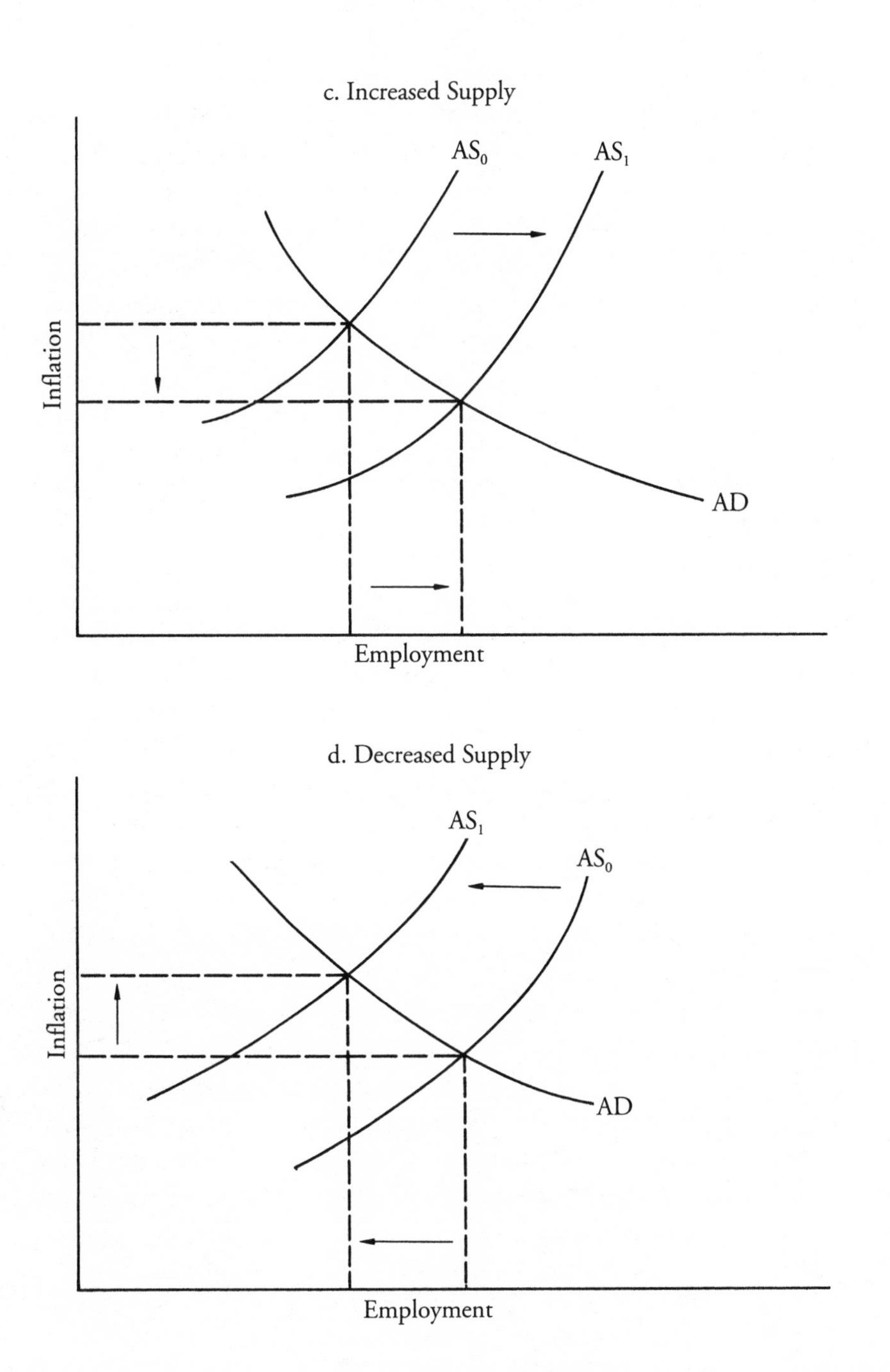

flation and higher employment; and *decreased supply* with higher inflation and lower employment.

We can use such analysis today to provide the economic context from which to make sense of the wide variety of economic circumstances that exist in the industrial world in the late 1990s. Today's supply shock is global in nature and stems from events that are largely outside the control of national policymakers: cheap labor in Asia and new technologies in transportation and communication. But most of the world's policymaking institutions have focused on the demand-based possibilities: increased demand with higher inflation and higher employment or decreased demand with lower inflation and lower employment. That policy mismatch means that our current global increase in supply was met differently in different countries. The result: different economic performance. Consider the three options policymakers faced—increase demand, decrease demand, and resist the supply shock—and the results in America, Japan, and Europe.

Option 1: Increase Demand. Figure 9-5 illustrates how such an increase in demand would affect an economy undergoing a positive supply shock. The actual results would depend on how much policymakers chose to increase demand in the face of an increase in supply. For the sake of discussion, one could imagine the entire supply shock's being transformed into increased output and higher employment levels. In this scenario, the authorities offset the downward pressure on the inflation rate that results from the supply shock by increasing purchases. Their objective would be to take the "mix" of news—lower prices and higher output—and emphasize the "higher output" part of the policy outcome.

Consider how that would work in practice. Suppose a supply shock came along that lowered the cost of production in a number of key sectors of the economy. The policymakers could take advantage of those lower costs in some areas by allowing labor markets to be somewhat tighter than usual, thus creating rising costs and higher prices in some other sectors. The key would be to focus on the overall price level in the economy—allowing falling prices in some areas to offset rising prices in others.

Figure 9-5
Increased Demand and Increased Supply

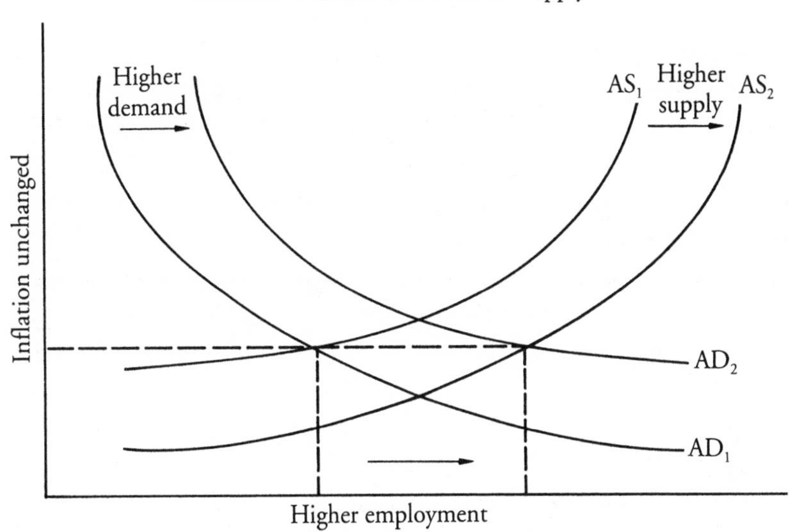

An increase in the size of the work force that competes in the global marketplace causes part of the current supply shock hitting the global economy. Workers in China and southeast Asia now produce many of the labor-intensive, low-value goods such as apparel, which low-wage workers in the more developed countries used to produce. Those low-wage workers are unemployed as a result of the competition from Asia. But by running a stimulative demand policy, other sectors of the economy that are not subject to import competition, such as health care and home construction, can expand. The expanding sectors not only can absorb all the workers laid off from the import-competing sectors but also can absorb new workers without causing higher inflation because prices are actually falling in the industries that those workers are leaving. The total number of jobs in society can rise, and the unemployment rate can fall without producing an acceleration of inflation.

Of course, pushing unemployment down below the levels that traditionally cause inflation does produce increased wage pressure. At first, that increased wage pressure is held down as the workers laid off in the import-competing industry seek work. That pressure may be held down further as workers who are not traditionally employed decide that jobs are available. But a tighter labor market is eventually bound to put upward pressure on wages. Even that can be absorbed, however, without increasing the underlying rate of inflation. True, prices will rise more in the sector that does not compete with goods produced abroad. But prices will rise less (inflation will be falling) in the import-competing sector. So the average rate of inflation in the economy could remain unchanged.

We can tell a similar, but somewhat different, story about a favorable supply shock when an economy deregulates, cuts taxes, and thereby makes more productive use of its existing capital stock. Aggregate supply increases. If it is accompanied by an increase in aggregate demand (which may happen automatically with a tax cut), then the total level of employment in the economy may rise without putting any upward pressure on the overall rate of inflation. That results because disinflation, a widespread phenomenon of falling inflation rates, is occurring in the sectors that the supply shock favorably affected. Such a situation tended to characterize American policy in the 1980s and is what probably predisposed policymakers to follow the same course in the 1990s.

Option 2: Decrease Demand. Figure 9-6 illustrates how cutting demand would affect an economy undergoing a favorable global supply shock. As in the case above, the actual results would depend on how much policymakers chose to decrease demand in the face of an increase in supply. But, as a limiting case, one could imagine the entire supply shock's being transformed into a reduction in the rate of inflation. In this scenario, the authorities offset the upward pressure on employment and output that results from the supply shock by manipulating the demand policy tools at their disposal.

Consider how this would work in practice. A supply shock comes along that lowers the cost of production in a number of key sectors of the economy. But unlike the case above, the policymakers take advantage of those lower costs in the disinflating sectors but do not allow labor markets to be any tighter than usual. If they simply left demand alone, labor markets would tighten somewhat because the real wealth of consumers in the economy had increased. In effect, when the goods in the sector affected by the supply shock fell in price, consumers would have more money to spend on other goods. That would allow employ-

Figure 9-6
Decreased Demand and Increased Supply

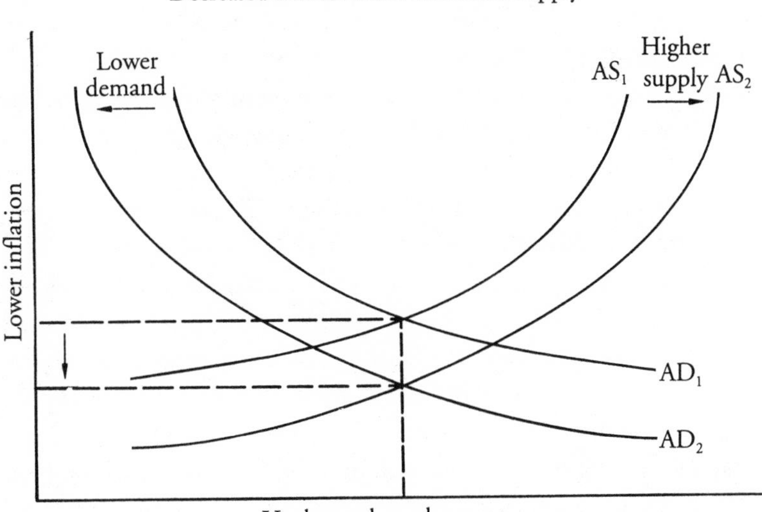

ment to expand in those sectors in which consumers spent their higher real incomes.

Of course, policymakers could leave demand unchanged and take that compromise between higher output and lower inflation. But they could also take advantage of the increased real wealth of consumers by tightening demand policy still further without producing any additional unemployment. They could, for example, raise taxes just enough to offset the greater spending power consumers had from the supply shock. That would allow the underlying inflation rate in the economy to fall still further without noticeably increasing the rate of unemployment.

It is important to stress that we should not yet reach normative judgments about whether that is a good or a bad policy. I'm sure that many Anglo-Saxon readers would consider option 2 to be so "bad" from a political point of view as to be unthinkable in practice. But different paradigms of political economy might approach that option differently. As a practical matter, policymakers in both Europe and Japan followed that option to varying degrees.

Generically, a number of reasons may make it reasonable to cut demand, even as supply increases. One possibility might be that inflation is higher than policymakers like but that those same policymakers might find the political cost of reducing inflation through any increase in unemployment unthinkable. In effect, those policymakers might view the favorable supply curve as manna from heaven. Here is the opportunity they have been waiting for to obtain their policy objective of lower inflation without the political cost of higher unemployment.

In the United States during the mid-1990s, for example, the Fed discussed a policy of opportunistic disinflation.[8] The argument was that monetary policymakers should not take any action (such as causing a recession) to drive inflation down further but should take advantage of such a drop in inflation if the drop came along, even if a recession caused the drop. The opportunistic disinflation discussion really came in the context of a world in which only the aggregate demand curve moved and the cut in demand that lowered inflation resulted from a nonmonetary factor. But opportunistic disinflation during a supply shock is an even more attractive option since there is no sacrifice at all in terms of higher unemployment. If such a possibility were entertained in the United States during a period in which inflation was running about 3 percent, we can certainly easily understand the motivations of policymakers in countries in which the inflation rate was much higher.

The Maastricht Treaty, which is driving policy, includes a Europewide agreement to move to lower inflation rates. That agreement constrained European policymakers to adopt a strict disinflationary course of action in the past few years. We discussed that in detail in chapters 6 and 7. In practice, global trends allowed Europeans to have both lower inflation and a tighter fiscal policy with less loss in employment than would otherwise have been the case. The Maastricht Treaty left little choice except for Europe to adopt option 2 during most of the late 1990s.

The second reason that policymakers might opt to tighten demand in the face of a supply shock has to do with fiscal policy. Policymakers may want to move their national treasuries closer to balance. But, as in the case of unemployment, it may be politically impossible either to cut government spending or to reduce the real living standards of voters through a tax increase under normal circumstances. But a favorable supply shock increases the real incomes of the electorate. Policymakers may appropriate that increased real wealth of their society to improve the fiscal position of their governments.

Recall that a good deal of the development of aggregate demand policy has to do with the composition of demand as well as its level. Policymakers established institutions to monitor the fiscal position of the government, and it became increasingly fashionable to consider limiting the government's fiscal deficit as an objective in itself. In the United States, attaining a balanced budget became one of the core objectives of both political parties. In Europe, the Maastricht criteria on growth convergence placed a limit on the allowed size of national fiscal deficits as well as on inflation rates.

In Japan, the Ministry of Finance saw restraining fiscal deficits as one of the key long-term planning objectives of society—notably involving the aging of the population. The Ministry of Finance thus pushed for a big increase in taxes—a two-point rise in the sales tax and an end to a temporary income tax cut. Those measures took effect in March 1997 and were central to the sudden collapse of the Japanese economy.

On an international basis, it became quite common for the International Monetary Fund and the World Bank to advocate deficit reduction as a part of the economic reform and development process. Not only had the Keynesian notion of fiscal deficits as a stabilizing force been discredited, but balanced budgets came to be considered a positive objective in their own right. Given this, a reduction in demand to improve the government's fiscal position in the face of an increase in supply is a natural outgrowth of that traditional demand-management debate. Thus, even though we may view the choice of demand policy as wrongheaded, societies certainly had many reasons to decrease demand in recent years.

Option 3: Resist the Supply Shock. The final option available to policymakers is to implement policies that limit the impact of the supply shock on the economy. Again, the actual outcome of that policy depends on the extent to which the supply shock is offset. In the limiting case, we could imagine the economy's returning to its situation before the supply shock. In practice, that would be very difficult, but setting up that possibility as a limiting case shows what could happen; the degree of implementation is all that is in dispute.

Again, the reader might ask whether, as a practical matter, any government would ever do such a thing. Why would a government prohibit implementing a lower-cost alternative to existing production arrangements? The plain answer is that governments do this all the time. Indeed, economic history suggests that with rare exceptions (mostly in the past 200 years), the dominant economic objective of government has been to protect the economic status quo and limit the options available to both producers and consumers. The objective of ancient emperors, medieval guilds, and modern despots is the same.

Today, even in most modern "market" economies, the state is almost invariably a force against change: quotas, tariffs, regulations on corporate ownership, price controls, employment standards, and the like. By and large opinion makers consider such policies on a case-by-case basis. So even in a market-oriented economy such as the United States, where leading opinion is rhetorically "promarket," policymakers may adopt such measures as increasing the minimum wage and may make well-intentioned exceptions to the general disposition to let markets work. In the early 1980s, improvement in automobile production technology was met with de facto import restrictions by the promarket Reagan administration as Japanese producers had a head start over their American counterparts.

But there is another reason as well. We should recall the challenge Alan Greenspan now faces: mastering the process of creative destruction. The tale is a cautionary one. Sure, a new technology or a new product is a good thing. But as we saw in chapter 3, fear and greed create enormous financial and economic damage, even from a positive development.

First comes the growing disparity between those lucky enough to be in industries benefiting from the supply shock and those in dead-end jobs in industries left behind. Then we see the speculative excess and the example of people getting rich just by being in the right place at the right time. We experience the regional recessions, which turn into regional depressions unless handled with care. Widespread bank failures develop that end either with depositors' being wiped out or taxpayers' financing a "bailout." If that is such a familiar tale, why do we never learn? It would seem eminently rational to "resist" the supply shock if at all possible.

One can already hear the critics of capitalism claiming that unrestrained markets and speculative lending have caused our current problems. Those voices will get louder as time passes. Many of the loudest voices belong to despots, near despots, or would-be despots who don't like market forces' challenging their cozy view of the world in which they pull all the levers. Be it a Suharto of Indonesia, a Mahathir of Malaysia, or a Jean-Marie Le Pen in France, the opponents of market-based change are ascendant. We can easily see then why existing governments try to resist a supply shock. The economic change it brings also threatens social and political upheaval.

Bad As It Is, Consider the Alternative

We capitalists should also admit that those critics of capitalism are not totally wrong. The decisions of individuals drive markets, and emotions as well as rational calculation drive individuals. One does not have to be as skeptical as George Soros about markets. But even if Soros himself acts as if markets are reflexive and not rational, then by definition an element of something other than rational calculation exists in their behavior. All that markets can do is to hold the individuals who made the failed decisions responsible after the fact for their judgment. That may be cold comfort to those who find their hopes and dreams disrupted by these boom-bust cycles. The critics of capitalism make their pitch to those disaffected people.

But those who advocate that governments implement rules to prevent that process from happening miss two important points. The first point is that the evidence is overwhelming that the state would not have done that job any better. State planning in the former Soviet Union and Eastern Europe created excess steel and other industrial plants in such abundance that there was no market for the output. The human emotion of greed and dreams of grandeur do not disappear simply because someone becomes an employee of the state or carries a party card.

Nor are such problems limited to communist systems. Much of the problem we have witnessed in Asia results from government policies' carrying on the creation of ever more productive capacity well beyond the period when the markets—imperfect though they are—would simply have said no. Some of the critics of capitalism in Asia are really the cause of their country's problems, as they foisted grand but noneconomic projects on their economies.

In Japan, as we saw, the mandarin system created an economy that was far too overborrowed. Firms borrowed too much from banks that were themselves overextended. That was not the product of capitalism but the deliberate strategy of the mandarins who ran economic policy. In part they chose that course because it made the most of scarce capital after the Second World War. But the mandarins kept that system in place long after Japan became a capital-rich nation. They did so not just for economically sensible reasons, but because doing so extended and enhanced their control.

Many of those same people now resent the supposedly ruthless consequences of the market. Do they feel sorry for the powerless losers? Or is it for themselves, who are now seeing the reins of power slip from their grasp? Those individuals had their chance, and they could not do any better. In fact, they did demonstrably worse.

The second reason the critics of capitalism are wrong is that they miss a very important, although somewhat subtle, point about capitalism and its process of creative destruction. Would we have been better off if those cycles had never occurred? In the case of the Cancer Cure story of chapter 3, critics would say that the product was fine but the market should have been developed in a "controlled" fashion. Controlled by whom? When those critics are pressed, the answer is by the critics themselves, of course, since "controlled" would have naturally meant that fewer cancer pills would have been produced and that the market would have developed more slowly. "Controlled development" would have meant more cancer deaths.

But, of course, we aren't talking about a cancer cure in the current Asian crisis or in any number of real estate cycles, are we? Instead, we are talking about microprocessor chips, automobiles, shoes, children's clothes and toys, and office buildings. So controlled development (assuming the market's critics could actually do a better job) would have meant that millions of newly middle-class people around the world would have had to wait for their first PC, their first car, or for toys and clothes for their children.

Consider one of the most poignant tales I saw last year in my travels around the world. In the shopping district of Buenos Aires, I saw $30 children's toys on sale for ten monthly installments of $3. It is certainly heart-wrenching to imagine having to purchase toys for children "on time." But would the advocates of controlling the market suggest that these parents simply say no to their children as they have had to for countless generations before? Or would they walk away as I did, wishing for even faster growth and more unbridled capitalism, so that toys need not be bought on the installment plan? Like democracy, creative destruction is a messy process. But it is not just as Churchill once said of democracy as a form of government: that all the other systems are so much worse. It is also true in the positive sense—the world is incomparably better off because of creative destruction.

We can make the same case for real estate cycles and their "creative destruction" counterparts. Nearly all the buildings in our cities, particularly those sporting the architecture of which we are most proud, were constructed during one of the up phases of those cycles. Because hope springs eternal in the human spirit, someone is willing to take the risks and go through the headaches involved in building something new and uplifting. The key point that the critics miss in all such cycles is that there is no alternative to creative destruction for fermenting economic growth in our societies.

What Should the Puppetmaster Do?

What this highlights is one of the key limits to economic management: often there is no "right" thing to do. Exactly what lever of power would you, the reader, have an economic decisionmaker pull to make things different? Would you raise interest rates to make the development of new office buildings—or new cures for cancer—less affordable? Or cut rates, thus ensuring that the resulting economic bubble got larger, with ever greater downside consequences once the bubble burst? Would you raise taxes so fewer people could buy the cancer cure or have a massive health care scheme to ensure unlimited demand? If so, what would you do with the extra pills and pill factories?

If you follow this logic far enough, you ultimately find yourself at a classic fork in the road. The path to the left is to reestablish bureaucratic control. Much of the world opted for this in the 1920s and 1930s.

The state could make sure that disruptive innovations did not upset the plan. It could control every facet of economic life as in Stalin's Russia or Hitler's Germany. Or it could simply control the commanding heights as in pre-Thatcher Britain or postwar India. But, if we have learned anything from the past seventy years, it is that this path ends in tears.

The path to the right looks vaguely like a capitulation to endless boom-bust cycles and rule by predatory robber barons. If the path to the left looks like a smoothly paved superhighway, which we know thanks to Friedrich A. Hayek as the *Road to Serfdom*, the path to the right looks deeply rutted and full of obstacles, even though it is the road to freedom and prosperity. One does not opt for that course if he believes in Utopias or the omniscience of planners. Freedom requires that one build a vehicle with a strong set of shock absorbers before beginning. In particular, one should establish the role of the contrarian in the economy and pick some sober and sensible drivers like Alan Greenspan. That is the course on which we now seem headed.

Summing Up

The world seems to be in the midst of a supply shock of the kind Chairman Greenspan said occurs one or twice in a century. This supply shock produces enormous benefits and higher living standards. But, in the short run, creative destruction increases the risks to society. Sensible monetary and fiscal policies are needed to maximize the benefits to society from the process of a supply shock. But even those sensible policies cannot change the central fact that fear, greed, and changing economic circumstances create a dynamic over which even economic puppetmasters have only limited control.

Without any question, the economy that seems to have best recognized that fact is the United States. We now take a closer look at American economic policy and how it evolved to produce its current relatively successful arrangements. But we should not forget that those arrangements are only relatively better. The road ahead is bumpy, indeed, and while we have a strong set of shock absorbers, we also need leaders with clear vision who keep their eyes on the road for the dangers ahead.

10

The Criteria for Successful Economic Management

If not us, who? And if not now, when?

—*Ronald Reagan*[1]

Limitations on the economic puppetmasters of our world seem to have become the order of the day. In each of the major economies of the world, policymakers have reached the point where the clear-cut management options of the past no longer seem to suffice. One can no longer just pull some strings to accomplish one's policy objective. Often, those limitations are institutional. Existing arrangements for economic management have reached a point where the puppetmaster simply lacks the right strings to pull by himself or with his institution. While that shortcoming is not necessarily fatal, it does increase the overall risk to the national and global economies.

In the United States, which has by far the most successful economy at present, a modus vivendi of economic policy had been established to meld those institutional limitations with the political demands of society. Fiscal policy, hamstrung by a complex constitutional process, has been abandoned as a method of fine-tuning the economic engine. Instead, that role has been left to the monetary authorities. Although immensely capable, those authorities find themselves limited in their ability to provide both economic stability and stable financial markets. A financial market bubble developed, and the policymakers seem to lack the mandate to end the bubble without sacrificing their more traditional missions.

In Japan, the entire panoply of economic institutions, which were designed to make maximum use of available capital and labor in the headlong rush to rebuild after the war, are still in place. But it is increasingly obvious to all that many of those institutions are anachronisms. Unfortunately, the decisionmaking structure has a vested interest in maintaining the status quo, and no obvious alternative is in sight. While the dominance of economic management by the bureaucracy is increasingly unpopular, the political arrangements by the Japanese that can end that dominance are far from apparent. So Japan suffers under both political and economic ennui.

A lot is at stake. Even under relatively optimistic assumptions, Japan is likely to suffer an entire decade of subpar economic growth. During most of the 1980s and 1990s, the decisions of the Japanese bureaucracy were subject to only the most muted of market-based tests. Strict limits existed on the international capital flows of the yen, but they have been eased over time. The government also made massive interventions in both the foreign exchange and equity markets to control and mute the price signals being given by investors. As a result, a continuous market test was lacking, and the result was a significantly worse set of economic choices than could have been made.

The loss to the typical Japanese citizen is potentially enormous. For example, had the Japanese enjoyed American levels of economic growth in the 1990s, instead of what actually occurred, they would have been much richer. Even under an optimistic set of assumptions about the course of Japan over the rest of the 1990s, that difference will amount to roughly $5,000 of annual output per capita by 2000. Furthermore, even if growth returns to its normal pace, the loss in terms of living standards will be permanent. So a baby born in Japan in the year 2000 will have lost, in present value terms, the equivalent of $150,000 in wealth owing to the economic policies of the 1990s.[2]

In Germany, at the heart of Europe, two of the political imperatives of history are coming into conflict. On the one hand, the need to prevent yet another war among the various European powers is causing them to develop political and economic arrangements that will bring them closer together. The current unifying force is the single currency.

Yet Germany has had nothing but bad experiences with a politically managed currency. The thought that politicians—particularly non-German politicians—will control the currency is anathema to the German middle class. The result is going to be, at least in the short run, an enormous increase in the uncertainty regarding the bases under which European economic policy is run.

Meanwhile, Europe continues to suffer from near-record-high unemployment. The loss in long-term well-being to the typical European from the mismatched policies of the 1990s is not so different from the typical Japanese. Collectively, the world is losing trillions of dollars of output owing to poor economic management.

While economic management truly is of great aid and comfort if it is well conducted, it can become a heavy cross borne by the workers, taxpayers, and consumers of a country when it is mismanaged. Markets now have the power regularly to second-guess decisionmakers and score their performance. But that does not make the increased power of markets to second-guess policymakers' decisions popular with the governments that are open to question. Politicians would much prefer that their performance be subject to only occasional tests, at the ballot box, under conditions with which they are familiar and rules that they have mastered. They are decidedly uncomfortable with a world in which their decisions are subject to a constant and instantaneous judgment by markets.

In chapter 8, George Soros expressed a view that any believer in good government would share: "Of course, it would be better if the authorities were responsible to their own citizens." Today, with the triumph of democracy and economic freedom, we may have thought that we had solved our economic and political problems. We plainly have not. We have yet to find a way of making authorities "deliver the goods" in terms of sound economic policy.

But we do know some things. First, the evidence is clear that America has a huge advantage over its counterparts in knowing how to get policies right. We can attribute that success to establishing the contrarian role in government. If American policy has any potential shortcoming, it is that contrarian power is centered among unelected officials at the Federal Reserve. They face legal and political constraints (as well as economic doubts) that limit their ability to deal with a prospective financial bubble and the process of creative destruction.

Second, it would be far better if those with direct political authority exercised some contrarian behavior. It would be useful to have an elected official act as contrarian because he would be far more credible as someone out to change things, given an electoral mandate. Unfortunately, America's leader has chosen the exact opposite tack—to stay popular by elevating empathy to be the main presidential emotion.

The far more severe problems in Japan and Europe are too deeply rooted in the past to be solved by anything other than an elected official acting credibly as a contrarian. Getting one is not so simple. America produced such a leader in Ronald Reagan. It would be useful considering his legacy as a model on how to effect needed changes. Lest readers "on the left" take offense, it is important to note that a key reason for Reagan's success was his adoption of an essentially Keynesian role for himself, including a willingness to use a key Keynesian tool—deficit spending—as a temporary expedient.

The last chapter ended by observing that the statist road to the left has been discredited. The market-oriented road is the only alternative, but it is bumpy, and proceeding on it will require strong shock absorbers. Remarkably, Reagan did just that in 1981 in America. He took the bumpy road to the right, but in a vehicle modified with an extra strong suspension system. Obviously, Reagan was a man who is not replicable and might not even be the right man at a different place or time. We consider the details of his policies not because of their complete applicability but because they give us the best road map in existence on how to proceed.

Reagan as a Credible Contrarian

Ronald Reagan turned out to be that elusive product that Keynes really felt an economy needed at a time of crisis: a politician who was willing to act as a contrarian. Reagan did not abandon Keynesian economics, but he reshaped it in a way that allowed the government the capacity to regain its contrarian role. That was the cause of substantial misunderstanding, particularly by the economic and political establishment.

According to the received wisdom of the time, one of the key centerpieces of Reagan's campaign, an across-the-board tax cut, would be

Figure 10-1
Reaganomics and a Positive Supply Shock: Inflation and Unemployment, 1980–1996

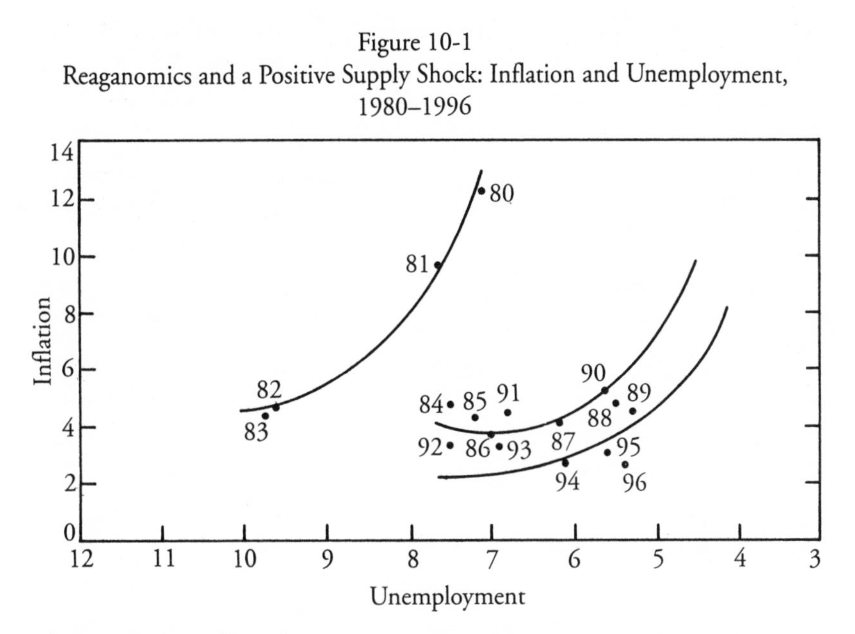

Source: Data are from the *Economic Report of the President* (Washington, D.C.: Government Printing Office, 1997), tables B-40 and B-61.

yet another increase in the aggregate demand curve and thus only make things worse. William Miller, Jimmy Carter's Treasury secretary, argued against then–candidate Reagan's policies during the 1980 campaign. "Hasty tax cutting now could be counterproductive. It would be a great hoax on the American people to promise a tax cut that sets off a new price spiral," said Miller. Walter Heller, a leading Keynesian economist, warned, "[A] $114 billion tax cut in three years would simply overwhelm our existing productive capacity with a tidal wave of increased demand and sweep away all hopes of curbing deficits and containing inflation."[3]

But the views of Messrs. Miller and Heller had ceased to be those of economic contrarians and instead had become a predictable set of policymaker reactions. It is undoubtedly the case that the tax cut proposals of Reagan increased aggregate demand. But, as figure 10-1 makes clear, the Reagan era was also one in which the aggregate supply curve stopped its headlong retreat of the 1970s and reversed direction. The administration accomplished that by reversing many government policies that had hard-wired the predictable path of a guaranteed-demand safety net. The result of this was exactly what policymakers in Europe and Japan most desire today: an improvement in the *menu* of choices between unemployment and inflation.

That Reaganomics proved successful is best illustrated by two key economic indicators: inflation and unemployment. Reaganomics reversed the long deterioration of the aggregate supply curve during the 1970s. By the time Reagan left office, the rate of consumer price inflation had fallen to 4.6 percent from 12.5 percent the year he was elected. The rate of unemployment fell from 7.1 percent to 5.3 percent. Reagan was the first president since World War II to complete his term in office with both inflation and unemployment lower than when he was first elected.[4] Furthermore, important structural changes in both policy and the economy have meant that continued positive supply-side developments outlasted his tenure in office. As of mid-1998, unemployment was nearly a full point lower than when Reagan left office, and inflation was over two and a half points lower.

But the reinvigoration of a contrarian role for policymakers is evidenced by the fact that Reaganomics also seems to have been successful at stabilization policy, which was supposed to have been Keynes's forte. In terms of mitigating the business cycle, the period since 1981 was even more remarkable than the period between World War II and the start of the Reagan administration. If one includes the 1982 recession in the analysis, in the past seventeen years we have seen only two years in which real disposable personal income per capita was lower than the year before: and one was a decline of less than one-tenth of a percent. The 1945–1980 period had seven such years, plus two more years in which incomes rose but not enough to recover their levels two years prior. Even if you exclude from that record the Truman administration, which had to deal with the demobilization from World War II, the United States still had four one-year declines plus a fifth year in which income didn't rise to its level two years prior, all in a span of twenty-seven years. While real per capita disposable personal income grew at roughly the same 1.7 percent annual rate in both parts of the post–World War II era, the years since 1981 have unequivocally seen a diminution of the variations in the business cycle.[5]

Those figures understate the actual performance of Reaganomics. The recession of 1982 was primarily an economic detoxification from the inflationary effects of earlier policies. Since then, we have had a continuous sixteen-year period of sustained economic expansion broken only by a single short and relatively mild recession. Such a performance is unprecedented in American history and is far better than the 1945–1980 period. The key question is why.

A good deal of that improvement might well be credited to a change in expectations. But we cannot ascribe that change in expectations to a simple change in demand-management policies. Reagan's critics predicted that his policies were likely to worsen inflation. What Reagan did was to attack some of the key structural rigidities in the economy in taxation, regulation, and labor markets that were impeding the smooth functioning of markets. The essence of Reaganomics was that well-functioning markets, free of privately created or governmentally imposed barriers to entry and trade, would cause society's resources to be used most efficiently. An improvement in the efficiency with which society's resources are used will mean that we can enjoy a higher rate of resource utilization and lower unemployment without creating pricing pressures.

Making underlying structural changes facilitates the process of changing the expectations of decisionmakers. As economists in the late 1970s noted, the more rapidly expectations adjust to new realities, the less painful will be the ultimate adjustment. A new and very important word crept into the economic jargon of the time—*credibility.* While the neo-Keynesians in the Carter administration had talked about a variety of anti-inflation strategies, the markets simply did not believe them. The aggregate supply curve continued to shift backward, reflecting the private decisionmakers' view that the same old policies would remain in place.

Reagan was different. His rhetoric was different. No one would ever confuse him with the established or conventional view. While this meant that he was criticized by some as a simplistic ideologue, his image helped lend him a credibility that no one else in the political or economic establishment could project. Dinesh D'Souza, best-selling author and John M. Olin Fellow at the American Enterprise Institute, recounts a story in his book *Ronald Reagan: How an Ordinary Man Became an Extraordinary Leader,* which shows that this contrarian image was precisely what Reagan intended.

A few weeks into the start of Reagan's administration, Alexander

Haig, the secretary of state, was seeking to have the president's blessing for continued discussions for the Law of the Sea treaty, which had been going on for many years. Reagan said that he would not support the treaty and asked for negotiations to be suspended. Haig tried his best, noting how both parties had been working for many years on that treaty:

> "Well yes," Reagan said, "but you see, Al, that's what the last election was all about."
>
> "What?" Haig sneered. "About the Law of the Sea treaty?"
>
> "No," Reagan replied. "It was about not doing things just because that's the way they've been done before."[6]

This exchange conveys the essence of a policymaker determined to break with the conventional wisdom and to use that break to alter the expectations of economic decisionmakers throughout the nation. Reagan chose a set of key structural changes likely to have a major impact and coupled them with a credible resolve that proved immensely successful. Two particular issues—attitudes toward labor markets and tax indexation—are particularly important to consider, because they indicate an analytic break with the past as well as a difference in policy.

Labor Markets. One of Reagan's most decisive acts in his first year in office had nothing to do with demand management or even the supply curve per se. It was the firing of the Professional Air Traffic Controllers Organization (PATCO) workers, the air traffic controllers for the nation. The union was demanding a bigger wage settlement than the government was prepared to meet. The union felt, not without good reason, that it was in an immensely powerful position—its members were vital to the air traffic system. That system was of enormous importance, not only to the economy, but to a segment of the public that was probably key to the political constituency of the incoming president: the flying public in general and business travelers in particular. Furthermore, PATCO had been one of the few unions that had supported Reagan in the general election.

The union called a strike, an illegal act under existing public employment law. All air traffic controllers, as government employees, had signed an oath never to strike against the government. Reagan gave them an ultimatum to return to work and fired all those who did not. The strike gradually fizzled out, and union demands switched to rehiring the fired workers. Reagan stood firm despite enormous public pressure. No single act could have established more credibility for the president as being serious about inflation or undermined the sense of wage increases as a "one-sided bet" than this one. Wage psychology changed virtually overnight, and inflationary pressures rapidly abated.

The data on the number of strikes bear this out. The number of work days lost to strikes exceeded 20 million in each year of the Carter administration. It averaged less than 10 million during Reagan's eight years and has continued to decline ever since.[7]

Reagan also failed to increase the minimum wage, allowing it to decline in real terms by 36 percent during his administration.[8] That was an interesting policy decision. On the one hand, some of Reagan's economic advisers certainly believed that the minimum wage was an impediment to a smoothly functioning labor market and was artificially creating unemployment, particularly among younger and lower-skilled workers. That led those advisers to consider repealing the minimum wage.

But refusing to increase the minimum wage while keeping it actively in place may well have had a greater effect on anti-inflationary psychology. Here was a key price in the economy, posted in the newspapers, actively being discussed on television, that was not going to be automatically increased with inflation! Under normal political and economic dynamics, the minimum wage was a natural to be "indexed," because it took the issue off the table. Low-income workers would get an automatic increase, but employers did not risk having to pay an even greater increase that was legislatively mandated. Repealing the minimum wage would have looked like an act of ideologues and not one of trying to hold the line on wages and prices.

Tax Policy. The centerpiece of Reagan's first-term economics policy was the Economic Recovery Tax Act, an across-the-board reduction in personal rates coupled with saving and investment incentives for both businesses and individuals. Today, a general consensus exists that tax rates were too high before the Reagan reductions. It is worth recalling, for example, that in 1980 a family of four earning $60,000, or about twice the median income, was in the 49 percent federal income tax bracket. Just fifteen years earlier, a similarly situated family was in the 22 percent tax bracket.[9] The high rates induced a wide variety of distortions in labor-supply decisions, type of compensation, and in the level and form of saving.

But the debate over income tax indexing in 1981 gives the prime example of how an antiquated mode of analysis can impede reform. Keynesian demand siders simply refused to understand how high rates and a progressive tax structure combine to exacerbate wage negotiation decisions. In an inflationary environment, the resulting dynamics create pressures for a cost-push inflationary spiral and a constantly upward-shifting aggregate supply curve.

Consider a worker earning $1,000 per week in the 50 percent marginal tax bracket with an average rate of 30 percent. In other words, he is taking home $700 per week but keeps only half of any pay increase. Suppose a "real" productivity increase of 2 percent is the norm and that inflation is running at 8 percent. If this worker were to get the 10 percent nominal wage increase to $1,100 per week that economic theory suggests, the government would take half, leaving him with just a $50 increase in his take-home pay. But he would have needed at least a $56 increase in his real take-home pay to keep up with the 8 percent inflation, with no room for a "real" pay increase. To get what he feels he deserves, the worker would need a 14 percent wage boost, or $140. The government would have taken $70, leaving him with a 10 percent after-tax increase, $56 to cover inflation and $14 to cover his real 2 percent wage hike.

That provides a tax-driven explanation of why the aggregate supply curve was shifting back even more quickly than the aggregate demand curve was increasing. If you think of that worker's position, he needs a pay boost well above the inflation rate just to stay even. To get compensated for the fact that he is more productive, he needs a pay boost dramatically above the inflation rate. As the aggregate supply curve shows, how much of a wage increase that worker (and the millions like him) needs to supply just as much labor and output as before clearly requires an upward shift in the curve.

Thus, the most important structural reform in the Economic Recovery Tax Act was the indexing of personal income tax brackets for inflation. In the case described above, the worker would need only an 8 percent increase in nominal wages—the same as the inflation rate—to maintain the purchasing power of his take-home pay. This removed the incentives for a tax-induced, cost-push inflation spiral that were a regular part of wage negotiations before the enactment of indexation.

All of this was completely lost on the Keynesian-oriented economic establishment. Indeed, no issue differentiated the Reagan emphasis on structural distortions in markets from the purely Keynesian emphasis on aggregate demand more than did indexation. Actually, the Carter administration saw the *lack* of indexation as an anti-inflationary tool. It reasoned that after-tax compensation would rise more slowly as a result of bracket creep, and that would put a damper on consumers' ability to spend. The Carter administration's 1980 *Economic Report of the President* stated:

> Fighting inflation continues to be the top priority of economic policy. . . . Since individuals will be moving into higher tax brackets as their incomes increase, the share of personal income taken by Federal income taxes will rise. . . . The resulting rise in effective tax rates, combined with limited growth of Federal outlays, will cause the Federal budget to move significantly toward restraint in the next fiscal year.[10]

Here was a group totally lost in a demand-side analysis of the economy. Their view was that a shrinking federal deficit was the key measurement of the effect of government policies on the underlying rate of inflation. The Keynesian ideal of the government's acting as a nimble contrarian had metamorphosed into a government with rigid rules that helped hard-wire private-sector decisionmaking. The income tax indexing issue is merely an example of how true believers in the status quo can be blind to the actual consequences of their actions.

Direct Applicability to Japan and Europe

As noted earlier, today policymakers in both Japan and Europe are also totally lost in demand-side analysis. Both economies suffer from excessively high tax rates. Both societies refuse to cut them for a host of reasons that echo Reagan's many critics. In Europe and Japan, successful people must often share more than half their income with the tax collector. Similarly, both societies have labor markets in desperate need of restructuring. Again, no leader is willing, as Reagan was, to face down those who wish to maintain noneconomic work rules. I suggest that those wishing to change their systems take a close look at the PATCO strike.

At different times in the past, both Germany and Japan have taken drastic measures to rebuild. Ludwig Erhard, minister of economics in post–World War II Germany, was as much a credible contrarian as Ronald Reagan. He defied not just conventional wisdom, but the military powers occupying his country. The same can be said of early post–World War II Japan.

At the end of the Second World War, the per capita GDP levels in Japan were just twice those in India.[11] In fact, India had more natural resources and a larger intact industrial base. India would also gain political independence before General MacArthur left Japan. Though both countries were effectively controlled by bureaucratic elites that democratic governance only lightly checked, those elites chose different growth paths: Japan was outward-looking and capitalistic; India was inward-looking and socialistic. Within two generations, per capita GDP levels in Japan were fourteen times those of India.[12]

Though geopolitical tact prevents the frequent statement of the obvious—that the Indian model was a failure—imitation remains the sincerest form of flattery. While many nations sought to import the Japanese model as a basis for their own development, no leader has ever told his electorate that he is going to bring them the glories of the Indian model. In the short run, politically correct spin may paper over results. But, over time, which system is economically dynamic and which is not become abundantly clear to all observers.

All that may sound like a recipe for just letting markets do their damage unmitigated by government. Laissez-faire works in markets. Markets still need the strong shock absorbers of a sound macroeconomic management, however. While the current global supply shock is largely driven by forces outside the control of policymakers, Reagan's was not. It was deliberate. Change in Europe and Japan will, in fact, require that a policy-induced supply shock be loaded on top of that which is occurring anyway. Indeed, that makes the key lesson from Reaganomics even more applicable to Europe and Japan today. If you're going to have a supply shock, use an aggressive fiscal policy.

The "Keynesian" side of Reagan's fiscal policy was to provide a demand-side insurance policy in case the economy were to suffer a sudden collapse while undergoing a rapid transformation. In Reagan's case, disinflation was clearly needed, but recent experience had suggested to policymakers that it might prove extremely costly.

Consider what happened in America in early 1980. In January consumer prices rose 1.4 percent, a rate of monthly increase that exceeded even the average annual rate during most of the 1950s and early 1960s.[13] Had it continued at that pace for the year, inflation would have been 18.2 percent. President Carter urged consumers to stop using their credit cards. Some limited credit controls were imposed. Demand collapsed. In the second quarter of 1980, GDP fell at an annual rate of 9.9 percent, exceeding the average rate of collapse during the Great Depression.[14] The number of unemployed rose 1.4 million in just two months.[15]

With deflationary risks of that magnitude, some kind of demand-side safety net was a useful precaution. Structural changes, including disinflations, can often be quite disruptive. Investments that were made based on ever-rising prices of fixed assets ceased to be profitable. The debt that often financed such investments was unsound. Supply shocks, even favorable ones, can cause their share of economic disruption. As we learned earlier, the government could respond to those supply shocks by either expanding demand or contracting demand. The expansive demand-side policies of the 1980s made the economic transition of that decade to a more flexible, low-inflation economy far easier than it otherwise might have been.

One can never rerun history, and so it is impossible to know what would have happened had this demand-side insurance policy not been taken out. But we have some striking evidence that even the Reagan administration failed to appreciate just how quickly inflation would come down. That is, the administration underestimated how quickly the positive supply shock it initiated would take hold. Shortly after coming to office in 1981, the administration issued its *Program for Economic Recovery,* outlining its fiscal policy and underlying economic assumptions. Later, it was called the "Rosy Scenario" because the economy simply had not grown as fast as expected. While nominal GDP grew 35 percent in the five years from 1982 to 1986, the administration had expected 68 percent growth. As things turned out, both real growth and inflation were much lower than the administration expected: real growth turned out 9 percent lower and inflation was 14 percent lower than the administration forecast over that period.[16]

During the 1980s, Reagan was criticized for having put such a supposedly aggressive fiscal policy into place: his budget deficits were too large. A fair question would be, What if he hadn't? If there is any validity at all in Keynesian theory—and the postwar results at economic stabilization suggests that there is—we know that nominal GDP growth (the combination of inflation and real growth) would have been even lower. Furthermore, both supply-side and Keynesian analysis of the lagged effects of policy suggest that *most of the lower growth would have been in real GDP.* In short, the wrenching transition to a lower inflation economy would have been far worse had the Reagan administration not taken out a Keynesian-type fiscal insurance policy.

True, that policy had one key difference from any of the pre-Reagan stimulus policies. With the Fed tightly controlling the rate of growth of money, and therefore nominal GDP, the chance that this fiscal stimulus could get out of hand was remote. The "upside" part of fiscal policy was therefore truncated. Prohibitive interest rates would quickly choke off an expansion that got too far ahead of itself. But the demand-side insurance policy still was in effect in case the disinflationary and other structural changes threatened the economy on the downside. Today, independent central banks around the world still can play the key role that the Fed played in the 1980s.

Interestingly, Keynes would have probably understood all that perfectly well. But his self-proclaimed disciples in the 1980s were part of the establishment that Reagan was attacking. Furthermore, the Reagan people could never dare say anything kind about Keynesian policy because Keynes was the name associated with the failed policies of the 1970s. Politics conspires to keep that lesson from America a secret, so we need to repeat it here so that Japanese and European policymakers have no doubt: *If you're going to have a major supply shock, use an aggressive fiscal policy as some economic insurance.*

A Deemphasis on Crisis Management

My travels around the globe have led me to another conclusion about the corridors of power: a marked deemphasis on crisis management pervades. One of the key lessons that East Asia will be learning from its current travails is that no matter how dynamic an economy, major crises can wipe out years of hard work and economic development. To give some idea of what's involved, consider the effect of the Great Depression on the United States. Real per capita incomes in the United States reached a peak in 1929, fell thereafter, and did not regain their 1929 level again until 1940, when the Second World War had already begun in much of the world. In the decade before that time, real per capita incomes had been growing at roughly 2 percent per year.[17] The effect of the depression was therefore not only to cause a decade of misery, but to permanently lower the incomes of the American people by 25 percent from their predepression growth path. While those extrapolations are perilous, one could conclude that per capita incomes in the United States might be $7,000 higher today had the Great Depression not occurred. Stated in terms of economic dynamism, it would take an extra six-tenths of a percent real growth in each year of a forty-year working life to get back what was lost as a result of that major economic crisis.

No wonder, then, that so many of the economic institutional arrangements of the United States are in place to attempt to make sure that the Great Depression never happens again. Rational calculations of that sort indicate that a society should demand roughly as much attention to the ability of its economic managers to limit successfully the damage of a crisis as they do to making sure that their economy can grow up to its potential.

The capacity for crisis management is much more difficult to monitor effectively than is the growth rate of an economy. Fortunately, major crises do not happen frequently. An electorate often doesn't know how its system can handle a crisis until it's too late. Of course, minor crises happen a bit more frequently and give some indication of a nation's capacity to handle a crisis. One could consider the effect of the oil shocks of the 1970s as a test of different countries' abilities to handle a severe economic shock. The same could be said of military threats, either to the country or to its vital economic interests. The 1990 Gulf War was certainly one of those situations.

Of course, both economic dynamism and the capacity to handle a crisis are not easily quantifiable. But a look at postwar history in the world's major economies gives some good indication of the rough direction in which those economies have been headed. For illustrative purposes, we shall consider the analysis of each country graphically, with

Figure 10-2
Economic Dynamism and Crisis Management in the United States

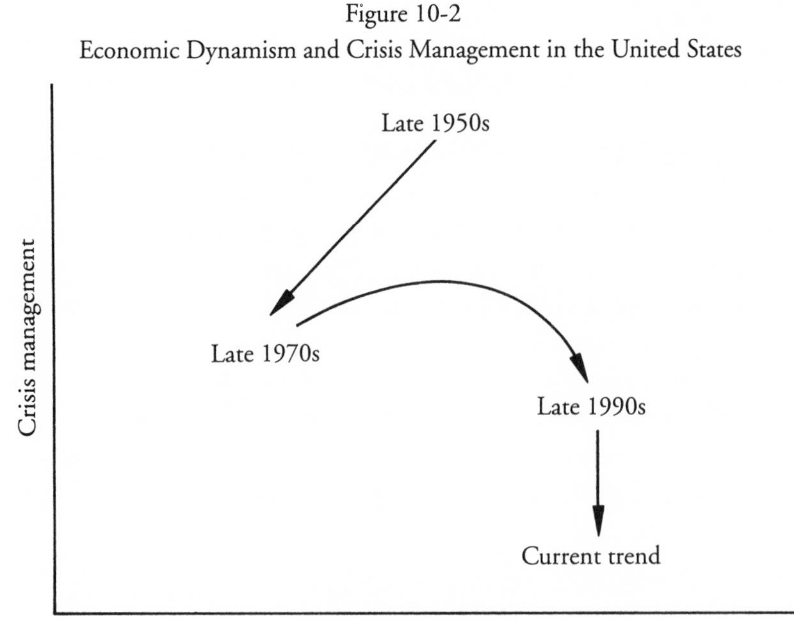

our two objectives—crisis management potential and economic dynamism—on the axes of a single graph. The most desirable direction is to move "northeast," to a point where an economic system can both be more dynamic and handle crises as well as possible.

The United States

Figure 10-2 depicts economic dynamism and crisis management in the United States. In the late 1950s, the capacity of the United States to handle a crisis was probably at a historic peak. History demanded that this be so. Economically, memories of the Great Depression were still dominant in the minds of the electorate. More important, the country was fighting for its life in the midst of the cold war. Universal conscription of young males coupled with defense expenditures equal to nearly one-tenth of national output produced a country not only ready to deal with a crisis but expecting one to happen at any time.[18]

Most important for estimating crisis management is the capacity of the system to recognize a crisis, make the necessary decisions, and implement its actions in a timely fashion. In the context of the U.S. government, that really boils down to the relative ability of the president to make tough decisions quickly and get the cooperation (or at least the noninterference) of Congress. We have little doubt that this was the case in the late 1950s. The president could and did commit troops as he saw fit. A nonpartisan foreign policy meant that having Congress controlled by a different party than that of the president did not inhibit his freedom of action. And, on the economic front, the announcement of a major change in economic direction (as occurred in 1963 with the passage of a massive package of tax cuts) was still possible and could be led only by the president.

The price for this was that the president did not interfere in decisionmaking about issues that were not viewed as central to national economic or foreign policy performance. Eisenhower permitted the Democratic Congress to maintain and even expand much of the New Deal orientation of government. Even on pressing national concerns such as civil rights, action by the president (both Eisenhower and Kennedy) was quite limited and only took place when a national crisis was looming, such as defiance of a Supreme Court decision on segregation. One can clearly view that as a limitation or drawback to those with an expansive view of the presidency. It would have been unthinkable for Truman, Eisenhower, or even Kennedy to have taken a leadership role on the kind of lifestyle issues, ranging from teen smoking to school uniforms to how long a mother should stay in the hospital after delivering her newborn child, that now preoccupy the president. The current emphasis on having an "issue of the day" would have been unthinkable. There simply were not 365 issues worthy of presidential attention. If a list that long were produced, most commentators would have considered most issues on the list beneath the office.

The presidency, and with it the ability to manage a crisis, reached a peak during the Kennedy administration when the new administration mastered television as a way of moving public opinion in a crisis. Crisis management then was put in a long decline as the costs of an "imperial president" in foreign affairs became evident in the Johnson and Nixon administrations as the Vietnam War dragged on. The apparent failure of Johnson's domestic program and Nixon's Watergate problems hastened that progress. By the time of the oil crisis of the late 1970s, the inability of the U.S. president to act decisively was televised to all when President Carter addressed the nation in a heavy sweater. Later, when inflation seemed to be rising out of control, his prescription was that we all stop using our credit cards. Sadly, even the ability to take decisive foreign policy action seemed to have hit a new low when American helicopters, on a mission to rescue diplomatic hostages in Tehran, crashed in the Iranian desert.

The dynamism of the economy also declined during that period. Economists measure that with a marked reduction in the rate of productivity increase. A good deal of that was due to the change in energy prices. More was attributable to regulations designed to "purchase" items such as cleaner air and water, which are not measured correctly in the GDP accounts. Still more was attributable to regulations designed to redress social imbalances. By the late 1970s, the U.S. economy was in a deep malaise.

The changes that followed have been lumped together under the rubric "Reaganomics." To a large extent, Reagan restored economic dynamism. Measured productivity changes, which do not happen immediately when policy changes are made, have begun to accelerate. Small business creation, technological innovation, and even real wages began to increase starting in 1983. That increase in economic dynamism seems to have continued to the present, although the rate of increase may now be slowing.

The decisive actions in the areas of fiscal and monetary policy in the early 1980s seem to suggest that the ability of the country to deal decisively with a crisis increased. Similarly, ability to take decisive military action in the midst of a crisis was renewed with the positioning of intermediate-range missiles in central Europe—and ultimately by the successful defeat of the Soviet empire. In the foreign policy arena, the success of President Bush at organizing an international coalition to combat Iraqi aggression against Kuwait indicated that the power of the presidency in the midst of a crisis was higher than it had been under Carter.

But that revival of the presidency had its limits. After 1986, Congress and the presidency were once again in the hands of different parties. That led to an increase in tensions and a return to a Watergate-style congressional emphasis on checking the executive through scandal. Faced with the Kuwaiti crisis, Bush elected to imitate the implicit compromise of the late 1950s, letting Congress have the upper hand on domestic issues, while he used the presidency to resolve a foreign crisis. Congressional acceptance of that arrangement was only grudging, and narrow approval of a resolution supportive of the war effort occurred on a highly partisan vote.[19] Even after successful conduct of the war, the president was unable, some might say unwilling, to regain the policymaking initiative.

The capacity of the president to confront a major crisis has remained untested since the Gulf War, but the signs are not auspicious. During the 1992 election campaign, President Clinton promised to refocus the presidency away from foreign policy matters and onto the domestic situation, and we have every indication that he has more than fulfilled his promise. In addition, the partisan positioning of Congress and the presidency—in both institutional and philosophical conflict—which was established in 1986, has continued. Not only is the political scene inauspicious, but the tangible measures of power, including military readiness, are in jeopardy.[20]

On the economic front, policy has taken on a remarkable degree of passivity. While both Congress and the president remind voters that the federal budget is balanced for the first time in thirty years, they neglect to mention that most of the improvement in the budgetary situation was due to factors outside of policy. According to the Congressional Budget Office, some 60 percent of the budgetary reduction was due to "technical" or "economic" factors.[21] Although the direction of the trend is favorable, the fact remains that the direction of fiscal events is largely randomly determined and is not under the control of policymakers. Thus, from the view of crisis management, nothing has changed on the fiscal front.

On the monetary front, we have discussed both the success and the limitations of current monetary policy. While Greenspan and the Fed have been enormously successful at their mission to stabilize the U.S. economy, their capacity to act as a contrarian with regard to financial markets is still in question. On that front is the "crisis management" potential of current American policy arrangements most likely to be tested.

Figure 10-3
Economic Dynamism and Crisis Management in Japan

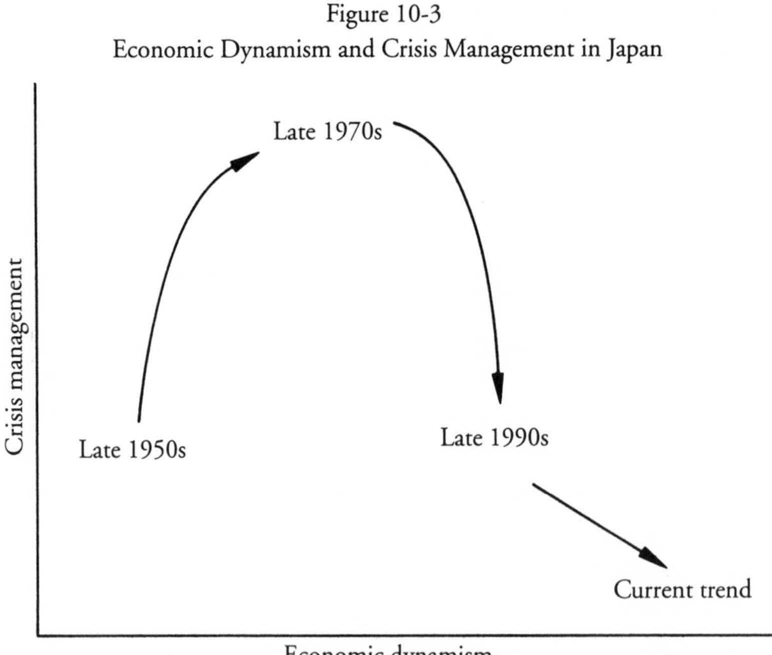

Japan

Figure 10-3 depicts economic dynamism and crisis management in Japan. In the late 1950s Japan was still trying to regain its bearings as a nation. The turning point came in 1960 when Prime Minister Kishi left office and the new prime minister, Ikeda, announced the start of the income-doubling plan. We have little question that the economic dynamism of the Japanese economy began to climb, as annual growth rates in the 10 percent range became commonplace. What is unusual is that this corresponded to an increase in the ability of the economy's decisionmakers to manage crisis. Stated differently, this was the heyday of the bureaucracy and the maximum extent of its capacity to "administratively guide" the economy.

Under most circumstances, bureaucratic control and economic dynamism do not mix. But it is worth recapping the conditions in Japan that made such a combination possible. Many factors come together to make economic growth—capital formation, the training and use of skilled labor, and technological innovation are the three catchall terms that economists use to sum up what is involved. Bureaucratic control greatly assisted the process of capital formation, particularly the harnessing of the banking sector and the money-creation process. A well-educated labor force had long been a Japanese asset. The development of the lifetime employment system gave firms (and indirectly the development process) a leg up in its utilization. Again, the bureaucratic control of the economy assisted that. The final factor, technological innovation, was less important as Japan could obtain key technologies from abroad.

Bureaucratic control, particularly if such control is centrally administered, can have other advantages. Obstacles to growth can arise in the form of local opposition to major national objectives. We now call this the NIMBY phenomenon—not in my back yard. Bureaucratic control can overcome NIMBY since the central authority can overcome local democratic and private property interests. At the stage of economic development in which large infrastructure projects and production facilities are important—a point at which Japan found itself in 1960—that can be particularly crucial. It was symbolic of the reassertion of NIMBY that, in the 1970s, the construction of Tokyo's Narita International Airport was a very costly and time-consuming victory for the central government. Today, bureaucrats shy away from taking on similar projects for the same reason. Even at Narita, local opposition blocked construction of a second major runway for an extended period.

The crisis management potential of the Japanese also became apparent during the oil shocks of the 1970s. Although far more dependent on imported oil than the United States, Japan was able to rebound from those shocks more easily than the United States. While the special economic interests of various regions, industries, and consumers kept the United States attempting to protect its economy from the effects of higher energy prices, the Japanese bureaucracy was largely able to resist such pressures. The result was that Japanese industry quickly adjusted to new global energy realities while the United States dragged out its own adjustment process.

On our graphical depiction of those trends, it is instructive that the overall direction of the United States was to move "southwest" on our chart, while Japan moved in the optimal "northeast" direction. That led to an enormous sense of exuberance about the Japanese model, in both Japan and the United States. Japan watchers such as Herman Kahn and Ezra Vogel began to proclaim the *Emerging Japanese Superstate* and *Japan As Number One.* The extrapolation of the trends of the 1960s and 1970s certainly might justify those conclusions.

But, beginning in the 1980s, the limitations of the Japanese model began to affect the country's performance. The key is that centralized bureaucratic control can impose costs, as well as benefits, on a society. Among the biggest problems Japan faced was its enormous excess savings rate. The bureaucratically designed capital allocation system had been a net asset to Japanese development during the 1960s and 1970s. By the 1980s, the large captive pool of saving began to become a problem. But nothing was done—for probably two reasons.

First, that captive pool of saving was not recognized as a "problem," because the excess saving found an outlet in the creation of a large bubble in both equities and land prices. Decisionmakers, as well as the public at large, considered that rise in the value of Japanese assets to be a tribute to Japan—just compensation for the hard work and talents of the Japanese people and for the sound management of the Japanese bureaucracy.

Second, even if some had recognized the excess saving as a problem, the bureaucracy would have been quite reticent about making fundamental changes because the existing arrangements were the key to its power. We saw in chapter 5 how the attitudes of one of Japan's leading bureaucrats stressed next steps that involved the need for continued bureaucratic control—not what he considered unbridled capitalism—to reform the system so as to save it. Those attitudes are entirely understandable, even if they might not be the solution to Japan's current problems.

The failure to recognize the problem and a deep-seated reluctance to deal fundamentally with it have precipitated a decade-long plunge in Japanese economic performance. After the bubble burst at the start of the 1990s, Japan found both its crisis management capability and the dynamism of its economy retarded. The effects on economic dynamism have been somewhat muted because of the large backlog of global technological advantages that Japan had amassed. But that dynamism is being eroded because of the banking difficulties and a hangover from the highly leveraged policies of the past that continue to prevent the formation of new businesses. Unless changes come soon, the decline in the dynamism of the Japanese economy is likely to accelerate.

The biggest effect of the problems of the 1990s has been on the decisionmaking institutions of Japan. As we noted, the Mandate of Heaven has been withdrawn from the bureaucracy. At present, nothing has taken its place, however. So, as the crisis deepens, the ability to deal with the crisis has diminished. Existing decisionmaking institutions are continuously discredited as new failures emerge and old practices are exposed. Today, Japan finds itself in as deep a decisionmaking crisis as it did when Prime Minister Ikeda assumed power in 1960. The problem is that an Ikeda does not seem to be waiting in the wings to take over.

In the near term, that is likely to have one salutary effect. The dynamism of the Japanese economy is likely to increase. With the hand of the bureaucracy removed from many of the levers of control, new ideas are beginning to emerge in both the capital and labor markets. Foreign enterprises are slowly buying their way into the Japanese economy—particularly its financial sector. Gradually, the dynamism of the Japanese economy will increase. Unfortunately, the lag between the start of that process and the point at which the Japanese economy as a whole will turn around will be long. The Japanese still have to make enormous changes in many of the arrangements that have guided their country during the past fifty years.

Europe

Figure 10-4 depicts economic dynamism and crisis management in Europe. One of the problems with evaluating Europe is that it is not a single political or economic entity, although that is changing. The highly refined power of the centralized state to manage a crisis in DeGaulle's Fifth Republic contrasts with the situation in most of Italy's postwar history, in which the term *Italian government* became an oxymoron. The term *dynamism* certainly applied to the German economy during

Figure 10-4
Economic Dynamism and Crisis Management in Europe

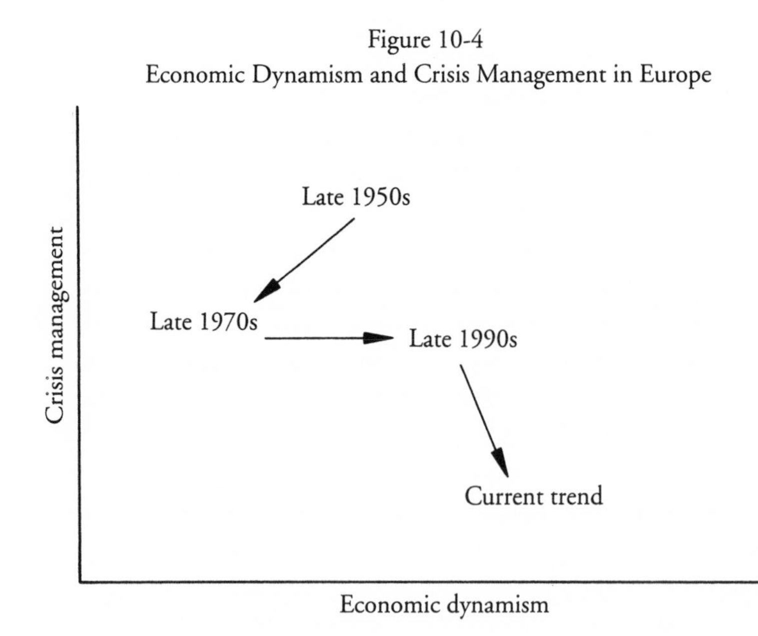

the 1950s and 1960s. No one would ascribe the same term to the British at that time.

The unification of Europe and the centralization of decisionmaking also produce conflicting objectives. Most Italians see unelected governance from Brussels as a salvation from elected government from Rome, in terms of both dynamism and crisis management. On the other hand, most post-Thatcher Britons have the opposite view, as probably do most Germans.

Complicating that issue is the role of the United States. Many Europeans looked to Washington for leadership in a crisis during the postwar period. That is certainly less true today. It is therefore hard to compare Europe's ability to manage a crisis in the 1950s—when much of what was involved was following Washington's leadership—to a modern European summit in which the heads of state of fifteen separate nations must reach a consensus.

By and large, economic dynamism on both sides of the Atlantic ran in close parallel. The rise of social regulation and the breakdown in labor-management cooperation during the late 1960s and 1970s certainly produced less dynamic economies on both sides of the Atlantic.

Similarly, the challenge to overcome those problems led to increased dynamism in much of Europe during the 1980s and 1990s, although the trend on average was certainly much less dramatic than in the United States. Today, Europe's double-digit unemployment rate stands in marked contrast to America's full employment and is ample testimony to the relative decline in the dynamism of Europe.

What of the future? The integration of Europe is likely to continue to produce a mixed trend. For example, the single currency is certain to produce some clear-cut advantages in the area of trade. After all, the need to convert currencies, even if such currencies are trading at fixed parities, imposes a cost on intra-European trade. On the other hand, as we discussed in chapter 7, the need to reach a monetary policy compromise for the widely diverse economies of Europe should, on net, produce less flexibility and, therefore, greater costs for regional business cycles. On net, it is probably best to give Europe the benefit of the doubt on those arrangements and look forward to a modest increase in European dynamism in the near future.

On the other hand, it is difficult to see how the new arrangements can facilitate crisis management. The scope of the consensus necessary to take bold and decisive action has certainly increased. The need to assemble the leaders of widely diverse electorates and for them to agree on a course of action reminds one of the arrangements under the Articles of Confederation in the early history of the United States. Certainly, that is a halfway house to some other arrangement—either a genuine continental government or a return to nation-based decisionmaking on many issues.

The capacity for crisis management on the monetary front has also been reduced. The official mandate of the new European Central Bank is extremely narrow—focused exclusively on price stability. That sharply circumscribes the official ability to intervene in a financial crisis. The central bank has no capacity to intervene in a regional (that is, national) financial crisis, either. Some of the provisions of the Maastricht Treaty strictly circumscribe such behavior. In addition, the political forces are already forming to have substantial input into the decisionmaking of the central bank, thereby further constraining dramatic action. Those arrangements may make a banking crisis in Europe extremely painful, should one ever develop.

Conclusion

George Soros saw the current economic situation as a victory for global capitalism. Perhaps. If that is the case, then the world will clearly benefit from having a more dynamic economy. But global capitalism by itself cannot prevent crises from developing or from spreading. The essence of global capitalism is a disaggregation of economic decisionmaking into many hands. It is the economic parallel of democracy. But having power in many hands means that reaching a consensus is more difficult.

Globally, the limits on economic management may be reaching a new high. Alternatively, one might see this as a new nadir in the capacity to manage a crisis. While this analysis of the economic dynamism of the global economy has shown some ups and downs over the past fifty years, the trend for crisis management has been virtually unremittingly downward.

If correct, that trend means that economic growth today is the least of our worries. We have an abundance of new technologies that will improve the lives of all of us. The introduction of those new technologies into the real economy is not going to be riskless. In all likelihood, the path of introduction is likely to follow the model driven by highly leveraged bank loans that we described in the story of the cancer cure pill. When the world is introducing new products in a wide variety of areas—biotechnology and medicine, communication and information processing, transportation, and energy production—the chances of a financial miscue in one of those industries is high. At the same time, the entrance of many new nations into mainstream global commerce is likely to increase the chances that a regional financial crisis will emerge.

We may therefore be entering an era not unlike the period before the First World War. Then, an earlier version of today's global capitalism was spreading. New technologies were emerging. Banking crises were frequent. Global economic progress, at least in those areas of the world that were participating, was one of two or three steps forward and one step back. From the point of view of the "typical" citizen, it was a time of enormous promise and improvement in living standards, but also a time of significant risk. It was a time of growing personal liberty; one could travel worldwide virtually unobstructed by regulation—and in many cases even without a passport. It was also a time in which the economic difference between those participating in the global market and those who were not was growing. Politically, it was felt that governments could not do a lot about economic crises, although the demand that they do something was growing.

Today, electorates have significantly discounted the need for crisis management skills in their officials. Politicians are responding by focusing on their ability to deliver the goods to the local constituency—to assert that they care about things that matter in people's everyday lives. That is as true in Japan, where Tanaka's Construction State still exists, as it is in the United States, where the president must feel the typical citizen's pain, and as it is in Europe, where much of the electorate is choosing to waste its vote on extreme parties with no chance to govern, simply to register a protest. In all three areas participation is declining, a trend that reflects a further disinterest in politics.

In part, those trends result from electorates' feeling that the politicians can't do much about the big issues. In part, those trends emerge because things have been quite good (that is, relatively crisis-free) for a long time. If, in fact, the world is headed for a period of increased crisis, that myopia will turn out to be unfortunate and much regretted. Then, the search will be on—for new leaders—or failing that, for scapegoats on whom to blame the deepening crisis. In an age of limited capacity for decisionmakers to manage and in the age of ever-expanding democracy, the main relevance of Mervyn King's comment at the Bank of England was that it was "we," in the broadest sense, who didn't see it coming.

Notes

Chapter 1: Masters of the System—Or Its Servants?

1. Epigraph: Winston Churchill, Winston Churchill home page [database online] [cited 10 February 1998]; available from: http://www.winstonchurchill.org.

2. Bob Davis and David Wessel, *Prosperity* (New York: Random House, 1998), and James K. Glassman and Kevin A. Hassett, "Are Stocks Overvalued? Not a Chance," *Wall Street Journal*, March 30, 1998.

3. "Asia Economic Forecast Summary," Bear Stearns, August 1998.

4. "A High-Rise Bust," *Economist*, June 27, 1998, p. 40.

5. Glyn Davies, *A History of Money* (Cardiff: University of Wales Press, 1996) [database online] [cited 10 February 1998]; available from: http://www.ex.ac.uk/~Rdavies/arian/amser/chrono.html. The pound has not had to be replaced in 1,300 years.

6. "Annual Trends: 1995," *Nikkei Net* [database online] [cited 14 July 1998]; available from: http://www.nikkei.co.jp/enews/TNKS/stox/historical.

7. Frederick Lewis Allen, *Only Yesterday* (New York: Harper & Row, 1931), p. 242.

8. Gregory Zuckerman, "Economists Warn Bonds Won't Sustain Recent Rally," *Wall Street Journal*, January 12, 1998, p. C1.

9. "Asian Crisis Causing Jitters about Inflation to Wane, Rivlin Says," *Wall Street Journal*, December 10, 1997, p. A24.

10. Jacob M. Schlesinger, "Is Asian Crisis a Boon to U.S. or First Whiff of the

Next Recession?" *Wall Street Journal,* December 29, 1997, p. A1.

11. Bob Davis, "IMF Says Asian Crisis Won't Hurt U.S.," *Wall Street Journal,* December 22, 1997, p. A2.

12. U.S. House of Representatives, Committee on Banking and Financial Services, *Hearing on East Asian Economic Conditions, Part 2,* January 30, 1998, [database online] [cited 16 July 1998]; available from: http://commdocs.house.gov/committees/bank/hba46637.000/hba46637_0.HTM#95, p. 40.

13. David Wessel and Thomas T. Vogel, Jr., "Market Watcher: Arcane World of Bonds Is Guide and Beacon to a Populist President," *Wall Street Journal,* February 25, 1993, p. A1.

14. William Shakespeare, *Julius Caesar* 1.2.

15. *Voter Turnout from 1945 to 1997: A Global Report* (Stockholm: International Institute for Democracy and Electoral Assistance, 1998), pp. 63–84.

16. Conversation with Professor Marco Vitale of Bocconi University.

17. Dick Morris, *Behind the Oval Office: Winning the Presidency in the Nineties* (New York: Random House, 1997), pp. 9–13.

18. Schlesinger, "Is Asian Crisis a Boon to U.S. or First Whiff of the Next Recession?"

Chapter 2: The Contrarian at the Center

1. Epigraph: John Maynard Keynes, *General Theory of Employment, Interest, and Money* (New York: Harcourt, Brace & World, 1964), p. 383.

2. Lawrence H. Summers, "American Global Leadership: The Denver Summit and Beyond," World Trade Conference, Denver, Colo., June 10, 1997 [database online] [cited 24 July 1997]; available from: http://www.ustreas.gov/treasury/speech/sp061097.html.

3. William Greider, *Secrets of the Temple* (New York: Simon and Schuster, 1989).

4. All quotations of Chairman Greenspan are from an interview I conducted with him on April 23, 1998.

5. Radio broadcast, October 1, 1939, quoted in John Bartlett and Justin Kaplan, *Bartlett's Familiar Quotations,* 16th ed. (Boston: Little Brown & Co., 1992), p. 620.

6. John Maynard Keynes, *The General Theory of Employment, Interest, and Money* (New York: Harcourt, Brace & World, 1964), p. 162.

7. Ibid., p. 129.

8. The data are as of March 1998. Council of Economic Advisers, *Economic Indicators, March 1998* (Washington, D.C.: Government Printing Office, 1998), p. 12.

9. Michael Lewis, "Beyond Economics, Beyond Politics, Beyond Accountability," *Worth,* May 1995 [database online] [cited 7 May 1998]; available from: http://www.worth.com.

10. Ibid.

11. Joan Warner, "A Kinder, Gentler Business Cycle?" *BusinessWeek*, March 6, 1989, pp. 50–51.

Chapter 3: Supply Shocks and Creative Destruction

1. Epigraph: George Bernard Shaw, *The Intelligent Woman's Guide to Socialism and Capitalism*, quoted in *Respectfully Quoted* (Washington, D.C.: Library of Congress, 1989), p. 34.

2. "America's Bubble Economy" and "America Bubbles Over," *Economist*, April 18, 1998, pp. 15, 67; "Addressing the U.S. Bubble," editorial, *Financial Times*, April 22, 1998, p. 15.

3. Joseph A. Schumpeter, *Capitalism, Socialism, and Democracy* (New York: Harper & Brothers Publishers, 1942), p. 83.

4. Frederick Lewis Allen, *Only Yesterday* (New York: Harper & Row, 1931), p. 133.

5. *Economic Report of the President* (Washington, D.C.: Government Printing Office, 1997), table B-2, and *Economic Report of the President* (Washington, D.C.: Government Printing Office, 1998), table B-2.

6. *Economic Report of the President* (Washington, D.C.: Government Printing Office, 1998), table B-30, and the National Bureau of Economic Research, "U.S. Business Cycle Expansions and Contractions" [database online] [cited 5 March 1998]; available from: http://www.nber.org/cycles.html.

7. *Economic Report of the President* (Washington, D.C.: Government Printing Office, 1998), table B-103, and *Economic Report of the President* (Washington, D.C.: Government Printing Office, 1992), table B-99.

8. Board of Governors of the Federal Reserve System, "U.S. Weighted Average Exchange Rate of the Dollar, Weighted by G-10 Countries" [database online] [cited 5 March 1998]; available from: http://www.bog.frb.fed.us/releases/H10/hist; *Economic Report of the President* (Washington, D.C.: Government Printing Office, 1998), table B-103.

9. Mollie Dickenson, "The Real S&L Scandal," *Worth*, September 1994 [database online] [cited 23 February 1998]; available from: http://www.worth.com/articles.

10. U.S. Department of Energy, Energy Information Administration, "World Oil Market and Oil Price Chronologies, 1970–1996" [database online] [cited 12 December 1997]; available from: http://eiainfo.eia.doe.gov/emeu/cabs/chron.html; Susan H. Holte, "Annual Energy Outlook Forecast Evaluation," in *Issues in Midterm Analysis and Forecasting, 1997* [database online] [cited 6 March 1998]; available from: http://www.eia.doe.gov/oiaf/issues97/aeoeval.html/#introd.

11. Conversation with Robert McTeer, president, Federal Reserve Bank of Dallas, December 12, 1997.

12. See Brian Arthur, "Competing Technologies, Increasing Returns, and Lock-

In by Historical Small Events," in *Increasing Returns and Path Dependence in the Economy* (Ann Arbor: University of Michigan Press, 1994), pp. 13–32; Paul Krugman and Elhanan Helpman, *Market Structure and Foreign Trade: Increasing Returns, Imperfect Competition, and the International Economy* (Cambridge: MIT Press, 1985); and Victor Norman and Avinash K. Dixit, *Theory of International Trade: A Dual, General Equilibrium Approach* (Cambridge: Cambridge University Press, 1980).

13. Alan Greenspan, Francis Boyer Lecture, American Enterprise Institute, December 5, 1996.

14. In the fall of 1998, financial conditions forced Greenspan to cut rates. As of this writing, the market was up more than 1,000 points as the result of a fifty-basis-point rate reduction. Greenspan's dilemma continues.

Chapter 4: The Mandarin

1. Epigraph: Plato, *The Republic* 4.425, trans. Benjamin Jowett (New York: Vintage Books, 1991), p. 136.

2. Nicholas D. Kristof, "Hubris and Humility as U.S. Waxes and Asia Wanes," *New York Times*, March 22, 1998.

3. Sara Webb and Silvia Ascarelli, "Global Markets Sink, but U.S. Shares Rebound," *Wall Street Journal*, January 13, 1998, p. C1. After the spring rally caused by Sakakibara's reforms, the market resumed its decline, falling below 13,000 in September 1998.

4. Bloomberg News, "Japan's Cabinet Clears Huge Bank Bailout," *New York Times*, January 20, 1998, p. D2.

5. DKB International, *Economic Briefing*, April 8, 1998, and "Average Household Can Expect Tax Rebate Totaling 65,000 Yen," *Daily Yomiuri*, December 18, 1997, p. 1.

6. Gillian Tett, "The Day Japan Let a Flagship Go Under," *Financial Times*, January 14, 1998, p. 6.

7. Many Japanese households maintain savings accounts or buy certificates of deposit at their local post office. The postal saving system then invests that money. A substantial portion of Japanese household saving is done through the postal system.

8. Michiyo Nakamoto, "Tokyo Falls on Lack of Support," *Financial Times*, March 31, 1998, p. 42. The net swing is measured by the difference between the peak and the close of the Nikkei on March 30, 1998.

9. Jathon Sapsford and Sara Webb, "Tokyo Market's Current Slogan: We Are No. 3," *Wall Street Journal*, March 31, 1998, p. C1. The market capitalization figure is according to Goldman Sachs.

10. I am indebted to the work of Patrick Smith, W. G. Beasely, Jacob Schlesinger, and Ezra F. Vogel for their comprehensive and fascinating look at Japan and its history. Patrick Smith, *Japan: A Reinterpretation* (New York: Pantheon Books, 1997), pp. 69–70.

11. *The Autobiography of Fukuzawa Yukichi* (Tokyo: 1934), quoted in W. G. Beasely, *The Modern History of Japan* (New York: Praeger Publishers, 1963), pp. 152–53.

12. Smith, *Japan: A Reinterpretation*, p. 90.

13. John Creighton Campbell, "Democracy and Bureaucracy in Japan," quoted in Jacob M. Schlesinger, *Shadow Shoguns* (New York: Simon & Schuster, 1997), p. 132.

14. Ezra F. Vogel, *Japan As Number One: Lessons for America* (New York: Harper Colophon Books, 1979), p. 55.

15. William S. Dietrich, *In the Shadow of the Rising Sun* (University Park: Pennsylvania State University Press, 1991), p. 82.

16. Vogel, *Japan As Number One*, p. 36.

17. Ibid., p. 54.

18. Schlesinger, *Shadow Shoguns*, p. 132.

19. Jon Livingston, Joe Moore, and Felicia Oldfather, eds., *Postwar Japan: 1945 to the Present*, quoted in Schlesinger, *Shadow Shoguns*, p. 31.

20. Smith, *Japan: A Reinterpretation*, p. 14.

21. Eisuke Sakakibara, *Beyond Capitalism: The Japanese Model of Market Economics* (New York: University Press of America, 1993), p. 114.

22. Herman Kahn, *The Emerging Japanese Superstate: Challenge and Response* (Englewood Cliffs, N.J.: Prentice-Hall, 1970), pp. 4, 94; *Economic Eye*, Winter 1989 and Summer 1990, quoted in Glyn Davies, *A History of Money* (Cardiff: University of Wales Press, 1994), p. 590; *Economic Report of the President* (Washington, D.C.: Government Printing Office, 1998), table B-31.

23. Conversation with Tomohiro Sugita of Jiji Press, March 1998.

24. Kahn, *The Emerging Japanese Superstate*, p. 3.

25. Schlesinger, *Shadow Shoguns*, p. 48.

26. Ibid., p. 50.

27. Ibid., p. 48, and Davies, *A History of Money*, p. 589.

28. *Economic Report of the President* (Washington, D.C.: Government Printing Office, 1998), table B-31.

29. Smith, *Japan: A Reinterpretation*, p. 13.

30. Chalmers Johnson, *MITI and the Japanese Miracle* (Stanford, Calif.: Stanford University Press, 1982), p. 49.

31. *Economist*, "Consider Japan" (London: Gerald Duckworth & Co., Ltd., 1963), quoted in Kahn, *The Emerging Japanese Superstate*, p. 80.

32. Vogel, *Japan As Number One*, p. 75.

33. Kahn, *The Emerging Japanese Superstate*, p. 105, and Dietrich, *In the Shadow of the Rising Sun*, p. 96.

34. James McCormack, "The Japanese Way: The Relationship between Financial Institutions and Nonfinancial Firms," Canadian Department of Foreign Affairs and International Trade, Policy Staff Paper #94/16, June 1994 [database online] [cited 21 April 1998]; available from: http://www.dfait-maeci.gc.ca/english/foreignp/dfait/policy-1/94_16_e/s5.html.

35. Johnson, *MITI and the Japanese Miracle*, p. 10.

36. Bank of Japan, Money Stock, January 1998 [database online] [cited 1 May 1998]; available from: http://www.boj.or.jp/en/siryo/stat/ms9801.htm; Japanese Ministry of Finance, *Leading Economic and Financial Indicators* [database online] [cited 15 April 1998]; available from: http://www.mof.go.jp/english/apec-jei.htm; and *Economic Report of the President* (Washington, D.C.: Government Printing Office, 1998), tables B-1 and B-70.

37. For example, consider an initial deposit of ¥100 in a system in which 80 percent of each deposit is re-lent. The bank receiving the initial deposit lends ¥80, which is deposited in some other bank. That bank relends 80 percent of the ¥80 or ¥64. The bank receiving the deposit of that ¥64 lends 80 percent of that, and so on. Math shows that the money multiplier is the reciprocal of the fraction that is not re-lent, that is $1/(1 - r)$, where r is the fraction that is re-lent.

38. Gillian Tett and Bethan Hutton, "Japan Tries to Stop Run on Banks," *Financial Times*, November 29, 1997, p. 3.

39. Charles W. Calomiris, *The Postmodern Bank Safety Net* (Washington, D.C.: AEI Press), p. 16.

40. Dietrich, *In the Shadow of the Rising Sun*, p. 98.

41. Quoted in Albert M. Craig, "Functional and Dysfunctional Aspects of Government Bureaucracy," in Ezra F. Vogel, ed., *Modern Japanese Organization and Decision Making*; quoted in Dietrich, *In the Shadow of the Rising Sun*, p. 113.

42. Sakakibara, *Beyond Capitalism*, p. 114.

43. Ibid., p. 112.

44. Ibid., p. 113.

45. Kahn, *The Emerging Japanese Superstate*, pp. 64–65.

46. Dietrich, *In the Shadow of the Rising Sun*, pp. 81–82.

47. Schlesinger, *Shadow Shoguns*, pp. 51–52.

Chapter 5: Mandate of Heaven Withdrawn

1. Epigraph: Milton Friedman, "Bureaucracy Scorned," *Newsweek*, December 29, 1975.

2. This statement is based on purchasing power parity: $27,821 in the United States, $23,235 in Japan, and $19,333 in Europe. If we use exchange rates, there is some variation: $36,509 in Japan, $27,821 in the United States, and $23,042 in Europe. *OECD National Accounts, Main Aggregates*, vol. 1 (January 1998) [database online] [cited 1 May 1998]; available from: http://www.oecd.org/std/gdpperca.htm.

3. For example, see Robert Reich, *The Next American Frontier*, quoted in Richard B. McKenzie, "Fashionable Myths of National Industrial Policy," *Policy Review*, Fall 1983; and J. Bradford Delong and Lawrence Summers, "Equipment Investment and Economic Growth," National Bureau of Economic Research Working Paper No. 3515, November 1990.

4. Tip O'Neill with William Novak, *Man of the House* (New York: Random House, 1987), pp. 25–26.

5. For an in-depth and fascinating look at this period in Japanese history, see Jacob M. Schlesinger, *Shadow Shoguns* (New York: Simon & Schuster, 1997).

6. Ibid., p. 56.

7. Ibid., pp. 110–12.

8. Ibid., p. 131.

9. Ibid., p. 140.

10. Ibid., p. 247.

11. Eisuke Sakakibara, *Beyond Capitalism: The Japanese Model of Market Economics* (New York: University Press of America, 1993), p. 66.

12. Ibid., pp. 29, 31.

13. Ibid., p. 45.

14. See the Japanese Statistics Bureau, *Japan in Figures*, charts on population and the number of establishments by form of organization and industry [database online] [cited 15 April 1998]; available from: http://www.stat.go.jp/1611m.htm; Schlesinger, *Shadow Shoguns*, p. 141; and Japanese Ministry of Finance, *Leading Economic and Financial Indicators* [database online] [cited 15 April 1998]; available from: http://www.mof.go.jp/english/apec-jei.htm.

15. Nicholas D. Kristof, "Hubris and Humility as U.S. Waxes and Asia Wanes," *New York Times*, March 22, 1998.

16. Steven S. Weiler, Jardine Fleming Securities (Asia), Tokyo.

17. David Atkinson and David Richards, "Risk Loan Growth, 1985–1995," Goldman Sachs Research Report, January 31, 1996, p. 5.

18. Weiler, Jardin Fleming Securities.

19. Atkinson and Richards, "Risk Loan Growth, 1985–1995," p. 7.

20. Japanese Ministry of Health and Welfare, "Summary of Vital Statistics" [database online] [cited 29 April 1998 and 12 May 1998]; available from: http://www.mhw.go.jp/english/database/populate/pop1.html and pop4.html.

21. Anthony Karydakis, "U.S. Market Analysis," First Chicago Capital Markets, Inc., May 28, 1998; *Economic Report of the President* (Washington, D.C.: Government Printing Office, 1998), table B-36.

22. U.S. Department of Commerce, Bureau of Economic Analysis, and various news reports. U.S. real gross domestic product (GDP) increased $85.6 billion in the first quarter of 1998. Contemporaneous news reports indicate that Microsoft's market capitalization increased some $40 billion over the same period.

23. See the Japanese Statistics Bureau, *Japan in Figures*, chart on Japanese living abroad [database online]; available from: http://www.stat.go.jp/1611m.htm.

24. Eisuke Sakakibara, "The Once and Future Boom," *Economist*, March 22, 1997, p. 89.

25. Ibid.

26. Eisuke Sakakibara, "The End of Progressivism," *Foreign Affairs*, September/October 1995, p. 10.

27. Ibid., pp. 8–9.
28. Ibid., p. 11.
29. Ibid., p. 12.
30. Ibid., p. 13.
31. Ibid., p. 14.
32. Sakakibara, *Beyond Capitalism*, p. 141.
33. Ibid.
34. Ibid., p. 142.

Chapter 6: The Dictates of History

1. Epigraph: Niccolo Machiavelli, quoted in Franklin C. Baer, *Baertracks* [database online] [cited 31 August 1998]; available from: http://www.bemorecreative.com.
2. Correspondence with Walter Kohl, Helmut Kohl's son.
3. Ibid.
4. Ibid.
5. Ibid. and Eric Solsten, ed., *Germany: A Country Study* (Washington, D.C.: Government Printing Office, 1996), p. 419.
6. My thinking on the subject of Germany was greatly influenced by the work of David Marsh, *The Most Powerful Bank: Inside Germany's Bundesbank* (New York: Times Books, 1992). Montgomery's observation appears in Aidan Crawley, *The Rise of Western Germany, 1945–1972*, quoted in Marsh, *The Most Powerful Bank,* p. 120.
7. "The Effects of Strategic Bombing on the German War Economy," *United States Strategic Bombing Survey* (October 31, 1945), quoted in John Kenneth Galbraith, *A Life in Our Times* (Boston: Houghton Mifflin Co., 1981), p. 205.
8. Correspondence with Walter Kohl.
9. Haus der Geschichte der Bundesrepublik Deutschland (History Museum of the German Federal Republic).
10. Solsten, *Germany, A Country Study,* pp. 77, 525.
11. Conversation with Walter Kohl.
12. Ibid.
13. Haus der Geschichte der Bundesrepublik Deutschland (History Museum of the German Federal Republic).
14. United Nations, *World Economic Report 1949–50* (New York: United Nations, Department of Economic Affairs, 1951), p. 49; Michael Balfour, *Germany: The Tides of Power* (London: Routledge, 1992), p. 110; Dipl. Phys. Peter Majer, Universitat Gottingen [database online] [cited 10 May 1998]; available from: http://www.gwdg.de/~pmajer/timeseries/Data/economic/macro/UnEmploy.dat.
15. Erhard, *Wohlstand fur Alle,* quoted in Marsh, *The Most Powerful Bank,* p. 22.
16. Marsh, *The Most Powerful Bank*, pp. 81–83.
17. Conversation with Walter Kohl.

18. Letter dated January 26, 1939, BDC CF/Brinkmann, quoted in Marsh, *The Most Powerful Bank*, p. 102.

19. Marsh, *The Most Powerful Bank*, pp. 113, 117.

20. Report by the Reichsbankleitstelle (head office), January 1947, quoted in ibid., p. 120.

21. Ibid., pp. 131–32, 276.

22. Radio address by Ludwig Erhard, June 21, 1948, quoted in ibid., p. 102.

23. Law on Bank deutscher Lander, 1948, quoted in ibid., p. 123.

24. Letter from Vocke to Adenauer, October 31, 1949, BB CF/Vocke, quoted in ibid., p. 120; letter to Fritz Schaffer, finance minister, March 7, 1950, BB CF/Vocke, quoted in ibid., p. 224.

25. Speech to the Federation of German Industry in Cologne, May 23, 1956, quoted in ibid., p. 45; remarks during Bundesbank council meeting on March 3, 1961, Bundesbank minutes, quoted in ibid., p. 144; an interview by Marsh with former Chancellor Schmidt in Hamburg, June 4, 1991, quoted in ibid., p. 45.

26. Ibid, p. 141; Glyn Davies, *A History of Money* (Cardiff: University of Wales Press, 1996), pp. 393, 564; and International Monetary Fund, *International Financial Statistics, 1989.*

27. *Economic Report of the President* (Washington, D.C.: Government Printing Office, 1997), table B-108.

28. "France Out of Work, Out of Sorts," *Economist*, January 17, 1998, p. 43.

29. Eurostat, *1996, Facts through Figures: A Statistical Portrait of the European Union*, p. 18.

30. "Spend, Spend, Spend," *Economist,* September 20, 1997, pp. 7–8.

31. OECD, "Latest Trends in Consumer Prices," January 16, 1996, and April 22, 1998 [database online] [cited 28 April 1998]; available from: http://www.oecd.org.

32. Central Intelligence Agency, *World Fact Book, 1997* [database online] [cited 28 June 1998]; available from: http://www.odci.gov/cia/publications/factbook.

33. Ibid. and *Economic Report of the President* (Washington, D.C.: Government Printing Office, 1998), tables B-26 and B-103.

34. "Small Beginnings," *Economist*, November 23, 1996, pp. 13–14.

35. John Templeman, Karen Lowry Miller, and David Woodruff, "Reform at Last?" *BusinessWeek*, September 23, 1996, p. 50.

36. "Chirac Rallies to Defend French Icon, la Baguette," *Reuters, Ltd.*, January 13, 1997, and David Buchan, "Chirac Hits at Superstores," *Financial Times*, May 2, 1996, p. 2.

37. "Open up!" *Economist*, March 14, 1998, p. 59.

38. Peter Ford, "France Cuts Hours to Make Jobs," *Christian Science Monitor*, February 11, 1998.

39. Charles Fleming, "French Disagree on Shorter Workweek," *Wall Street Journal*, February 12, 1998.

40. Charles Lambroschini, "L'Exception Française," *Le Figaro*, June 7, 1997, p. 1.

41. "A Fortress against Change," *Economist*, November 23, 1996, Business in Europe Survey, p. 3.

42. Marsh, *The Most Powerful Bank*, p. 6.

43. Thane Peterson, "The World Economy Could Use a Lift. Hello? Europe?" *BusinessWeek*, January 26, 1998, p. 45.

44. Dominique Moisi, "End in Sight for Mr. Eternity," *Financial Times*, March 10, 1998, p. 22.

Chapter 7: Europe's Great Experiment

1. Epigraph: Hans Tietmeyer, "Fifty Years of the Deutsche Mark: A Currency and Its Consequences." Address in the Paulskirche, Frankfurt am Main, June 20, 1998.

2. Bank for International Settlements, press release, "Consolidated International Banking Statistics for End-1997," May 25, 1998 [database online]; available from: http://www.bis.org.

3. Lionel Barber, "Europe Takes Its New Currency to the Marketplace," *Financial Times*, Spetember 30, 1997, p. 2.

4. Johann Wilhelm Gaddum, "Economic and Monetary Union," in *Economic and Monetary Union: The Euro's Challenge to the Dollar and the Yen,* Symposium on Economic and Monetary Union (Tokyo: Institute for International Monetary Affairs, April 1997), p. 18.

5. "Financial Indicators," *Economist*, February 21, 1998, and February 28, 1998, pp. 109 and 111, respectively.

6. David Marsh, *The Most Powerful Bank: Inside Germany's Bundesbank* (New York: Times Books, 1992), appendix, p. 307.

7. U.S. Census Bureau, *1997 Statistical Abstract of the United States*, "Mobility Status of the Population, by Selected Characteristics: 1980 to 1996," p. 32; *1995 Statistical Abstract of the United States*, "Components of Population Change—States: 1990 to 1994," p. 30, and U.S. Department of Labor, Bureau of Labor Statistics, "State and Area Employment, Hours, and Earnings, Utah" [database online] [cited 24 April 1996]; available from: http://stats.bls.gov:80.

8. Patrick Fleenor, ed., *Facts and Figures on Government Finance* (Washington, D.C.: Tax Foundation, 1995), tables B3 and C26, pp. 28 and 84.

9. Only five regional bank presidents vote at any given time on a rotational basis. The Federal Reserve Bank of New York is the exception as it has a permanent vote.

10. George Jones and Christopher Lockwood, "Jospin Says Seat on Euro Bank Will Be Kept Warm for Britain," *Daily Telegraph*, November 8, 1997, p. 4.

11. Gerard Lyons, "History Shows EMU's Success May Depend on Political Union," DKB International, *Economic Note*, December 3, 1997.

Chapter 8: On a Clear Day You Can See Forever

1. Epigraph: Benjamin Disraeli, letter to Mrs. Sarah Brydges Willyams, October 17, 1863, quoted in *Respectfully Quoted* (Washington, D.C.: Library of Congress, 1989), p. 249.

2. All quotations of George Soros are from an interview I conducted with him on April 22, 1998.

Chapter 9: An Intellectual Confusion between Supply and Demand

1. Epigraph: Gertrude Stein, quoted in Robert Andrews, *Cassell Dictionary of Contemporary Quotations* (London: Cassell, 1996), p. 382.

2. Richard W. Stevenson, "An Old School Inflation Fighter; Fed Official Resists Notion of a New Era in Economics," *New York Times*, September 18, 1997, p. D1.

3. Alan Greenspan, "Monetary Policy Testimony and Report to Congress," July 22, 1997 [database online] [cited 13 February 1998]; available from: http://www.bog.frb.fed.us/boarddocs/hh/default.htm.

4. Economic journals have been filled with discussions of those details. It is not our purpose to replicate those detailed arguments here. Rather, we assume that it is intuitively plausible that the higher national output can be obtained only through higher inflation, just as higher output of a product can be obtained only through higher prices.

5. This notion of equilibrium is obtained by considering what would happen if the economy were not at equilibrium. First, consider what would happen if inflation were "too high," that is, above equilibrium. If the prevailing inflation rate is higher than that implied by the intersection of supply and demand, then *real* (inflation-adjusted) household wealth is too low to sustain much spending. Demand will be lower as a result. On the other hand, prices and wages are so high that they are causing firms to produce flat out. The resulting glut on the market (excessive supply, insufficient demand) will cause price cutting, and the underlying inflation rate will fall to equilibrium. If, on the other hand, the prevailing inflation rate is below equilibrium, then real household wealth is high and consumers are spending aggressively. Suppliers are not enjoying the kind of price and wage increases they want and consequently are holding back goods from the market. The resulting shortage will drive wages, prices, and inflation up to the equilibrium level.

6. Paul A. Samuelson, *Economics,* 8th ed. (New York: McGraw-Hill Book Company, 1970), p. 812.

7. See "Crash, Dammit," *Economist,* October 18, 1997, p. 13.

8. See Athanasios Orphanides, David H. Small, Voker Wieland, and David W. Wilcox, "A Quantitative Exploration of the Opportunistic Approach to Disinflation," Finance and Economics Discussion Series (Washington, D.C.: Fed-

eral Reserve Board, June 1997), and Athanasios Orphanides and David Wilcox, "The Opportunistic Approach to Disinflation," Finance and Economics Discussion Series (Washington, D.C.: Federal Reserve Board, 1996).

Chapter 10: The Criteria for Successful Economic Management

1. Epigraph: Ronald Reagan, "Inaugural Address," Public Papers of the Presidents of the United States: Ronald Reagan, 1985, vol. 1 (Washington, D.C.: Government Printing Office, 1985), pp. 55–58.

2. This assumes a 3 percent real discount rate and an eighty-year life expectancy.

3. Lawrence B. Lindsey, *The Growth Experiment: How the New Tax Policy Is Transforming the U.S. Economy* (New York: Basic Books, 1990), p. 103.

4. *Economic Report of the President* (Washington, D.C.: Government Printing Office, 1997), tables B-40, B-61, and B-62.

5. *Economic Report of the President* (Washington, D.C.: Government Printing Office, 1991), table B-27; *Economic Report of the President* (Washington, D.C.: Government Printing Office, 1998), table B-31; and National Bureau of Economic Research, "U.S. Business Cycle Expansions and Contractions" [database online] [cited 5 March 1998]; available from: http://www.nber.org/cycles.html.

6. Dinesh D'Souza, *Ronald Reagan: How an Ordinary Man Became an Extraordinary Leader* (New York: Free Press, 1997), p. 230.

7. U.S. Department of Labor, Bureau of Labor Statistics, *Work Stoppage Data* [database online] [cited 31 March 1998]; available from: http://stats.bls.gov.

8. U.S. Department of Labor, "Value of the Minimum Wage over the Last 40 Years" [database online] [cited 29 July 1997]; available from: http://www.dol.gov/dol/esa/public/minwage/chart2.htm.

9. Lindsey, *The Growth Experiment*, p. 42.

10. *Economic Report of the President* (Washington, D.C.: Government Printing Office, 1980), p. 68.

11. Per capita GDP is expressed in 1990 Geary-Khamis dollars. In 1945 India's per capita GDP was 665 and Japan's was 1,295. In 1990 India's per capita GDP was 1,316 and Japan's was 18,548. Angus Maddison, *Monitoring the World Economy, 1820–1992* (Paris: OECD, 1995), pp. 197, 204–5. Maddison describes Geary-Khamis dollars on p. 163.

12. Ibid.

13. *Economic Report of the President* (Washington, D.C.: Government Printing Office, 1981), table B-53.

14. Ibid., table B-2, and Herbert Stein, *Presidential Economics* (Washington, D.C.: AEI Press, 1994), p. 452.

15. *Economic Report of the President* (Washington, D.C.: Government Printing Office, 1981), table B-28.

16. White House, Office of the Press Secretary, "A Program for Economic Recovery," February 18, 1981, p. 25; *Economic Report of the President* (Washington, D.C.: Government Printing Office, 1988), tables B-2, B-8, and B-58.

17. *Economic Report of the President* (Washington, D.C.: Government Printing Office, 1947), table 6; Simon Kuznets, *National Income: A Summary of Findings* (New York: National Bureau of Economic Research, 1946), p. 32.

18. *Economic Report of the President* (Washington, D.C.: Government Printing Office, 1982), table B-1.

19. Federation of American Scientists, "Congress Approves Using Force against Iraq" [database online] [cited 11 May 1998]; available from: http//www.fas.org/news/iraq/1991/910113-168336.htm.

20. U.S. House of Representatives, Committee on National Security, "Military Readiness 1997: Rhetoric and Reality" [database online] [cited May 1998]; available from: http://www.house.gov/nsc.

21. Senate Budget Committee, "Sources of Deficit Reduction 1993–1997," chart, February 1998.

Index

About the Author

Lawrence B. Lindsey is a resident scholar and holder of the Arthur F. Burns Chair in Economics at the American Enterprise Institute in Washington, D.C. He is also managing director of Economic Strategies, an economic advisory service based in New York City.

Mr. Lindsey served as a member of the Board of Governors of the Federal Reserve System for five years from November 1991 to February 1997. Additionally, he was chairman of the board of the Neighborhood Reinvestment Corporation, a national public-private community redevelopment organization, from 1993 until his departure from the Federal Reserve. Before joining the Federal Reserve Board, Mr. Lindsey was a special assistant to the president for policy development during the Bush administration. A former professor of economics at Harvard University, Mr. Lindsey also served for three years as senior staff economist for tax policy on the Council of Economic Advisers during the Reagan administration.

Mr. Lindsey received his A.B., magna cum laude, from Bowdoin College and his master's and Ph.D. in economics from Harvard University. He is the author of *The Growth Experiment: How the New Tax Policy Is Transforming the U.S. Economy* (Basic Books, 1990) and has contributed numerous articles to professional publications. His honors and awards include the Distinguished Public Service Award of the Boston Bar Association in 1994, an honorary juris doctor degree from Bowdoin College in 1993, selection as a Citicorp-Wriston Fellow for Economic Research in 1988, and the Outstanding Doctoral Dissertation Award from the National Tax Association in 1985.

The American Enterprise Institute for Public Policy Research

Founded in 1943, AEI is a nonpartisan, nonprofit, research and educational organization based in Washington, D. C. The Institute sponsors research, conducts seminars and conferences, and publishes books and periodicals.

AEI's research is carried out under three major programs: Economic Policy Studies; Foreign Policy and Defense Studies; and Social and Political Studies. The resident scholars and fellows listed in these pages are part of a network that also includes ninety adjunct scholars at leading universities throughout the United States and in several foreign countries.

The views expressed in AEI publications are those of the authors and do not necessarily reflect the views of the staff, advisory panels, officers, or trustees.

This book was edited by
Leigh Tripoli of the publications staff
of the American Enterprise Institute.
The text was set in Garamond.
Alice Anne English designed the book.
Nancy Rosenberg prepared the index.
Susanna Huang set the type,
and Edwards Brothers, Incorporated,
of Lillington, North Carolina,
printed and bound the book,
using permanent acid-free paper.

The AEI Press is the publisher for the American Enterprise Institute for Public Policy Research, 1150 Seventeenth Street, N.W., Washington, D.C. 20036; Christopher DeMuth, publisher; Leigh Tripoli, acting director; Ann Petty, editor; Cheryl Weissman, editor; Alice Anne English, managing editor; Susanna Huang editorial production assistant.